WHERE TO GO IN GREECE

A New Look

TREVOR WEBSTER

SETTLE PRESS

© 1985 Trevor Webster
Third reprint 1986
Revised edition 1986
Totally enlarged and updated edition 1992
Revised edition 1994

First published by Settle Press
10 Boyne Terrace Mews
London W11 3LR

ISBN   1 872876 15 3

Printed by Villiers Publications Ltd
19 Sylvan Avenue, London N3 2LE

Contents

Foreword

When the opportunity first arose to be associated with 'Where to Go in Greece', we were particularly delighted. Trevor Webster has produced a very readable book packed not only with practical information about Greece and her islands, but also with the sort of personal observations that add that special dash of flavour. In this new edition he has revised, updated and expanded previous information, while still retaining the essential charm of Greece.

As the leading holiday company operating in Greece, we recognise the need for detailed information and guidance for the would-be traveller. Here is a book covering over 70 islands, which answers all the questions, written in the impartial and highly personalised style of someone who knows and loves this unique country.

Whether you are a committed Grecophile or a potential first-timer, we are sure you will find this book invaluable in helping you to plan your next holiday in Greece.

Thomson Holidays

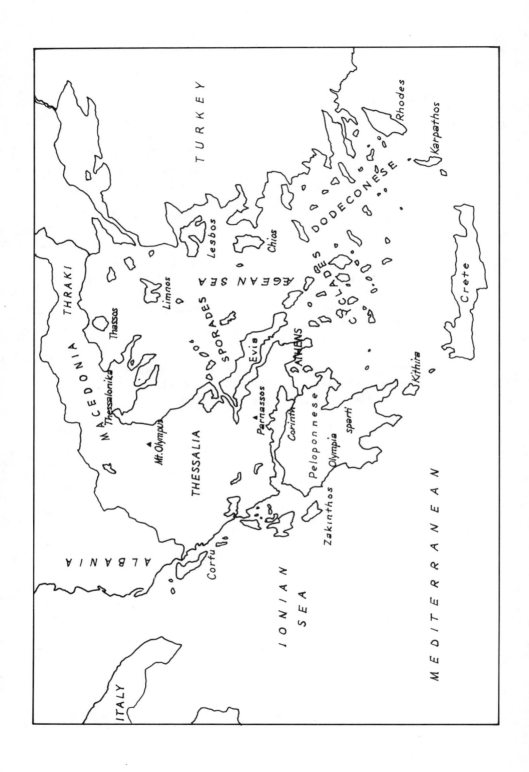

1. Greece in the 1990's

Greece has a timeless appeal and a magic that stems from its unique history, hot climate and its hundreds of scattered islands.

After a decade in the Common Market its formal trappings and its standard of living have been transformed into those of a modern West European democracy. Yet little has changed on the islands, in the villages or in the countryside to spoil its special quality.

The march of time has brought a few bonuses for tourists in Greece which were not available when the first edition of this book was written ten years ago. Those who travelled through Greece in the 1960's and 1970's will notice changes in accommodation, food, transport and the countryside that are almost wholly for the better.

Greece has followed the fashion of the Western Mediterranean and Canary Islands for self-catering. So there is now an abundance of apartments and even hotel rooms with bathrooms, small kitchens and big balconies.

The bathrooms are no longer such bad jokes and they have hot water, mostly from solar heating, while electric lights usually work nowadays and their bulbs are covered with shades more often than not.

Restaurant food is more varied, the service is faster, and meals are almost always served hot. So much so that Greek cuisine is rising in places to gourmet standards that deserve praise from the most jaded food writers.

Travel within the country has been transformed by the expansion of the Olympic Airways network between the islands, the arrival of a major competitor in South East European Airways (partnered by Virgin), the spread of hydrofoils and catamarans – which more than halve the travelling times of ships – and far more local buses and taxis.

Most amazing of all to seasoned travellers in Greece is that it is going green. Rubbish baskets have appeared where there were none before and there is much less garbage strewn across beaches and hillsides.

This silent revolution in standards owes much to the package tour trade and it has exacted a price. Airports can be crowded and there are now areas of strip development with discos and cocktail bars that are a bit of an eyesore to most visitors.

But the country has proved big enough and flexible enough to restrict such developments so that, miraculously, they haven't spoiled its essential charm and that of its people.

The Glory that is Greece

Greece is more exotic than other Mediterranean sunspots such as France, Spain and Italy. It is a hot country with scrub hillsides, palm trees, Byzantine churches and over

1,000 islands, which has cultural links with the Bible lands of the Middle East and climatic links with North Africa.

Donkeys still provide transport in country areas, goats roam the hillsides, and bananas, peaches, melons and grapes grow alongside colder weather crops like corn, potatoes and tomatoes.

Both sky and sea are usually the bright blue of postcards and buildings can be just as bright. On the islands whole villages are painted brilliant white and window frames are picked out in green, blue, red or brown.

The climate shows off the colours. Greece is the hottest country in Europe with its southern isles on the same level as north Africa, Syria and Iraq. Most areas record 300 days of sunshine a year and temperatures of 90 degrees are common from June to September.

The Greek Mainland

Tired of the islands and the tourists, or just looking for something different off the beaten track? Try the mainland.

It boasts four great holiday coasts in Halkidiki, the Peloponnese, Pelion and Epirus, with better beaches than most islands, plus better food, wine and sites.

The only thing it lacks is package tours. But that might be exactly what you are looking for.

It is a stunning country to look at, with wide plains and high mountains in the north and rocky islands with sandy bays scattered across the Ionian and Aegean seas in the south.

Thanks to the islands, Greece has the longest coastline in Europe and the scenery seems to constantly unfold and change around each headland. It also has the best beaches in Europe – safe, pleasing to the eye and more numerous that those in all the other Mediterranean countries put together. So you can always find a beach to yourself.

The Greek Islands

Greek islands are pure magic. They have an air of warmth, continuity and great age. And they give an immediate sense of belonging and having a stake in all you survey.

Each one is unique. If you ever find an island that reminds you of another, they are sure to be at opposite ends of the Aegean or Adriatic. The next one across the water always offers a complete contrast to the one you are on.

Last, but not least, Greece is cheap. Despite an inflation rate that always seems to be running over 20 per cent, you get a lot of drachmas for your money and they stretch a long way.

You can find a modest double room for £10 a night, an apartment for £12 to £20 and buy a splendid dinner for two for £12 to £15, including drinks. A bottle of beer costs around £1, a coffee 30p to 60p and a bottle of wine in a restaurant runs from £1 to £6.

Such prices more than make up for the irritating return of an airport departure tax of around £14 since November 1992 which has sometimes caused unnecessary queues and resentment in already-congested Greek airports during the summer months.

Weather in a land of all seasons

If you are planning a trip to Greece in

8

July or August, especially late July or early August, take plenty of sun cream, a tube of insect repellant and a hat. This is high season, and it can be hot.

The heat beckons alluringly to refugees from an English summer, but it is too easy to forget that most of Greece is on a level with North Africa. So, don't throw yourself upon Apollo's altar as a burnt sacrifice, especially if the meltemmi is blowing hard and disguising the full blast of the furnace.

The temperature is probably around 92 degrees in the sheltered shade. You can feel it well enough later that night when you lie turning on the spit in bed.

The best months of the year, to combine heat and perfect weather with a civilised choice of accommodation and more of the true Greek atmosphere are June and September. June is less crowded and the countryside is a blaze of flowers, but the sea is warmer in September. June has the first flush of hot weather fruit – strawberries, peaches and apricots. September has the grape season, figs and succulent melons.

May and October come close on all these counts, especially late May and early October. The weather is usually warm, particularly in the south Aegean; everywhere is less crowded; prices tend to fall or be negotiable. May has an abundance of flowers and the feel of a hot English summer. The sea stays warm through October.

November, December, March and April are ideal for people who want to flee the crowds, but still see the sites. The weather resembles a good English spring and March–April offer the added bonus of the Greek Easter festivals with flowers everywhere.

2. Personal Recommendations

Families — Corfu, Zakynthos, Rhodes, Kos, Paros, Crete, Skiathos, Siros, Halkidiki

Golfers — Corfu, Rhodes, Skiathos, Halkidiki

Tennis-players — Corfu, Kefalonia, Rhodes, Crete, Halkidiki

Windsurfers — Corfu, Rhodes, Kos, Paros, Crete, Mykonos, Skiathos, Thassos, Evia, Lefkas

Motorists — Corfu, Kefalonia, Rhodes, Crete, Evia, Kos, Peloponnese, Pelion, Lesvos, Halkidiki, Chios

Motor cyclists — Corfu, Kefalonia, Kos, Paros, Santorini, Samos, Thassos, Milos, Samos, Zakynthos

Cyclists — Zakynthos, Kos, Paros, Samos, Thassos, Milos, Andros

Walkers — Crete, Skiathos, Samos, Tilos, Serifos, Amorgos, Kithnos, Folegandros, Patmos, Nissiros, Skopelos, Ithaca, Kythera

Campers — Corfu, Rhodes, Kos, Crete, Paros, Thassos, Halkidiki

Back-packers — Corfu, Rhodes, Crete, Paros, Thassos, Evia

Naturalists — Corfu, Kefalonia, Zakynthos, Rhodes, Santorini, Crete, Nissiros, Milos, Pelion

Painters — Corfu, Zakynthos, Rhodes, Mykonos, Paros, Santorini

Wine Buffs — Kefalonia, Zakynthos, Rhodes, Kos, Santorini, Paros, Samos, Serifos, Halkidiki

Culture Vultures (Classical) — Rhodes, Kos, Crete, Santorini, Samos, Delos, Peloponnese, Athens, Delphi, Thessalonika, Macedonia

Culture Vultures (Byzantine) — Rhodes, Kos, Crete, Amorgos, Patmos, Meteora, Mount Athos, Peloponnese

Students — Corfu, Rhodes, Crete, Thassos, Peloponnese

Teeny-Boppers — Corfu, Kos, Paros, Thassos, Ios, Spetsai

Ravers — Corfu, Kos, Mykonos, Ios, Paros, Crete, Thassos, Spetsai, Rhodes

Nudists — Corfu, Rhodes, Mykonos, Crete, Skiathos, Thassos

Hermits — Crete, Anafi, Kastelorizo, Mount Athos

Gays — Mykonos, Hydra

Beach Bums — Corfu, Zakynthos, Rhodes, Kos, Crete, Paros, Naxos, Mykonos, Skiathos, Thassos

Trend-setters — Zakynthos, Simi, Skiathos, Samos, Thassos, Lesvos, Lefkas

Plutocrats — Corfu, Zakynthos, Rhodes, Mykonos, Santorini, Skiathos, Halkidiki

Honeymooners — Corfu, Zakynthos, Rhodes, Skiathos, Samos, Kefalonia, Halkidiki

Island-hoppers — Corfu, Kefalonia, Paros, Mykonos, Kos, Skiathos

Seasoned travellers — Samos, Lesvos, Santorini, Kefalonia, Zakynthos, Chios

Solitaries — Halki, Lipsi, Folegandros, Mount Athos, Elafonissos, Amouliani, Agios Efstratios

Gourmets — Corfu, Rhodes, Paros, Peloponnese, Pelion, Tilos, Naxos, Evia, Halkidiki

The rest of us — Zakynthos, Paros, Rhodes, Samos, Thassos, Evia, Pelion, Tilos, Milos, Folegandros, Chios, Halkidiki, Meganisi

3. Webster's Rating Tables

Which Island Guide

Odysseus, Jason, Theseus and the other heroes had the right idea. They sailed their ships over wine-dark seas, spurning the elements and inertia of their countrymen, to visit the beautiful islands of the Ionian and Aegean seas. Each had a quest and each was seeking his own idea of paradise and perfection.

Modern travellers to Greece can follow in the wake of the heroes and seek out the perfect Greek island. Probably they will never find it, but they will always find something special on the way.

By using the Which Island Guide you can pick out at a glance the right island for your Greek holiday this year. The 80 islands listed have been put into four groups:

Tourist Isles
Lesser Tourist Isles
Quiet Isles
Remote Isles

They all have star ratings for scenery, eating out and sites. All these plus Trevor Webster's personal rating for their beaches and overall appeal as a perfect Greek island.

Islands with Webster rating of 9 marks
Agios Efstratios
Amouliani
Folegandros
Inoussa
Milos
Paros
Patmos
Rhodes
Serifos
Tilos
Fourni
Elafonissos
Chios
Thassos

Mainland areas with 9 marks
Pelion
Halkidiki
Peloponnese

KEY

Scenery
★★★★ spectacular
★★★ special
★★ pretty
★ average

Eating out
★★★★ excellent variety of food and choice of restaurants
★★★ above-average food
★★ average

★ limited choice and/or few restaurants
O none, or extremely little food available

Sites
★★★★ spectacular
★★★ several interesting sites to see
★★ one or two sites
★ limited
O no sites at all, or none that are worth visiting

Which island guide
TOURIST ISLES

Webster rating
(max 10 marks)

	SCENERY	EATING OUT	SITES	SAND BEACHES	PEBBLE BEACHES	OVERALL ISLAND APPEAL
Aegina	★★	★★★	★	4	5	6
Corfu	★★★★	★★★★	★★	9	8	8
Crete	★★★	★★★	★★★	6	8	8
Cephalonia	★★★	★★	★	3	4	8
Delos	★★★	★★	★★★★	0	0	8
Hydra	★★★	★★★	○	0	4	6
Ios	★★★	★★	○	5	1	5
Kos	★★★	★★★	★★★	6	6	7
Mykonos	★★★	★★★★	○	9	2	8
Naxos	★★★	★★★	★	7	5	8
Paros	★★★	★★★★	★	9	2	9
Poros	★★	★★	★	1	2	4
Rhodes	★★★	★★★★	★★★★	9	8	9
Samos	★★★	★★★	★★	6	6	8
Santorini	★★★★	★★★	★★★★	5	4	8
Sifnos	★★★	★★	★★	5	2	6
Skiathos	★★★	★★★★	★	9	6	8
Spetse	★★	★★★	○	4	5	7
Thassos	★★★	★★★	★★★	8	7	9
Zakynthos	★★★	★★★★	★	7	2	8

Which island guide LESER TOURIST ISLES				Webster rating (max 10 marks)		
LESSER TOURIST ISLES	SCENERY	EATING OUT	SITES	SAND BEACHES	PEBBLE BEACHES	OVERALL ISLAND APPEAL
Alonissos	★★	★	○	1	6	4
Andros	★★	★★★	○	6	2	7
Antiparos	★★★	★★★	★	8	2	8
Chios	★★★	★★	★★★	6	5	9
Evia	★★★	★★★	★	7	6	8
Ithaca	★★	★★	★	3	4	6
Kalymnos	★★	★	○	4	2	5
Karpathos	★★★	★★	○	6	5	7
Kea	★★	★★	○	3	2	6
Lefkas	★★★	★★	○	4	5	7
Lemnos	★★	★★★	○	4	2	6
Lesvos	★★★	★★	★	4	5	8
Milos	★★	★★	★	8	4	9
Patmos	★★★	★★★	★★★	6	6	9
Paxos	★★	★★	○	2	4	6
Salamis	★	★	○	2	2	2
Siros	★★	★★★	○	6	2	7
Skopelos	★★	★★	○	2	5	6
Skyros	★★★	★★	★	6	2	6
Tinos	★★	★	★	3	2	5

Webster rating
(max 10 marks)

	SCENERY	EATING OUT	SITES	SAND BEACHES	PEBBLE BEACHES	OVERALL ISLAND APPEAL
Amorgos	★★★★	★★	★	5	4	8
Anafi	★★	★	○	2	2	4
Angistri	★★	★★	○	5	2	6
Astipalea	★★	★	○	4	2	7
Folegandros	★★★	★★★	○	6	4	9
Halki	★★	★★	○	4	2	6
Ikaria	★★	★	○	5	5	7
Kassos	★★	★★	○	1	5	5
Kimolos	★★	★★	○	8	2	8
Kithnos	★★★	★★	○	6	2	8
Kythera	★★★	★★	★	5	2	6
Leros	★★	★	○	1	5	4
Lipsi	★	★	○	2	2	8
Moni	★★	★★	○	2	2	6
Nissiros	★★★	★★	★★	2	4	7
Samothraki	★★	★	★	3	2	6
Serifos	★★★	★★	★	8	2	9
Sikinos	★★	★	○	2	2	4
Simi	★★	★★	★	1	3	5
Tilos	★★	★★	★	6	6	9

Which island guide
REMOTE ISLES

Webster rating
(max 10 marks)

	SCENERY	EATING OUT	SITES	SAND BEACHES	PEBBLE BEACHES	OVERALL ISLAND APPEAL
Agathonissi	★	★	○	2	2	4
Amouliani	★★	★★	○	3	2	9
Antikythera	★	★	○	2	2	2
Antipaxos	★	★	○	3	2	7
Agios Efstratios	★★	★★	○	6	2	9
Donoussa	★	★	○	4	2	6
Elafonissos	★	★★	○	7	2	9
Erikoussa	★★	★★	○	4	3	7
Fourni	★★	★★	○	5	2	9
Inoussa	★★	★★	○	6	2	9
Iraklia	★	★	○	2	2	4
Kastelorizo	★★	★	○	3	2	4
Keros	★	★	○	2	2	4
Koufonissi	★	★	○	2	2	6
Meganisi	★★	★	○	4	5	7
Poliegos	★	★	○	3	2	6
Psara	★	★★	○	2	2	6
Pserimos	★	★	○	3	2	6
Schinoussa	★	★	○	2	2	4
Telendos	★★	★	○	3	2	7
Yiali	★	★	○	6	2	7

Webster's Rating Tables — The Mainland

	BEACHES	SITES	SCENERY	EATING	Webster Rating (out of 10)
Athens		★★★	★	★★★	7
Piraeus				★	2
Attica	★	★	★★	★★	5
Delphi		★★★★	★★★★	★★★	8
Pelion	★★★		★★★★	★★★★	9
Meteora		★★★	★★★	★★	8
Peloponnese	★★★	★★★★	★★★	★★★	9
Halkidiki	★★★★	★★★★	★★★	★★★	9
Parga	★★★		★★	★★★	6
Epirus	★★★	★★	★★	★★★	7
Macedonia	★★★	★★★★	★★★	★★★	7

4. Which Site Guide

Greece is the striking point of the anvil of the ancient civilisation that stretched from Egypt to Mesopotamia. It has been at the cross roads of history ever since, and is endowed with historic and religious remains of a variety and quality given to few countries.

If Herodotus were alive today, he would be hard pushed to select only seven surviving Wonders of the Ancient World in Greece. Take Delos, Santorini, Mycenae, Delphi, Olympia, the Athenian acropolis, the Lindos acropolis, the Asclepion on Kos, Knossos, the amphitheatres of Epidavros and Dodoni, and the aquaduct and temple of Hera on Samos. They're a dozen to start with. And these are well matched by a collection of spectacular medieval or Byzantine sites in Mount Athos, Meteora, Patmos, Monemvasia, the turreted villages of the Mani, Mystras, the old towns of Rhodes and Kos, Naufplion, Dafni, Ossios Loukas and the Khozoviotissa monastery on Amorgos.

Most of the best sites are on the mainland or Peloponnese. True also of two of Greece's outstanding museums – those of Athens and Thessalonika.

The temples in Athens are well preserved despite the ravages of the Turks, who used the Parthenon successively as a brothel and gunpowder magazine during their occupation, and the British archaeologists like Elgin, who took the best bits of sculpture for the British Museum. But the Athenian acropolis and the surrounding Theseion, Forum, Temple of Zeus and Hadrian's gate lack something in atmosphere, surrounded as they are by the dust and heat of a busy city and the constant blaring of horns and squeal of tyres.

Thessalonika suffers the same fate. Its ancient city walls, the Arch of Galerius, his tomb and the old city baths are fringed by building sites and busy roads.

Most of the sites of old battles and scenes from mythology like Marathon, Thermopylae, Salamis, Mounts Olympus and Ida have nothing left to show for their place in history other than atmosphere.

If you have a keen taste for history, the best place to savour the ancient world is the Peloponnese, which boasts the citadel and beehive tombs of Mycenae, the amphitheatre of Epidavros, Olympia, Nestor's palace at Pylos, Tiryns, and the old cities of Argos, Corinth and Sparta. Climb the citadel of Mycenae at first light when there are no other tourists around and take a long look down the Argive plain towards Naufplion, where Agamemnon must have landed on his return from Troy. The Peloponnese gives easy access across the Gulf of Corinth to Delphi, scene of many similar crucial events. There are the smouldering ruins of the Mani, the Byzantine city of Mystras, the old

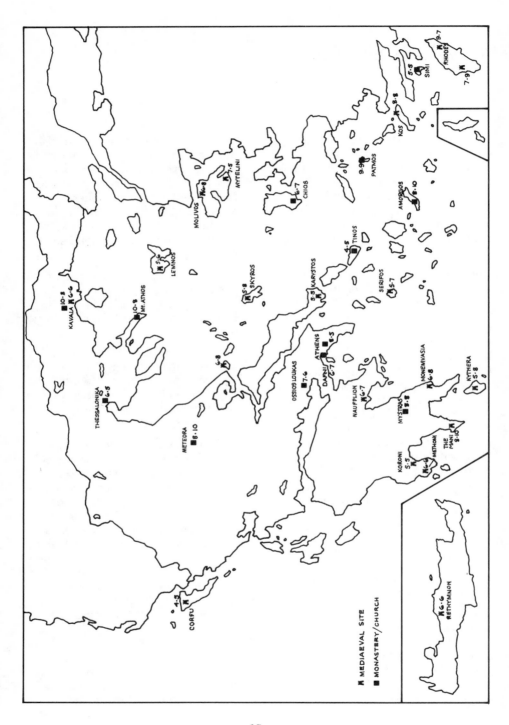

MEDIAEVAL SITE

MONASTERY/CHURCH

RHODES 9.7
SIMI 5.5
7.9

KOS 5.8 9.8
PATMOS 9.9
AMORGOS 8.10

MYTELLINI 7.5
MOLIVOS 9.8
CHIOS 6.7

TINOS 4.5
KARYSTOS 8.9
SERIFOS 5.7
SKYROS 5.8
LEMNOS 5.8

Mt. ATHOS 10.8
KAVALA 10.8 6.6

ATHENS 6.5
DAPHNI 6.7
OSSIOS LOUKAS 7.6
NAUFPLION 6.7
MONEMVASIA 9.8
KYTHERA 5.8

THESSALONIKA 6.5

METEORA 8.10

MYSTRAS 9.8
KORONI 5.5
METHONI 6.6
THE MANI 9.10

6.8

RETHYMNON 6.6

CORFU 4.5

town of Monemvasia and the castles of Methoni, Argos, Naufplion and Mystras.

Northern Greece is the nearest rival to the Peloponnese. It boasts Philippi – scene of a battle which decided the fate of the Roman Empire when Anthony defeated Caesar's murderers. Pella was the birthplace of Alexander the Great, and Vergina is believed to be the last resting place of Philip of Macedonia. Both are within easy reach of Thessalonika. If these sites are a trifle disappointing beside their Peloponnese rivals, the same cannot be said about the monasteries of Meteora and Mount Athos, which stand comparison with anything of their kind in the world.

You can take to Homer's wine dark sea and sail in the wake of the heroes on a cruise around the Greek islands, taking in both sites and beaches on the way. Almost every island has some remains from the distant past.

Follow wily Odysseus on his way around the Ionian Isles. Set off from Corfu where he was washed ashore on the long voyage from Troy. Wander down to his home island of Ithaca, which has a few relics of prehistory that may or may not belong to the hero, and call on the way at Cephalonia, whose cave is the nearest thing to the Styx I have seen. It is not a great archaeological tour, but good for conjuring up the past.

Or take the route of Jason and the Argonauts across the north Aegean to Lemnos, Thassos, Samothraki, Chios and Lesbos, bearing in mind that if you want to press on to the golden fleece country, you may have to enter Turkey via Chios or Samos. Thassos and Samothraki have their share of ancient temples and Chios, Lemnos

and Lesbos all have well preserved castles.

Theseus spent most of his time in Athens, but he also spent time on Naxos, Skyros and Crete, if the legends are to be believed. Naxos has ancient statues carved from the rock, Skyros the ruins of a castle and monastery, and you can now visit the labyrinth of Knossos on Crete without getting lost or tangling with the minotaur. It is also possible to call on the way at Santorini (where the famous eruption ended the Minoan rule) and see more local classical sites, plus the emerging Minoan city of Akrotiri.

The Greek heroes who sailed to besiege Troy also sailed across the North Aegean from Aulis around Evia and via Lesbos to the mainland. Again there are some interesting sites to see on the way, though you have to take one of the authorised trips to Turkey to see the site of the seven cities.

You could see more, though, by plotting your own archaeological journey across the central Aegean via Mykonos, Amorgos, Samos and Patmos to Kos and Rhodes. Delos is a satellite isle of Mykonos, and it and the other five islands share between them the most impressive sites in the Aegean – ancient and mediaeval. Rhodes has the acropolis of Lindos as well as three early Greek towns, while Patmos boasts the most splendid monastery on the islands.

One Greek hero, Perseus, had a novel way of travelling in those days. Instead of putting up with the rigours of sea travel, he strapped on a pair of golden sandals and flew to other islands from his home in Serifos. Icarus tried the same trick with wax wings, but came to grief when he flew too near the sun and was deposited in a pool of wax on

Ikaria. Those who find sea travel a problem can perform this ancient trick with a flight schedule from Olympic Airways as most of the big archaeological sites are linked to Athens by air.

SITES TO BUILD A JOURNEY ON

Webster rating (max 10 marks)

	BUILDINGS	SETTING
CLASSICAL		
Athens and the mainland		
Athens:		
Acropolis	9	8
Theseion	9	6
Temple of Zeus	6	5
Aeropagus/Pynx	3	6
Sounion	6	8
Thessalonika:		
Tomb and Arch of Galerius	6	5
Roman walls, baths and market	6	5
Delphi	8	9
Philippi	4	6
Vergina	7	6
Pella	7	5
Dodoni	9	9
Lefkadia	4	3
Olynthos	2	5
Peloponnese		
Corinth	7	6
Mycenae	6	9
Epidavros	8	5
Pylos	4	6
Vassae	8	7
Olympia	8	7
Ithomi	8	7
Tiryns	5	5
Argos	4	4
Evia		
Eretria	5	5
Cyclades		
Delos	8	10
Milos: catacombs	8	8
Naxos: Apollonia	5	5
Santorini:		
Akrotiri	9	5
Ancient Thira	6	5
North-east Aegean		
Samos	5	5
Samothraki	6	7
Thassos	8	8
Crete		
Knossos	7	5
Mallia	5	6
Phaistos	5	6
Zakros	7	7
Gournia	5	6
Itanos	4	7
Rhodes		
Lindos	9	10
Kamiros	7	8
Ialissos	5	7
Ancient Rhodes	4	5
Dodecanese		
Kos: Asclepion	7	7
Old Town	5	6
Saronic islands		
Aegina	7	7
Poros	5	5
Ionian islands		
Ithaca	4	6
MEDIEVAL		
Athens and the mainland		
Athens: churches	8	5
Dafni	6	7
Meteora	8	10
Mount Athos	10	9
Ossios Loukas	7	8
Thessalonika: churches	6	5
Kavala	6	6
Peloponnese		
Mystras	9	10
Monemvasia	6	9

Argos	5	6
Naufplion	6	7
The Mani	8	10
Methoni	8	7
Koroni	5	5
Evia		
Karystos	5	5
Dodecanese		
Patmos	9	9
Kos	8	8
Simi	5	5
Tilos	7	8
Rhodes		
Castle and old town	9	9
West coast castles	7	9
Crete		
Rethymnon	6	6
Frankocastello	9	9
Toplou	6	7
Kritsa	8	7
Cyclades		
Amorgos	8	10
Serifos	5	7
Tinos	4	5

Sporades		
Skiathos	6	8
Skyros	5	8
North-east Aegean		
Lemnos	5	6
Lesbos:		
Molivos	6	8
Mytileni	7	5
Chios	8	8
Ionian		
Corfu	4	5
Kythera	5	8

NATURAL WONDERS

Peloponnese	
Mani caves	7
Cyclades	
Santorini: volcano	10
Antiparos: cave	6
Ionian	
Cephalonia: caves	8
Dodecanese	
Nissiros: volcano	10

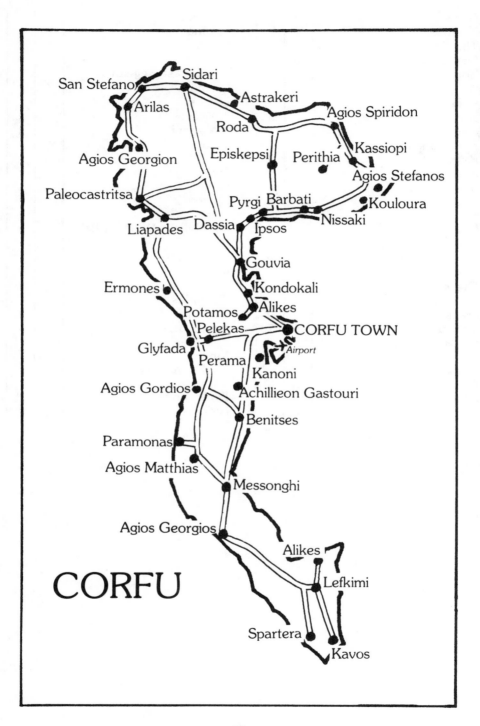

CORFU

5. The Big Three – Corfu, Crete and Rhodes

The Olive Isle – Corfu

Corfu or Kerkira is not only one of the most beautiful islands in Greece, it is one of the most beautiful in the world, ranking with the best of the Caribbean and the South Seas and outshining most of the other jewels of the Mediterranean.

It is a rich tapestry of green mountains, wooded hillsides, white villages and sandy beaches interwoven with the reds, yellows and blues of wild flowers and blossoms, and framed in the blue of the Ionian Sea. A Garden of Eden in modern Greece.

Corfu is an olive isle. Its dominant colour is olive green in light and dark shades, which are worn by herbs, shrubs and cypress trees after a winter's rain and a summer's sun. It is the greenest island in Greece.

Then there are the olives themselves. Every Greek island has olive trees, but none so many as Corfu. The Venetians, who occupied the island for four centuries, planted over a million of them and they have multiplied like the tribes of Israel.

You can see them everywhere on the island today, lining the roads and hillsides in serried groves. Whole families of gnarled and wizened old grandfather and grandmother trees surrounded by the mature fantastic shapes of their sons and daughters and their young straight thrusting offspring. At the last count there were over 4 million on the island.

Corfu is one of the most northern isles in Greece and also the most westerly, apart from three of its own small satellite isles, which helps to explain its lush fertility, and its cosmopolitan nature.

Thanks to the frequent showers of rain in the winter months it escapes the extremes of heat and dryness that burn many Greek islands bare and brown. It has always enjoyed an enormous number of visitors from Western Europe, who have found it easily accessible thanks to its position at the base of the Adriatic, directly across the Ionian Sea from the heel of Italy and Sicily, which was a vibrant part of the Greek world in ancient times.

Most visitors have come as conquerors – the Corinthians, the Romans, the Sicilians, the Venetians, the French, the Italians, the Germans and even the British, who were the only occupying power to quit voluntarily. Yet all of these races find a warm welcome on the island today, in the best traditions of the ancient people who welcomed Odysseus when he was washed ashore on his long voyage from Troy 32 centuries ago.

Corfu is the most popular holiday island in Greece, taking no less than a quarter of British package tourists. But it is big enough to absorb tourists without losing its true nature. And it has something for everyone.

Its most popular east coast resorts like

Benitses, Ipsos, Gouvia, Dassia, Kanoni, Perama, Kavos, Messonghi, Moraitika and Kontokali have been transformed in recent years by the development of villas, hotels, restaurants and discotheques to match the swelling crowds of summer tourists. Kassiopi, Rhoda and Sidari on the north coast and Paleocastritsa on the west coast are also fast-developing into multi-purpose tourist meccas.

If you want all the modern delights of a package holiday in the Med like wind-surfing, water-skiing, beach beds, a range of shops, restaurants serving English dishes, bars with cocktails and music, and a choice of discotheques, these are the places to aim for.

If you are yearning for peace and quiet, uncrowded beaches, and a refuge from motor-boats and piped music, try west coast resorts like Arillas, Agios Stefanos, Agios Georgiou (in the north and often called Agios Gorgeous), Glyfada, Agios Gordis, Agios Georgios (in the south) and San Barbara.

Often you can find a stretch of beach to yourself alongside or close to a resort with all the trimmings. Kavos has been expanding like crazy in recent years and now has 80 bars, most of them with music, but it also has two miles of sandy beach and you can quickly walk to an uncrowded seashore or unspoiled countryside.

It is always possible to get away from it all on Corfu. The interior of the island remains proud and unspoiled. The villages have barely been touched by tourism and the local people are friendly. And you can always find a healthy strip of beach to yourself somewhere on the island. Often a whole beach out of season.

Visit in May or October, when the weather is hot and sunny by the standards of English summers, and you may wonder that the island ever gets crowded. Wild flowers and magnificent sunsets are more noticeable than busy beaches or discotheques.

Corfu has a character and a culture that differs from all other Greek islands and has a curious British flavour that has not stemmed from the tourist flood of the past twenty years.

You can buy ginger beer along with Greek lemonade and resinated wine from the cafés flanking the main square in Corfu town and occasionally watch an afternoon cricket match where loud cheers are reserved for any batsman hitting a six into the crowded tables clustered beneath the arches of the town's fashionable Liston arcade. But by 8 p.m. in the evening the same square will be thronged with courting couples and Greek families with babies in prams indulging in the traditional Greek volta – an evening out walking the town.

Many Corfiots speak good English, especially in the town and the popular tourist resorts, and every schoolchild seems to learn 'Hello' and 'Goodbye' as soon as they have learned to walk. Two bars around the harbour area are called Dirty Dick's and the Spoty Dog. But if you mingle with local men in cafés where they sit sipping coffee and playing backgammon, you will hear animated conversation in Greek, which is often concerned with weather, fishing or local politics.

You will soon notice that half the men on the island are called Spiro after the island's patron saint, Saint Spiridon, who is paraded around the island four times a year on feast days and can also be viewed in his coffin in the church of the same name that towers over Corfu town.

Apart from the brief occupation in the 19th century, Corfu has many connections with Britain. it is renowned as the birthplace of the Duke of Edinburgh and was for years a favourite haunt of the Durrell family, which writers Lawrence and Gerald have celebrated in several books.

It is sometimes said that the island is 'not really Greek', usually by people who haven't visited much of the country, and it may have something to do with Corfu's lush green garb, which makes it look more like Capri or Majorca than the bare, burned Aegean islands. It looks as though it is rained on every other day. In fact, it rarely rains during the peak holiday months from May to October.

Corfu has the ambition to stay top of the pops on the British holiday market and will do so, thanks to its pleasant climate, beautiful landscape, friendly people and cheap prices stemming from a continuous devaluation of the Greek drachma in recent years.

The island has miraculously avoided the overdevelopment and the high-rise ghettos that scar slabs of the Spanish coastline and Sicily. You have only to walk 100 yards inland from any of the coast resorts to see a black-clad granny riding a donkey laden with firewood crossing herself as she passes a wayside shrine. You can walk along any harbourside and see fishermen drying their nets or beating a squid on the rocks to tenderise it for cooking. The old lives on alongside the new.

Long and narrow for most of its length with a wider head in the north, Corfu looks like a giant seahorse from the air. For a third of its length, the island faces Albania, and the gap between the two narrows to about 1½ miles in the north. The high shore in the north-east affords visitors a glimpse of that mysterious remote country, which is still living in the 1940's even though the Chinese and the Russians have long since let Capitalism rush into their countries.

From Corfu, it looks as though there is nobody stirring in Albania, but yachtsmen, fishermen and windsurfers can now stray across the channel into Albanian waters and there will soon be day excursions over there. Corfiots living in the north of the island sometimes tune in to TV programmes from Albania and also Yugoslavia and Italy, complaining that reception from mother Greece is difficult.

Ease of access from Western Europe, along with its natural beauty and friendliness, earns Corfu around 500,000 visitors a year, far more than any other Greek island, and two-thirds of them come from Britain. Tourism is rising at a rate of around 15 per cent a year and 100,000 people are now passing through Corfu Airport in a peak month like July. So it is hardly surprising that there are pressure points.

Although the British built some good roads by Greek island standards in the 19th century, some have too many potholes and narrow corners for today's tourist traffic. The airport terminal, at the head of Kanoni lagoon airstrip, which seemed such a dramatic improvement when it replaced a tiny shed in the 1970's, now bulges at the seams when two or three planes are landing or taking off around the same time.

However, there are plans to double

You can swim almost anywhere around the coast of Corfu, so you will never be far from a beach. But the beaches along the calmer east coast facing the mainland, which is popular with British holidaymakers, tend to be white shingle and pebble, with the odd strip of sand, while those along the surfy west coast facing the Ionian Sea are all of the yellow sand variety that dreams are made of. So are those on the north coast.

One guide to the island says that there are 6½ outstanding beaches on Corfu, but if you spend long enough there, you will be able to count up to ten times that number, and still have the three northern satellite islands of Mathraki, Othoni and Erikoussa to spare. The beaches are mostly easy to get to too, thanks to coastal roads running along the north and east coasts of the island and good signposting along the wilder west coast.

Corfu town has no beach worthy of the name and you swim at your peril off the long promenade around Garitsa Bay, which receives the effluent from some of the town's big hotels. It's safer to walk to Mon Repos beach at the southern end of town or to one of the strips just off Kanoni, close to the airport, but better still to travel 10–20 kilometres north or south of the town if you want to swim on the east coast.

South of the town lies the villa coast of Perama and Benitses, where there are dozens of small swimmable shingley coves – and a number of big hotels have sprung up. To the north lie the major resorts of Kontokali, Dassia,

Gouvia and Ipsos, boasting long beaches where pebble gives way to sand and you can find every kind of beach sport from windsurfing to paragliding. Nissaki also has the beach sports, but is more pebbly.

Gouvia's beach is almost always calm, whatever the weather, because it is sheltered by a big and almost enclosed bay. It is an unusual limpid scene with an old church on a sandpit contrasting strangely with all the water sports available on the beach.

If you go further north, to the coast that juts out towards Albania, as if it is trying to touch it, you are in Durrell country – the setting of Lawrence Durrell's 'Prospero's Cell' and Gerald Durrell's 'My Family and Other Animals'. There lie a succession of coves containing fishing hamlets and sheltered pebbly beaches under names like Koloura, Kalami, Kentrona and Agios Stefanos until you reach Kassiopi on the north-east tip, which has become a popular resort and gives the best view over to moody Albania. It has no great beaches, but there are pretty swimmable coves to rest off the revels of the night before, soak up the sun and cool off with the odd dip.

South of Benitses, there are more swimmable coves around Miramare, Moraitika and Messonghi, but the best beach on the whole east coast is the long stretch of sand at Kavos in the deep south. Kavos has grown into a major resort with hotels, restaurants and villas, and is visited by boats from higher up the coast, attracted by its long sandy beach, which stretches away towards the southern tip.

There is no need to travel so far, though, if you are staying in Corfu town or one of the east coast resorts close to it. The west coast abounds in beautiful strands and four of the most famous, Glyfada, Agios Gordis, Ermones and Myrtiotissa, are all within easy reach of the town.

In fact, Glyfada and Agois Gordis are growing into sizeable resorts on their own account, thanks to good roads, a string of restaurants and villas and a handful of big hotels that have opened in the past ten years, Glyfada, only 17 kilometres from Corfu town via the colourful village of Pelekas, and Agios Gordis, a slightly longer drive through some stunning coastal scenery, are both good family resorts with shallow waters and deep sand, and can be crowded in high season, but both are surrounded by cliffs and steep wooded slopes that helps to give a feeling of isolation.

Ermones is not such an impressive beach as the others, but it is a famous one. It is believed to be the bay where a ship-wrecked Odysseus was washed up and discovered by Nausicaa and her handmaidens on his long voyage from Troy. It has another claim to fame nowadays because it is the nearest beach to Corfu's Golf Club, a miniature Garden of Eden stretching down the Ropa Valley.

If you rise early enough, you can do 18 holes before lunch and swim in the afternoon in a bay where history, or at least mythology, was made. Though many golfers buy a week's golfing package, including transport, from Glyfada and might prefer that beach for relaxed swimming off perfect sand rather than Ermones.

Myrtiotissa has a different claim to fame. It is a narrow beach beneath a tiny whitewashed monastery and steep cliffs with big rocks rising from the sand. Remoteness from the road and bus stop long since suggested it as a nudist beach. Scandalised local peasants have regularly complained to the police and fines have been levied, but in between times the police turn a blind eye and the nudity lives on.

If you want to go topless on the west coast of Corfu, there are plenty of suitable places. Like the vast sands of Agios Georgios, which stretches down the south-west from the Korission Lagoon and the sand dunes lying on the seaside of Korission. This area now boasts half a dozen simple restaurants. A bus stops near a signposted side-road and you can drive a car or scooter closer to the beach, but beware of getting stuck in the sand.

It is the biggest and best beach on the island. The stretch by the lagoon is backed by sand dunes and the rest by high cliffs. There are now four access roads and two emerging resorts at Agios Georgios and San Barbara (or Marathia Beach) with a sprinkling of rooms to stay in. Even in mid-summer you can escape other tourists on this long beach, but there are no trees to shade the hot sun.

It has not developed as quickly as a beach of the same name, Agios Georgios Bay in the north-west, a superb curve of fine sand. It has a string of restaurants and a tarmac road, but is still long enough to absorb crowds of day trippers coming around by boat from Palaeocastritsa and allow you many yards of beach to yourself.

There are many other shorter sand beaches in the west. Paliokastritsa, the biggest resort on this coast, has its own quota of sandy bays, though they do become crowded with residents of the resort's many hotels. You can find less crowded beaches at Paramonas, reached through the 'black forest' of Agios Mattheos, Kontogialos immediately south of Glyfada reached by a short walk downhill from the village of Pelekas, and at a handful of small fishing villages now opening up as resorts in the north-west, Afionas, Arillas and Agios Stefanos.

Arillas has the best beach, a long thin stretch of sand. It also has caique trips to the deserted islet of Diaplo and a half hour walk across the cliffs brings you another beach in the neighbouring, but quite different, little resort of Agios Stefanos.

Paramonas makes a great day out if you have a car or scooter. It has a restaurant, an inn with a few rooms and a lovely sandy beach, which never seems to get crowded.

The north coast has the traditional resort of Sidari, which has strange sandstone rocks rising out of the sea clustering around one with a hole in it called the 'Canal D'Amour'. It is a haunt for lovers where a wish can come true and visitors often wade through the canal in hope and good faith.

Roda, also on the north coast, has grown into a resort from the small fishing village that has always been there, thanks to its long sandy bay that also encompasses the village of Anharavi. It is ideal for families, because the sea is so shallow and calm.

A third sandy stretch can be found on the north coast at Agios Spiridon, a small village off the main coast road which has a chapel in honour of the island's patron saint and also has a good beach for children. It makes a pleasant walk from Kassiopi.

There are also good beaches on the three small islets an hour by boat from Sidari. Erikoussa has dazzling sand beaches on two of its three sides.

What the east coast lacks in sand, it makes up in an exotic underwater seascape for snorkelling and spear-fishing, but most of the sand beaches of the west and north coasts are framed in clusters of rocks, which offer exciting sea life. Most of the big resorts, like Ipsos, Dassia, Gouvia, Perama, Benitses, Kavos, Paleocastritsa, Agios Georgios and Roda offer windsurfing and water-skiing and some have scuba-diving. Dassia and Ipsos have paragliding.

You can play golf on some of the greenest greens in Europe at Corfu's 18-hole course in the Ropa Valley close to Glyfada and Ermones. You can also take lessons and hire all the gear.

Corfu town has a tennis club, but few courts.

The best place to find tennis courts are in big hotels like the Roda Beach, the Corcyra Beach, the Kerkira Golf – which is on the opposite side of the island from the golf course and only 2 miles north of Corfu town – the Park at Gouvia, the Chandris as Dassia, the Dassia Beach, the Messonghi Beach and the Regency at Benitses. Many of the big hotels also offer riding.

Nightlife

Nightlife is not so formal or organised in Greece as in Western Europe, but almost everyone from old men to courting couples and families with babies in prams get involved in it. Usually outdoors and in a theatrical way that shows off the extrovert side of the Greeks.

If you scratch a Greek, he will open a bar or a restaurant and there are thousands on Corfu. Most of them have dozens of tables pouring out on to a pavement, a square or a harbourside, and they surge to life by night as people gather to drink beer, ouzo or coffee, to share a groaning table covered with tiny dishes, or in the case of ladies on their own to feast on sticky cakes.

Those who can find tables in the most popular spots such as the main square in Corfu town or the harboursides of the coastal resorts are then treated to a display of walking known as the volta. There are no fixed rules and no age and time limits. People walk up and down for hours seeking gentle exercise, showing off their new clothes, and stopping for an occasional chat with friends or to take a drink at one of the cafés on the side.

Wining and dining out is so cheap and full of fun that nightlife for most tourists is an evening in an outdoor restaurant preceded or followed by drinks in a bar.

In high summer many of the outdoor restaurants on Corfu, especially in the coastal resorts, have music to dine by, traditional Greek tunes mingled with slightly tarnished juke box melodies, and it is not unusual to see local people or even waiters start an impromptu syrtaki or group dance, which can involve every diner in the restaurant in time.

If you fail to come across this scene by yourself and want an evening of Greek dancing, you should always be able to find a tour going off one evening from any of the big hotels to a taverna specialising in Greek dancing and dining for an all-in price.

One place where you are certain to find it is 'The Village' – a place you mustn't leave Corfu without visiting, according to hundreds of signs along the roads. For an entry fee, which might include a drink, you can look over a recreated Greek village with handicraft shops and tavernas. The tavernas offer local delicacies, wine and Greek dancing often for an all-in price. Although it seems odd to create an artificial village on an island teeming with pretty villages, a visit to The Village can make an enjoyable evening out.

If you are staying outside Corfu town, it also makes sense to go into town for a night and eat at one of the old-established restaurants around the square such as the Aegli or the Averof where they serve a mixture of Greek and Italian dishes and a few Corfiot specialities which are not found everywhere in Greece such as sofrito and gouvetsi.

The Old Fort in Corfu town has sound and light performances and there are a number of open-air cinemas, which offer a mixture of old Hollywood hits and obscure Italian westerns with Greek subtitles and Greek comedies with elusive slapstick humour.

The most formal nightlife in Corfu is at the Casino a few kilometres uphill from the airport near the village of Gastouri, which can be reached by local bus or taxi. James Bond tried his luck at the table in 'For Your Eyes Only' and so can you so long as you are properly dressed (gentlemen with jackets and ties) and can pay the price of the entry ticket and your stake money.

The casino is set in the Achilleion Palace, built in an unusual mixture of styles by the sad Empress Elizabeth of Austria, which is often described as ugly, but for my money is the most beautiful casino in Greece. It stands proud and tall in a superb setting of formal gardens, surrounded by cypress trees, high in the hills with magic views of Corfu town way below.

If you don't fancy your luck at the tables, stroll down to the semi-circular restaurant a hundred yards down the road to eat in a romantic setting and watch the twinkling lights of Corfu and ships crossing the Ionian sea.

Another magic place to eat at night for good food and one of the world's great views is at the Belvedere Restaurant halfway up the winding zig-zag road leading to the Troumpeta Pass. Again you can see the bright lights of Corfu town and the coast resorts winking far below.

Greek discotheques wax and wane with the seasons and more often than not are housed in rough outdoor premises which would be unsuitable for winter use. There are exceptions in Corfu town and around the hotels in the big coastal resorts. Benitses, Gouvia, Ipsos, Dassia, Messonghi and Kanoni are resorts that have discos which all swing to the early hours through summer. Gouvia even has an underground disco, which is a rarity in Greece.

Not to be missed on Corfu

Corfu town ranks with Rhodes as the two most stylish towns in Greece, and both owe a lot to the Italians. Corfu's tall buildings, narrow alleys and peeling grandeur are reminiscent of Venice without the canals. The two forts have Venetian origins, and the main square or Esplanade with its pigeons and house martins has connotations with St Mark's Square.

It is a delightful town to stroll round, soaking up atmosphere, especially the bustling port, the grand sweep of Garitsa Bay and the Explanade (or Spianada) with its Liston arcade – so called in the days of British occupation because only people on the list of top families were allowed there. Pause at the Church of Saint Spyridon and look at the gold and silver votive offerings to the island's patron, and also at the 12th century church of Saints Jason and Sosipater.

Otherwise, it is not a great town for sights, other than the town itself. They are of the 'worth doing on a dull day' category. The two fortresses, or their remains, call for imagination rather than great staying power but they do give panoramic views of the town. The Palace of Saint Michael and Saint George, which originally housed the British High Commissioner and later the Greek royal family, has a small museum housing, of all things, an Asian art collection.

There is an archaeological museum in the town along the promenade of Garitsa Bay, just down from the Tourist Office, which is modern and airy and has two big finds, a Gorgon pediment from a Temple of Artemis dating back to the fifth century BC and an ancient lion of the same era. But the museum does not stand comparison with its rivals in Athens, Thessalonika or Crete. There is also the town cathedral, Mitropolis, which houses the headless remains of Saint Theodora, who arrived on the island with Saint Spyridon. But the real delights of Corfu are outside the town, reached either by bus from the station next to the New Fortress, by hired car, bicycle or scooter.

Scooters and bicycles can be hired in numerous shops towards the seafront of the old town, as well as in many beach resorts, but it is worth making sure before you quit the town that scooters are powerful enough to carry two people uphill and then take real care on unmade roads. You see too many tourists on Corfu with bandages around bloody ankles and Greek medical treatment is not so good that it is worth risking a road accident.

Immediately south of Corfu town – and reachable by bicycle – lie the island's most famous sights. First, Mon Repos, the villa where Prince Philip was born, then Mouse Island and the Achilleion Palace.

Mouse Island, or Pontikonissi, with its 13th century chapel, and its twin islet of Vlacherna, lie in Kanoni Bay and are almost a trade-mark of Corfu, much photographed by visitors and much seen on postcards. This idyllic scene lies only a few yards from the lagoon runway of Corfu airport, so the scene is also a familiar one to travellers arriving and departing by jet from colder climes.

The Achilleion lies a few kilometres beyond that and is easily the grandest building on Corfu. Many art experts have described the palace and the statues in its gardens as ugly, grotesque or misconceived, but their setting amid green hills, trees and gardens makes them one of the most beautiful sights on this and any other Greek island. Ignore the experts and enjoy the palace, the gardens and the statue of the dying Achilles, wounded in his heel, but still holding his warrior's spear. Spare a thought for the sad Empress Elizabeth who built this grand place and was assassinated by a crazy fanatic in Geneva.

Below the palace on the coast lies the Kaiser's Bridge, the remains of an old harbour built by the second owner of the palace, and it is worth exploring beyond there to the southern tip of the island. The old fishing village of Benitses has been transformed into a swinging resort, but bears no resemblance whatever to Palma, Majorca, and the road down to Kavos at the southern tip of the island passes through some delightful countryside and inland villages. In the south, the Korission lagoon is worth visiting and Kavos is another fishing village that has been turned into a thriving resort, with regular boats from Corfu town, the mainland and the island of Paxos to the south of Corfu.

While in the south, linger a little in Lefkimmi. It is a big, honest town with graceful mansions and a canal-like river stretching down to the sea. Pretty cafés are now springing up along its banks. It is a painter's delight and a strange contrast with the fleshpots of Kavos a few miles down the coast.

The coast north of Corfu town is even more developed with beach resorts such as Kondokali, Gouvia, Dassia and Ipsos, but is also a delightful tour as far as Kassiopi, pausing to visit the bays of Koloura and Agios Stefanos where the Durrells lived and to take a close look at Albania. The best view is probably from Kassiopi, where visitors can also look over traces of a Hellenistic town visited by Nero and a Byzantine fortress.

The most spectacular roads for high exotic scenery and pretty villages are those to the beach resorts of the west coast. Pelekas, with the Kaiser's Seat, where he used to watch the sunset, is a short trip and a rewarding one, while Paleocastritsa with its hills, sandy bays and 13th century castle is a delightful excursion. For the best view of the resort and its six bays, ascend the road that winds up from Paleocastritsa towards Makrades.

Even more spectacular is the high road over the Troumpeta Pass to Sidari and Roda. Pause at the little café at the summit for a coffee and the view.

That journey is strictly for car, scooter or bus, but there are many invigorating walks inland to pretty hill villages from the coastal resorts. Energetic climbers can tackle Mount Pantocrator, and a good alternative for the not-quite-so-energetic is a walk uphill to an abandoned hill village on the north slope of Pantocrator called Perithia.

It is reached by road inland from Kassiopi and Loutses, which is tarmaced for most of its way. When the tarmac runs out you have a stiff uphill walk for two hours or a 15-minute drive for a glimpse of what village life on Corfu was like 200 or 300 years ago. Most of the inhabitants have moved down to the coast and the place is now inhabited by only two families, but they do serve drinks from a tiny bar, which are most welcome after the climb.

Perithia makes an odd contrast with Kassiopi a few miles away, where the tavernas rock nightly to loud canned music and visitors sunbathe topless in adjoining bays.

Worth visiting off Corfu

If you fancy spending two or three days on one of the other big Ionian islands, Kefalonia or Zakynthos, you can island-hop in a light plane, which makes the trip in an amazingly short time.

Although the northern part of Corfu faces Albania, and it is now possible to travel across the Straits to that mysterious country, there are plenty of fascinating places to visit from Corfu. You can go north by boat from Sidari or sometimes Kassiopi to the three tiny satellite isles of Othoni, Erikoussa and Mathraki, south from Corfu town to the island of Paxos or east from the port by ferry to the mainland of Western Greece at Igoumenitsa.

The three northern islands are about an hour away by boat and seem more remote. Othoni has a medieval castle and a bay called Calypso where it is thought Odysseus might have stayed with the nymph of the same name on the voyage from Troy. All three are cute little isles and undeveloped, though a small two-storey hotel has recently been built on Erikoussa and there are two tavernas, so it is a comfortable place to stay and enjoy the good sandy beaches, which are almost continuous stretches on two sides of the island and hardly crowded.

Paxos is a jewel of an island, a good deal smaller than Corfu, but much bigger than the three northern islands, which takes about three hours by ship from Corfu town, but about half the time by boat from Kavos on the southern tip of Corfu. Boats also ply between Kavos and Parga.

Parga is the main seaside resort of Western Greece. Set between the towering hills of Epirus, it has three fine sandy beaches on separate bays with tiny islands offshore, and resembles an island port more than a mainland resort. Tourism has brought windsurfing, discotheques and regular boat trips to Corfu and Paxos, but just outside the town you are in wild countryside.

Epirus is a land of mountains, lakes and rivers with giant tortoises, birds of prey, occasional snakes and storks, which live on the steeples of churches in every town. It also boasts good roads, so it makes a good day's outing from Corfu by ferry with hired car or scooter.

If you want to see something grander

CORFU
The most famous landmark
— Mouse Island.

CORFU

Lunch al fresco.

CORFU

Perama panorama.

CRETE

The 'bottomless' inner harbour of
Agios Nikolaos.

than the seaside resort of Parga, drive inland to Dodoni, site of the oldest oracle and the best amphitheatre in Greece. It is a magnificent green glade, surrounded by high mountains, and the nearby restaurant offers much better fare than is usually found in such places serving archaeological sites.

If you drive east 100 kilometres, you will reach the main city of Western Greece, Ioannina, which is a bustling place set off a lake with a big part in Greek history of the past few centuries. It was the seat of the Turkish Governor and the castle promontory of Ali Pasha still dominates the lake.

There is a restaurant on the island and dozens more along the shore of the lake, where they serve frogs' legs, trout and eels from the lake. Zitza wine makes a good complement to this unusual Greek freshwater fare.

Just south of Parga off the main road to Preveza lies another of the great sights of Epirus, the Necromanteion. The mythical entrance to the underworld, the site of the Oracle of the Dead and Persephone's Grove visited by Odysseus in the Odyssey, it now comprises a few ruined buildings and an underground chamber. It makes up in eerie atmosphere what it lacks in size, enough to inspire regular day trips from Parga and Paxos.

If you lack time or don't fancy hiring a car or scooter, it is still worth taking the ferry crossing from Corfu to the mainland port of Igoumenitsa for the day. Igoumenitsa is a major ferry link with both Italy and Corfu and as much a harbour as a town, but it has good honest eating at restaurants along the quay and a respectable beach curving around the bay.

If you are staying on Corfu for a fortnight and want to see more of the mainland and its sights, it is not difficult to drive or take a bus beyond Ioannina to the monastery wonderland of Meteora, to drive down to Delphi on the north coast of the Gulf of Corinth, or even to visit some of the sites of the Peloponnese.
But plan a two-day trip with overnight stay to make the journey comfortable.

Zorba's Isle – Crete

Crete is easily the biggest island in Greece and the second most popular destination for British holidaymakers after Corfu. They are attracted by its popular beach resorts, wild mountainous landscape, moody atmosphere, and Minoan past; a past like the Minotaur, which shares its name, that is part history and part myth.

The 'Big Island' gave birth to Europe's first known civilisation, ruling the Eastern Mediterranean from grand palaces at Knossos, Phaistos, Zakros and Malia with colourful frescoes, modern drainage and a mysterious bull and axe cult. But there is no historical evidence for the dreadful Minotaur, a half-man, half-bull monster which enjoyed an annual diet of young men and women from faraway colonies like Athens. Nor are there any traces of the legendary King Minos, who started the dynasty, beyond the name.

There are modern myths and half-truths about Crete too. It is often described as the most Greek of Greek islands, blessed with picturesque towns, surrounded by superb beaches and wild scenery.

It is no more Greek than Paros, Naxos or Santorini – or, for that matter, Corfu, which is sometimes said to be 'unGreek' – and in fact joined the nation later than all of them.

The island's capital, Heraklion, is the ugliest town in the Aegean, but Crete's three other main towns, Chania, Rethymnon and Agios Nikolaos, are stunning. Much of the coastline is rocky, so that you sometimes have to travel miles for a good beach, but there are many long sandy stretches on all four shores.

Crete has wild scenery, but it is not as wild as it sounds. It is heavily populated with big towns and high-rise hotels along the north coast and more intensively cultivated inland. Its fertile valleys and plains, fed by rivers that run down from Mount Ida, the White Mountains and Mount Dikti, supply 90% of the Greek currant crop, a quarter of its olive oil, an eighth of its wine and a big slice of its tobacco. It has acres of ugly plastic greenhouses on the west and south coasts.

What is beyond dispute is that Crete has a unique history and character. And it is so big that it offers a great variety of places and scenery.

It has a good network of modern roads along all four coasts, including a motorway along the well-developed and windy north coast, where the Cretan Sea crashes on yellow sand, and along the south coast where the Libyan Sea is calmer, the sand is sometimes grey and the climate is warmer the year round thanks to the balmy breezes that drift across from Africa. It is also criss-crossed from north to south by good link roads that run down mountain passes and steep narrow gorges where the sky and valleys are squeezed between high mountains and the villages are often prettier than on the coast.

These mountains and ravines have witnessed many battles, right up to the Second World War when Crete was the focus of the German invasion of Greece. Cretan mountain men and shepherds can look wild and woolly in their traditional dress with long leather boots, headbands, drooping moustaches and long curved knives stuck in baggy trousers. Village weddings can be colourful affairs with both men and women in national dress performing the cyclical syrtos and the romantic sousta with endless drinking to the music of the lyre, mandolin and bagpipes (or tsabouna).

Crete is the land of the lotus-eaters and Zorba the Greek. It was the setting for the TV series, 'Who pays the Ferryman?', which helped kindle interest in the island in Britain. It has given birth to many famous sons, including the statesman, Eleftherios Venezelos – who shares his Christian name ('Freedom') with many other Cretans – and El Greco the painter whose great colourful religious works grace many art galleries in Spain and a room or two in London's National Gallery.

More than any other Greek island, it seems self-sufficient and able to support itself without tourism. But tourist development is well-established in Eastern Crete along the 'Cretan Riviera' in the nomos (or district) of Heraklion and that of Lassithi or Agios Nikolaos, while it is catching up fast in Western Crete in the nomos of Chania and that of Rethymnon.

Visitors who want to get away from it all should head away from the four big towns, especially Heraklion – after seeing Knossos and its beautiful archaeological museum – and head either inland or for the west and south coasts. As a general rule, Western Crete is less touristy than Eastern Crete.

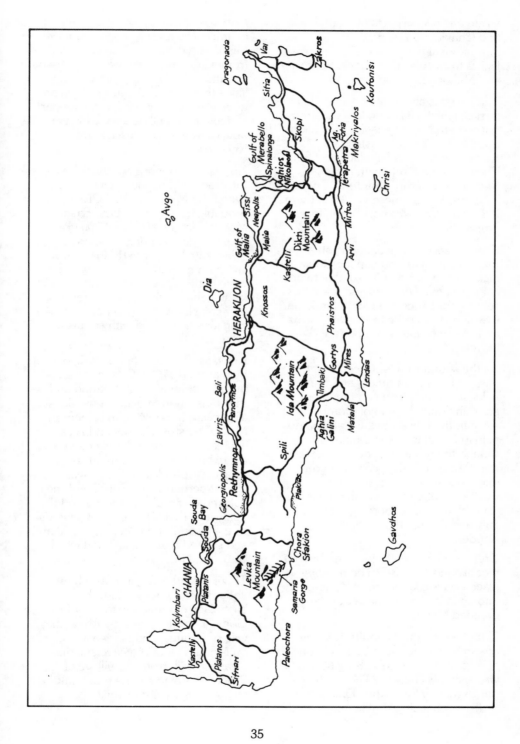

Crete has two airports at Heraklion and Chania, both served by international flights as well as internal flights from Athens, Rhodes, Santorini and Mykonos.

The island is also well-served by big ferries, which call at no less than five ports on the north coast – Heraklion, Souda (for Chania) Kastelli, Rethymnon, Agios Nikolaos and Sitia. They connect Crete with Piraeus, Rhodes, Karpathos, Santorini and the southern Peloponnese via Antikithera. It is also a frequent port of call for cruise ships.

Crete is easy to travel once you are there, so long as you can face long distances. It has a good road network linking all main centres and good bus services radiating out from Heraklion. Car hire is available in all main towns and so are scooters, mopeds and bicycles.

As the southernmost Greek island, it has the longest summers and the mildest winters. You can tan in hot sunshine until the end of October and swim in the Libyan Sea without undue pain in December and January, though the mountains attract more rain throughout the year than you might see on Rhodes, which is a fair way north of Crete, and the meltemmi wind blows harder across Crete in July and August than it does on Rhodes.

Crete is where mythology and history met around 1500 BC. The meeting place was the labyrinth of Knossos, known in legend as the lair of the dreaded Minotaur.

In mythology the Minotaur was the offspring of a bull sent by Poseidon and Pasifae, the wife of King Minos. It was slain by Theseus. The myth was put to rest by Sir Arthur Evans, the British archaeologist, who excavated Knossos around the turn of the century. His findings suggest that the Minoans did rule the known world from a labyrinthine palace at Knossos, and did exact tribute from colonies like Athens. Indeed young Athenians were trained as acrobats to take part in dangerous bull dances, which are now portrayed on frescoes at Knossos.

No island can more rightly claim to be the cradle of European civilisation. When the Minoans ruled Crete – and probably Santorini and the Eastern Mediterranean 3,000 to 4,000 years ago, they lived in richly-frescoed palaces with modern drainage and lavish entertainment. Their women wore make-up, jewellery and fashionable clothes, bared their breasts, plaited their hair and carried long jugs decorated with sophisticated patterns.

Knossos, the most famous Minoan site built around 1700 BC stands as a proud memorial to that period and that civilisation. It also shows signs, along with other Minoan palaces at Malia, Phaistos, Zakros and Agia Triada, of having suddenly been overwhelmed by a great natural disaster around 1500 BC. It was almost certainly the eruption of the volcano on nearby Santorini and the tidal wave that followed that gave rise to the legend of the lost city of Atlantis and started the Biblical flood which launched Noah's Ark.

There are other legends and myths about Crete. It was said to be the birthplace of Zeus, the father of the Gods, who was borne by Rhea, the wife of Cronus, and hidden in a cave on Mount Dikti. The cave still makes a pleasant walk from the village of Psychro, providing one more link between myth and history.

In the historic period that started around 1500 BC, Crete was invaded by the Myceneans, the Romans, the Venetians and the Turks. The Myceneans left linear B script, which was also found at Mycenae. The Romans left the remains of a handsome capital and a code of laws carved in stone, at Gortys south of Heraklion and a short way east of Phaistos. The Venetians left beautiful harbours at Chania, Heraklion and Rethymnon and promoted the Cretan School of Artists. The Turks built houses with wooden balconies around the harbours and left the memory of a bloody invasion from 1645 to 1669.

The Turks held Crete longer than most of their Aegean possessions and it only became part of Greece in 1913 after a long campaign by the island's best known statesman, Eleftherios Venezelos. Twenty-eight years later, in 1941, it was occupied again, this time by the Germans, when it became the focus of the Nazi invasion of Greece.

It was the site of the sea-borne Battle of Crete and a major retreat by British forces through the southern port of Chora Sfakion, which is marked by a memorial plaque on the harbour wall. It was also famous for the Cretan Resistance Movement, which was joined by a handful of British soldiers and stayed active in the mountains until the end of World War Two.

Eastern Crete

Eastern Crete contains the nomos (or district) of Heraklion, fanning out from the island capital of the same name, and that of Lassithi, which surrounds Agios Nikolaos, for years the main holiday centre of the island. The coast between the two towns is the main holiday coast of Crete and is often called the 'Cretan Riviera'.

It boasts a string of popular resorts like Agia Pelagia, Hersonisos, Sissi, Malia and Elounda opposite the islet of Spinalonga. They have all grown up over the past 20 years and now rival Agios Nikolaos for tourist developments, such as hotels, restaurants, discotheques and water sports. On this strip you get a fair quota of high-rise and crowds with your sandy beach.

East of Agios Nikolaos is a wilder region served by the Cretan ring road as far as Sitia, an honest but dull little town. The south coast, which is also served by the ring road, is a good deal quieter with Ierapetra and Matala its only major resorts.

The two nomoi also contain the six major Minoan sites on Crete – Knossos, Phaistos, Malia, Zakros, Gournia and Agia Triada, plus the fascinating Roman capital of Gortys and the pretty hill village of Kritsa. Which go a long way towards explaining why tourism flourished first at this end of the island.

They also abut Mount Dikti, with the cave where Zeus was reputedly born, and the Plain of Lassithi, famed for its thousands of tall windmills. Mount Ida forms a pivot for the whole of the island, dividing the nomos of Heraklion from that of Rethymnon and Eastern Crete from Western Crete.

Beaches on Eastern Crete

The most dazzling beaches in eastern Crete are between Vai and the south coast at Makriyalos, but there are several adequate stretches of sand on both sides of Heraklion and along the 'Cretan Riviera', which stretches east from the capital as far as Malia. There are windsurfers for hire and other watersports at all these resorts.

You can find a narrow sand beach around the long bay to the west of Heraklion and at Agia Pelagia on the next promontory. The only snags are the view of rusting ships and oil refineries around the bay and a slight feeling of claustrophobia at Agia Pelagia where a narrow strip of sand is sandwiched between a big package tour hotel complex and a series of bars and restaurants. East of Heraklion most people make for Amnissos just beyond the airport, which is a pay beach and tends to be crowded, but is good sand and is an easy bus ride from a stop by Heraklion harbour.

Like the Athenian Riviera, the Cretan Riviera becomes more scenic the further you travel along it. Another beach stretches from Chani Kokkini all the way along to Creta Camping or Gournes with a wilder look than Amnissos, but not such good sand. There are good sand beaches at Hersonissos and Stalis, though both are flanked by bustling promenades or bars, restaurants and discotheques.

Malia has an even longer stretch of sand, with dunes at one end, but it can get crowded. You can escape the crowds at Sissi, at the eastern end of the bay of Malia, though you have to walk 15 minutes from the harbour to find a series of three remote little sandy coves.

The main road turns inland after Malia and hits the coast again at Agios Nikolaos, which despite its reputation as a holiday centre has no beach of its own, other than three tiny imported strips of sand by the big beach hotels. There are, however, a number of cove beaches around the Gulf of Mirabello at Istro, Kalo Horio and Pachia Ammos south of Agios Nikolaos and 10 kilometres north at Elounda where

there is a good stretch of sand opposite the islet of Spinalonga with all the watersports and a good selection of restaurants.

Sitia has a long shingle beach, which stretches along the bay as far as Agia Fotia, but it is somehow a dull one. More exciting for those with transport is palm-fringed Vai just across the tip of eastern Crete's last spidery peninsula. It has superb sand, a good restaurant and a small island to swim out to and snorkel around. It looks divine at dawn and dusk. The only snags between those times are the crowds, who somehow find their way to this apparently remote place.

The east coast is barren and rocky, but it does have a pretty pebble beach at Kato Zakro east of the Minoan site flanked by a number of good simple rooms and tavernas.

My accolade for the best beaches in eastern Crete goes to those at the remote village of Xerokampos, reached by a dirt road from Zakros village, or if you have the stamina and the tyres via a poor mountain track from Lithines via Ziros.

It has rooms and restaurants and is a wonderful place to spend a few days. The runners-up are two beaches at Paleokastro, flanked by three restaurants with a lovely hotel a mile or so inland.

Those who find Vai too touristy should head up the coast two kilometres to Itanos where the fascinating old site boasts a remote beach. On the south coast Ierapetra is an honest town, with some sand, but there are good beaches stretching along the south coast all the way to Makriyalos and beyond. Windsurfing and watersports are available in places.

The south coast between Ierapetra and the Bay of Messara is mainly rocky, but it does have four or five isolated beach resorts which are notable more for their beauty than their sand. The most famous is at Matala, which has a greyish sand surrounded by rock caves where early Christians are said to have hidden and buried their dead. They were certainly occupied by hippies in the 1960's, but nowadays the village has developed a series of hotels and likes to coral its visitors into them or the nearby camping site.

The other beaches are at Arvi, Tsoutsouros, Lenda and Kali Limenes. They are all small villages with a couple of tavernas and the most fascinating is Kali Limenes. Although it is a long drive from Mires, and its beach is pebble, it is long and spectacular and has a pretty village nearby with a mysterious little island in the bay where NATO submarines refuel. It is also the place where Saint Paul landed on Crete. Well worth the drive in my view.

Nightlife on Eastern Crete

All four of Crete's big towns have a big selection of restaurants, bars and cinemas and a sprinkling of discotheques.

Heraklion is far from the prettiest town by day, but by night it acquires a certain glamour as its squares, alleyways and garden restaurants light up for the evening trade. There is plenty of activity around the cafés and restaurants of Platia Eleftherias by the archaeology museum and Platia Venezelou, while music can be heard in the cellar bars of narrow streets off Dikeosinis. There are also three or four discos near the middle of town.

But those who prefer to eat and drink cheaply without music should hunt the streets between the Venetian port and the market which are lined with good cheap restaurants spilling out on to the pavement.

Agios Nikolaos also boasts a good range of nightlife with a more sophisticated look than Heraklion in the open-air cafés, bars and restaurants clustered around the harbour and the lagoon. Here too you can find Greek music and dancing, spilling into discos.

Elounda, to the north of Agios Nikolaos, has its own brand of sophisticated nightlife with a handful of restaurants and a disco operating in summer. You can spend many a happy evening searching for the Shepherd's bar from 'Who Pays the Ferryman?'.

Other resorts in eastern Crete that feature nightlife beyond just eating out of doors are Matala, Ierapetra, Malia, Sitia, Stalis and Hersonissos. Malia has a string of bars, restaurants and discos, while Hersonissos seems to have been created for night owls. Its main promenade is one long series of bars, restaurants and discos on both sides of the street, aligned so closely that you can fall straight out of one and into another becoming quite confused about what music is playing on the way.

Visitors who value their sleep should make sure their hotel or room is well back from the seafront.

Not to be missed on Eastern Crete

As anyone who has been there will tell you, Heraklion is not one of the world's most beautiful cities, but it has a number of good things in it which make it well worth a visit. It has a super archaeological museum in the city's main square near the Tourist Office and Knossos is in a dusty suburb on the edge of town looking towards the hills in the centre of the island. There are frequent buses from the port.

The museum has the most precious finds from Knossos, including vases, frescoes, ceramics and jewellery, and others from other Minoan sites on Crete. It also has Roman remains from the island. Knossos evokes mixed feelings due to the way Sir Arthur Evans reconstructed its ruins and frescoes with bright paint to make concrete look like wood and colour up pillars, leaving only a few stone steps, big storage vases and the world's first flush toilet in their original state.

Personally, I don't relish the atmosphere as much as other sites like Phaistos and Zakros on Crete and Akrotiri on Santorini, but it has to be seen by anyone interested in archaeology or just plain humanity. The other sites on the island are complementary.

Heraklion also has thick Venetian walls over two miles in length with occasional forts, which you can hardly miss driving in and out of town. You can find the grave of Nikos Kazantzakis, author of 'Zorba the Greek' in the walls since he was agnostic and was denied a church burial. Appropriately for a Cretan, his tombstone carries the message: 'I believe in nothing and hope for nothing, but I am free.'

You can complete the Venetian era with a tour of the Historical Museum of Crete, which is near the Xenia hotel.

Eastern Crete has all the other major Minoan sites, and they all have points in their favour. Phaistos, almost due south of Heraklion, has a magnificent setting on a low hill overlooking the Messara Plain of southern Crete and is a lot more natural than Knossos. It is also within walking distance of the settlement of Agia Triada and only a short drive from the Roman capital of Gortys. Malia and Gournia to the east along the main road have less to show of their earlier glory, but Malia has a magnificent seaside location and Gournia the best outline of a Minoan town, while Zakros, latest to be excavated, lies remote on the east coast, but repays a long journey with its evocative remains and a pleasant little village to stay in nearby.

Gortys, about 12 kilometres east of Phaistos, is a neatly contained site of the old Roman capital of Crete, which boasts some of the best Roman remains in Greece. It has a pretty little theatre, odeon, the Governor's house and temples. The odeon contains the law code of Gortys written alternatively left to right and right to left.

If you have a day out at Phaistos, Agia Triada and Gortys, it is worth tacking on Matala on the coast nearby for a swim and a look at the caves above the beach, which were inhabited by early Christians.

The first real village past the sprawl of the Cretan Riviera is Milatos. It is a good rest stop away from the airport. Although the beach is poor, it has good restaurants, apartments with swimming pools and a pretty hill setting 7 kilometres off the motorway. It also has a cave.

Agios Nikolaos has no Minoan remains of its own, but it has its 'bottomless lake' or inner harbour and the frescoed 9th century church of

Agios Nikolaos, who is the patron saint of sailors. It also has a good museum with Minoan remains from Eastern Crete.

'Ag Nik', as it is called by many tourists, is a good starting point for the plain of Lassithi with its thousands of tall windmills or water pumps and the Diktean Cave where the infant Zeus is supposed to have been born. It is a short walk from the village of Psychro and a good imagination will reveal Rhea and her infant Zeus among the stalagmites. Another easy evening drive or taxi ride from Agios Nikolaos is the lovely hill village of Kritsa, which contains the splendid Medieval church of Kera Panagia and magnificent wall paintings of New Testament scenes.

Alas, Ag Nik has seen a lot of development in recent years. A less frantic place which is much more together is Elounda, 10 kilometres to the north. The Mykonos of Eastern Crete, it has kept marvellously white and elegant. It has a multitude of restaurants crowding around a cute little harbour and a number of apartment blocks and hotels, including the classy Elounda Beach, which has no real beach, but good swimming from steps beside the waterfront rooms.

Stay awhile if you have a long purse.

Those who like old Monasteries should make for Kroustellania on the edge of the Lassithi plain near Tzermiadon, and Toplou on the Gulf of Sitia on the road to Vai. Toplou is built like a fortress and held out against invading Turks with the monks pouring boiling oil on their attackers. It has colourful icons and an amazing quota of tourists. A much quieter place is Itanos, a little-known Minoan site with palm trees and sandy beach 2 kilometres north of Vai.

The road journey along the east coast is spectacular after Agios Nikolaos, as are the roads south through the mountains from Heraklion, the Bay of Mirabello and Sitia. The palm-fringed beach of Vai is unique, if a little wasp-blown, and the road across the Messara plain and on to Ierapetra is also spectacular once you are away from the plastic greenhouses.

Western Crete

Western Crete, which contains the nomos (or district) of Rethymnon and that of Chania, has far fewer 'sights' that the eastern end of the island and has developed much later and much less than the coast between Heraklion and Agios Nikolaos.

Its road network is also inferior to that of the east. It has a motorway along the north coast as far as Kastelli and three good roads running down between the mountains to the south coast. But the south coast is only served by road for a short way between Chora Sfakion and Agia Gallini and the road down the west coast peters out before it works its way down to Paliochora.

However, this end of Crete has far less high-rise and tourist strip. It also has better beaches. There is no lack of places to see, including the amazing Medieval castles of Frankocastello and Rethymnon, the two incomparable Venetian ports of Chania and Rethymnon, and the Samaria Gorge, which offers a 12-mile walk through a deep chasm from the White Mountains to the Libyan Sea.

Western Crete has a greater sense of 'isichia' – the peace and quiet and escape from the modern world that Greek islands offer better than anywhere else in the Mediterranean. And it has half a dozen charming natural beach resorts in Georgiopoulos, Kastelli, Falasarna, Plakias, Agia Gallini and Bali.

Beaches on Western Crete

Western Crete has more separate beaches than the east of the island, they are better sand and mostly in prettier, less touristy settings. Visitors who value beaches more than archaeological sites should make for this end of the island.

The two main towns of the area, Rethymnon and Chania, have long stretches of good sand reaching right into their suburbs and they go on for miles beyond. Visitors who want to run out of their downtown hotel straight into the sea should choose Rethymnon where the beach runs east of the town, but for sheer expanses of beach those reaching out to the west of Chania would win hands down because they run on for 20 kilometres as far as the mountainous Spathia or Rodopou peninsular.

A 5 or 10 minute bus ride from the port of Chania will take you to Neo Chora or Agia Marina, which have strings of tavernas, watersports and clean seas when the meltemmi is not blowing hard. Further west there are other stretches at Platanias, Maleme, Tavronitas and Kolimbari, all with hotels, restaurants, beach sports and camping.

There are good alternatives in both towns too. If you take the road west from Rethymnon you quickly reach the wide sweep of Georgiopoulos Bay, which stretches nearly 10 kilometres from the pretty village of the same name and has a wide

expanse of comfortable sand dunes to sleep the day away in, a handful of beach restaurants with above-average cooking in which to lunch and plenty of rooms in which to stay.

Similarly, if you head east out of Chania you can find a beach at Stavros on the tip of the Akrotiri peninsular, where Chania airport is sited and there are others along the main coast road around Kalives and Plaka towards the end of Souda Bay.

Georgiopoulos and Stavros are both good places to stay, if you want a spell on the beach and don't fancy the big towns. Two other good spots on the north coast west of Heraklion are Bali and Kastelli.

Bali is a tiny, pretty village only 45 kilometres west of Heraklion along the main motorway which you could easily pass by in a hurry, but it repays a stop with three tiny sand coves, a first-class beach hotel and a cluster of good restaurants in the centre of the village.

Kastelli or Kissamos is a spectacular, but quiet, little port in the far west, which has an expanse of orange sand to swim off, a number of good modest hotels and restaurants and occasional ferries to Antikithera and the Peloponnese.

Staying at Kastelli with a car or scooter can be a delight because it puts you within easy striking distance of the west coast of Crete across the spur-like peninsular of Grambousa and that way lie some of the best beaches on the whole island – perfect sand gently shelving into the sea in scenic coves which are nowhere near as crowded as the beaches on the doorstep of the big north coast towns.

Falasarna, immediately across the peninsular, is the Bay of Golden

Beaches. There are 4 or 5 separate coves set between craggy rocks with two small hotels and restaurants on tap. But the nearest bus stop is 5 kilometres away in Platanos. The other top spot on a coast that has a number of pleasant shingle beaches and remote places to stay like Sifnari and Kambos is below the Monastery of Chrisoskalitsa and opposite the islet of Elafonissos. You can wade across to the island and pick a cove to yourself on either side in a perfect natural setting spoilt only by a slightly tatty car park and the absence of a decent beach taverna or anywhere to stay nearer than the village by the monastery.

The south coast of Western Crete offers other beach delights. The most famous centres are Paleochora and Agia Gallini at opposite ends of the coast, and both have their disciples and good watersports, but they tend to be more trendy, pebbly and crowded than remarkable for the quality of their beaches. Better yellow sand beaches can be found at Frankocastello, where there are 4 or 5 separate stretches below the famous Medieval castle with some good restaurants, and a short way along the coast around Plakias. The village itself has a good stretch of sand, though it is becoming crowded as the small hotels and restaurants develop around the bay, and there are three others a stiff walk or easy taxi ride to the west at Damnoni, Amoudi and Preveli, which is now served by a couple of restaurants.

In the opposite direction Rodakino has a good sand beach with caves to escape the mid-day sun and rooms in the village.

Chora Sfakion has two or three pretty stretches of pebble. They do not rank as great beaches by those standards, but are worth knowing about if you are taking boats to or from the Samaria Gorge. The same goes for the long pebble stretch and the crowded sand strip at Paleochora, which is also a terminus for boats to the gorge and Agia Roumeli at the foot of the gorge also has a shining pebble beach which has brought great relief to thousands of people who have walked the gorge for 6 or 8 hours on a hot day.

Nightlife on Western Crete

Western Crete is not so strong on nightlife as the eastern end of the island, but both Chania and Rethymnon are lively in the evening, while smaller coast resorts like Paleochora, Plakias, Agia Gallini, Georgiopoulis, Platanias and Kastelli run to a little night music as well as a wide range of bars and restaurants.

Nightlife in Chania takes place mainly around the old harbour in restaurants, cafés and bars. There are one or two attractive garden restaurants in the backstreets close by and it is not hard to find music. There is also a sprinkling of discotheques and traditional dancing at the International Dance Festival, usually held in May.

As an alternative, take a bus or taxi a few kilometres along the coast to Neo Chora, Platanias or Galatas which is the birthplace of Mikis Theodorakis and usually lays on music as a reminder of its famous son.

Rethymnon has a delightful half-moon of fish restaurants along its harbourside and more in the backstreets close by. Here the bouzouki and the hi-fi are more common than the discotheque especially during the local wine festival, usually held in July. But there is one lively disco scene by the harbour in summer and another on the edge of town. Rumour has it that fish costs half as much in this town as in other parts of Crete because the nearby fishing grounds are particularly rich, but check the price on ordering to be on the safe side.

You can find a quieter, alternative night scene a short distance away to the west at Georgiopoulos along the main coast road, or even closer at Misiria 4 kilometres east of Rethymnon.

Paleochora, Plakias and Agia Gallini on the south coast all have a wide selection of restaurants along their seafronts and in the backstreets, where music and the odd disco are also to be found.

Kastelli (or Kissamos) is quieter than the other resorts, but has a lively line in restaurants around its main square and many of them serve the local Kastelli and Kissamos wines.

Not to be missed on Western Crete

When you enter Western Crete you wave goodbye to Minoan sites, but not to history. The Venetians left their most splendid towns and castles in this part of the island.

The splendour starts in Chania – formerly Candia and dubbed 'Candy' by Shakespeare. The Venetians chose this beautiful town as their capital and it has remained the capital of Crete, though it has often been called 'the Venice of the East'.

You can see why when you look at the old city walls, the splendid double-harbour the Venetians built, and the tall mansions that lie around it and have now been largely restored after wartime bombing, some as restaurants or small hotels. This is a much more 'together' town than Heraklion with a great sense of unity and style. Even the tourist office has found a special place on the quayside of the inner harbour in the domed Mosque of the Janissaries.

Chania has an archaeological museum with Minoan finds and a historical museum which contains the best relics from the Venetian period down to the present century. It also has the home and statue of Venezelos, the leading statesman.

Rethymnon, the other big town of western Crete is hardly less splendid. It is another Venetian town with its compact harbour sandwiched between a tall, handsome castle and the beach, which is flanked by a palm-shaded promenade. Around the curved harbour are a host of narrow streets containing both Venetian and Turkish houses with wooden balconies.

The Fortezza is one of the best-preserved Venetian castles in Greece, rivalling the Knights' castle in Rhodes town and challenged only by Frankocastello in Crete.

Frankocastello is on the south coast south-west of Rethymnon. It is a smaller castle, but has its own splendour because it stands proud and isolated on the seashore with only a beach and a restaurant for company, in such a good state of preservation that it must look much the same today as it did centuries ago when it was built.

It is believed to be haunted by Greek resistance fighters massacred by the Turks in 1829, who march from the castle into the sea at dawn each year on May 17. See it at dawn or dusk and you may well conjure up a vision of the slaughtered patriots.

Souda, the big port and NATO base east of Chania wins no prizes in the charm stakes, but the Akrotiri peninsular that rises above it is worth a visit. As well as the grave of Venezelos, it has the two monasteries of Agia Triada and Gouverneto and the stalactite cave of Katolikon where St John the Hermit lived. Another huge cave with stalactites and stalagmites can be found at Afrata, a few miles off the main coast road at the foot of the Spatha peninsular.

Kastelli has a castle built on the site of ancient Kissamos and Falasarna across the neck of the peninsular has Minoan remains, but they have to be searched out and neither compare with their competitors elsewhere on the island. The most memorable spot on the west coast is, in fact, the pretty little monastery (or nunnery) of Chrysoskalitissa – or 'golden stairway' – not far from Elafonissos islet.

On the south coast there is a castle at Paleochora, a pretty little wedding cake church at Agia Roumeli, and a handsome war memorial to British troops at Chora Sfakion. All these places could be on the route of people walking the Samaria Gorge.

The whole of western Crete is populated by pretty inland villages and deep gorges, making it a delight to drive down through the mountains on any of the roads that link the north coast with the south, but the deepest and best-known is the Samaria Gorge which stretches down from the White Mountains to the sea at Agia Roumeli and has become a special attraction to walkers.

It is 12 miles long and claimed to be the largest gorge in Europe. Anyone of moderate fitness with good shoes can walk its 12 miles of Castle Dracula scenery – towering peaks, rushing springs and stony pathways – in four to eight hours, especially if they set off on the early morning bus from Chania to the top of the gorge.

Agia Roumeli at the foot of the gorge has rooms and restaurants and motor boat connections along the coast to Chora Sfakion and Paleochora, which also have rooms, restaurants and return buses to Chania, but are worth a short stay.

Even if you get lost in the gorge, you won't be alone. It is well-walked even in mid-winter.

Along the north coast between Chania and Rethymnon, movie buffs may want to visit the hill village of Kokkino Chora (or 'red village') to see where 'Zorba the Greek' was filmed and eat in one of the cafés, which are almost shrines to Anthony Quinn who played the title role.

Georgiopoulos is a good place to linger for a meal or a swim between there and Rethymnon and Bali is a lovely little seaside place between Rethymnon and Heraklion.

The south coast between Frankocastello and the nomos of Heraklion has the Preveli monastery near the welcoming village of Plakias, which has been a great centre of resistance over the centuries and has two silver candlesticks given by grateful British servicemen. It also has Agia Gallini, a small fishing village which has mushroomed into a major resort with rooms and restaurants galore in recent years.

Worth visiting off Crete
It is hard to exhaust the delights of Crete because the island is so big, but there are a number of easy escapes to offshore islets by boat and to the other fully-fledged Greek islands by both

ferry and aeroplane. The Greek mainland is also near enough to combine with a holiday on Crete, using ferries or planes to transfer between the two.

Crete has around 20 satellite isles and there are ready-made boat trips to half a dozen of them, while you can wade across to Elafonissos off the west coast carrying your clothes, despite the amount of blue separating the main island and its tiny satellite on most maps.

Elafonissos is definitely an islet to make for if you like swimming off little desert island beaches surrounded by sand dunes and a number of nudists with not a beach umbrella or beach taverna in sight.

Spinalonga opposite Elounda in the bay of Mirabello is completely different – a place to hunt phantoms. Up to 30 years ago it was a leper colony and has a deserted old village with creepy creaks and bangs breaking the silence when the wind is blowing.

It was made an islet by Venetian engineers, who cut a channel to separate it from Crete and built a strong fortress. To such good effect that it held out against Turkish invaders for over 40 years. Nowadays it is easily accessible by caique from Elounda or from Agios Nikolaos, which sometimes takes in another small islet on the way. It has a small pebble beach and tavernas to cater for day trippers.

Another islet which held out for a long time against the Turks is tiny Nea Souda in Souda Bay, which was the last place in Crete surrendered to the Turks. It has a spectacular little fort and is easily reached by motor boat from Souda.

Agia Theodori is another small islet near the coast opposite the seaside resort of Agia Marina in the Bay of Chania. It too was fortified by the Venetians, but today it is worth visiting to see its huge cave and the wild Cretan goat, the kri kri, which is becoming hard to spot in the mountains of the main island.

Dia island, opposite Heraklion, is another barren island which plays host to the kri kri, but is not as easy to get to as it looks from the island capital.

The triangular island of Gavdos, however, is easy to get to if you don't mind a four-hour sea crossing from Paleochora, and is thinly-populated. It is the most southerly island in Greece, and is reputed to have been the island of the nymph Calypso who seduced Odysseus to tarry in the 'Odyssey' on his way home from Troy. It is worth tarrying there today because it is a charming, rocky island with a little modest accommodation, a castle in the Hora and two or three pretty shingley beaches near the port.

You can easily combine a visit to Crete with one to Athens and the Peloponnese, thanks to overnight ferries, which do the journey in 12 hours, and Olympic Airways, which do it in an hour. It is worth thinking about for a classical tour.

It is equally easy to combine Crete with Rhodes for glimpses of two big and contrasting islands, or with Karpathos and Kassos, which lie between Crete and Rhodes. There are flights to Rhodes and ferries to the other Cycladic islands and to Rhodes from all the eastern ports of Crete.

You can also fly to Cycladic islands like Santorini, if you want to do the complete Minoan tour, and Mykonos, if you want to visit a small, gay, sophisticated island in the middle of the Aegean, while the ferries run to Piraeus and the southern Peloponnese from Heraklion, Chania and Kastelli. You can also sail easily to the barren island of Antikithera from Kastelli, but it is not a particularly inviting island. Better to stay aboard and go as far as Kithera.

Crusaders' Isle – Rhodes

Rhodes is the island of Apollo, the Sun God, and the Colossus, one of the Seven Wonders of the Ancient World. It is also the Crusaders' isle where the Knights of St John headquartered after retreating from the Holy Land and built a string of castle strongholds to keep the Turks at bay when they attacked the island.

Modern crusaders flock to Rhodes more in the cause of Apollo than that of the Holy Land. The sun shines nearly every day of the year and hot weather shrubs like rhododendron, bougainvillea and hibiscus blossom everywhere along with fruits like oranges, lemons, apricots and figs. The beaches of the island are baked brown by the sun, and most visitors too if they indulge in sun worship.

The Colossus which once bestrode the harbour of Rhodes town now exists only on postcards, having fallen victim to an earthquake in 225 BC, but Rhodes has a strong historical background and sites to match. Apart from the Crusader castles dominating Rhodes town, strung along the hilltops of the east coast as far as Lindos and the west coast as far as Monolithos, the island boasts four ancient cities, Lindos, Kamiros, Ialyssos and Rodos.

The island vies with Corfu in natural beauty. Although it is browner and less lush in appearance, it has a

painter's landscape with pine-clad hills and mountains rising in the interior around the 4,000 foot peak of Mount Ataviros and white villages sprinkled around the coast, often in grand bays between high cliffs, like that at Lindos which once provided anchorage for one of the world's biggest fleets.

Rhodes has provided a rich natural setting for many films, including 'Guns of Navarone' and 'Escape to Athena'.

Rhodes town itself offers two towns in one, with the old town contained in an amazing state of preservation within the castle walls, and the new town, the loveliest modern conurbation in Greece. A unique blend of Italian town-planning and Greek style, it is rivalled only by Corfu town. Not to be outdone, Lindos is all white like a bride in her wedding dress crowned by the most beautiful acropolis in Greece.

There are plenty of cool, green places in the interior of the island, where pinewoods and valleys are fed by streams and olive and cyprus trees grown in profusion beside fruit farms. The new town is also green with pine, plane and blossom trees lining its broad avenues and waterfront, complementing the arched public buildings and grand harbour, legacies of the Italian occupation which lasted until 1948.

It has been called 'the island of Eternal summer' and boasts an 8 or 10-month season, a good two–three months longer than Corfu and other northern islands of Greece. You can swim in the sea in December, if you are determined and don't linger long, and can find over 200 hours of sun in March, half the 420 hour average of June, July and August. With such impressive statistics, you won't be surprised to learn that Rhodes has the best sunshine record in Greece.

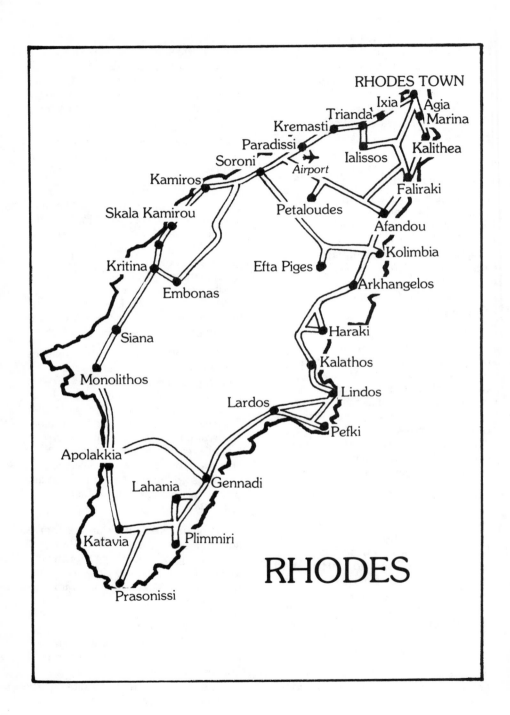

RHODES TOWN
Ixia
Agia
Marina
Trianda
Kremasti
Kalithea
Paradissi
Ialissos
Soroni
Airport
Faliraki
Kamiros
Petaloudes
Afandou
Skala Kamirou
Kolimbia
Efta Piges
Kritina
Arkhangelos
Embonas
Haraki
Siana
Kalathos
Monolithos
Lindos
Lardos
Pefki
Apolakkia
Lahania
Gennadi
Katavia
Plimmiri
RHODES
Prasonissi

The weather, the spectacular landscape and the history are three good reasons why the island draws northern Europeans in droves from Scandinavia and Germany as well as Britain. But Rhodes also boasts long, sandy beaches most of the way around its coast, divinely peaceful places in the south of the island, and modern tourist attractions like tennis courts, a golf course, a casino, nightclubs, foreign restaurants, windsurfing, water-skiing and easy boat trips to its many beaches as well as to other islands in the Dodecanese chain.

Its most popular coastal resorts like Rhodes town, Faliraki, Lindos, Agia Marina, Kallithea, Trianda, Ixia and Paradissi have been transformed in recent years by developments of hotels, villas, restaurants and discotheques to match the rising influx of tourists and the busloads of cruise ship passengers that pour down the coast roads from Rhodes town to Lindos and Kamiros.

Yet Rhodes town remains the only big town in Greece surrounded by a clean, sandy beach and the island has oases of quiet between the big resorts and throughout the south below Lindos in the east and Kamiros in the west. Down there, it is not hard to find a long, broad sandy beach to yourself or to walk along through unchartered countryside. Accommodation can be found in small pensions, village houses or apartments. The deep south is easily accessible thanks to a ring road 200 kilometres long running right around the island.

Rhodes is cheap for tourists, cheaper than most Greek islands, despite its sophistication, casino and big hotels. It boasts low prices for drink, food products, imported goods and

transport like hired motorbikes. They stem partly from the island's duty-free status.

This is the big Greek island with everything. Yet it is not quite so well known as Corfu and Crete to British holidaymakers. It is not surprising that it has soared in popularity in recent years, rising to rank among the top British package tour destinations, close behind Corfu and Crete.

There are scheduled and charter flights from Britain to Rhodes.

It is also possible to fly to and from Rhodes and other Greek islands, including Karpathos, Kos, Santorini and Crete, each flight taking roughly half an hour.

There are daily ships from Piraeus, the port of Athens, but it can be a depressingly long journey taking between 24 and 30 hours and calling almost everywhere, so it is only for people with plenty of time who want a glimpse of many islands.

The shipping line that runs down the Dodecanese is businesslike, but calls at almost every island, so again time and patience are needed. Fortunately, recent years and calm coastal seas have brought a hydrofoil service to the Dodecanese and island-hoppers should pray that it keeps on running.

It runs from Samos to Patmos, Patmos to Kos and Kos to Rhodes, taking 1½ hours for each leg, so it more than halves travelling time, yet still gives you a glimpse of passing islands if you brave spray and vibration to travel on deck.

There are also shipping services connecting Rhodes with Symi, Kastelorizo, Halki, the Cyclades and Cyprus that do not always run to the rest of the Dodecanese, and an intermittent service across to Marmaris in Turkey.

Long and broad for most of its length, Rhodes resembles a giant fish in shape with Lindos on its fin. For most of its length it faces the Turkish mainland, though it is too far away to be seen clearly from the island.

Legend says that Rhodes was still rising from the sea when it was selected by Apollo or Helios, the sun god, as his share of Greece from Zeus, the father of the gods, who was distributing it among his children. Apollo named it after his beloved nymph, Rhodos, the daughter of Aphrodite, and the Dorians who ruled the island called their three big cities after the sons of Apollo and Rhodos – Lindos, Ialyssos and Kamiros.

Ancient Rhodes ordered a giant statue of Apollo, its patron and protector, from its most famous sculptor, Chares of Lindos. It stood around 100 feet tall, almost the height of New York's Statue of Liberty, took 12 years to cast in sections and was reputedly mounted with its legs astride the harbour mouth for ships to pass underneath with a torch in one hand to guide them home at night. It is not surprising that it became known as the Colossus of Rhodes and was ranked among the Seven Wonders of the Ancient World.

Alas, the Colossus was short-lived and met an untimely end. It was erected in 290 BC and fell victim to an earthquake in 225 BC. It lay in pieces for eight centuries and was sold off for scrap to a Jewish merchant who carried it off to Syria.

The Apostle Paul came to the island, around 42 AD, and converted many of the Rhodians to Christianity.

The Knights of St John retreated from Jerusalem via Cyprus to Rhodes in 1306 AD and gave the island two more centuries of security, prosperity and relative independence.

The order of the Knights was founded in the 11th century by a family from Amalfi. They never numbered more than 600 and were usually ruled by a French Grand Master. They bought the island from Genoese pirates and won it fully in a long siege of the Byzantine garrison. They then set about ensuring that they would be secure there by fortifying Rhodes town with high walls and building other castle strongholds at key strategic points along the coast of the island and on other neighbouring islands of the Dodecanese. In the town itself they built a hospital and eight inns, representing the eight 'tongues' of the order – those of France, England, Germany, Italy, Castile, Aragon, Auverge and Provence – who each had a portion of the city walls to defend.

They did their work and their fighting so well that they managed to keep the Turks at bay for the next 200 years, including two particularly determined assaults in 1444 and 1480. But they were finally unseated in 1522 when Suleiman the Magnificent was so angry that the Knights were attacking Moslem pilgrim ships that he laid siege to the island for six months with a huge force. Although he lost 50,000 troops, Suleiman finally persuaded the Knights to surrender and allowed the survivors to move on to Malta.

The Italians ruled from 1912 to 1948. They were not welcome as occupiers since they tried to suppress the Greek language and the Orthodox church, but they did give a start to tourism, beautified Rhodes town with noble civic buildings and built good roads. Their legacy is evident today in the new town, while the ghosts of the Knights ride through the old town and stalk every hilltop citadel on the island. Little remains of the Turkish occupation other than two or three small mosques and a fountain in the old town, but there is plenty to see of the ancient Greek cities of Rhodes, Lindos, Kamiros and Ialyssos. This unique combination makes Rhodes a fascinating island for sight-seeing without peer in the whole of Greece.

Beaches

Rhodes is almost one long beach. Even Rhodes town at the northern tip of the island is surrounded by sand and it runs on for bay after bay with a few exceptions right to the southern tip of the island, but the west coast is a lot windier, more shingley, and there are places between Skala Kamiros and Apolakia where the coast is not easily accessible.

The town has good sandy beaches on both sides of its promontory and they are enough to satisfy many of its summer visitors, who crowd together beneath colourful beach umbrellas in serried ranks only a few yards away from their big hotels and the restaurants where they take lunch and dinner. It is an easy life and it stretches along as far as Mandraki Harbour on the east coast and for three or four kilometres to Ixia on the west side with windsurfing, water-skiing and pedaloes on the calmer stretches. But there are greater treasures, and calmer seas, to be found further down the east coast for those prepared to travel.

The first resort that is separate from Rhodes town is Agia Marina, which has a passable beach with

watersports, then comes Kallithea, a thermal health spa with waters that are believed to work wonders on internal problems and rheumatism. The Italian-built spa buildings have seen better days, but the waters are still there and the bay offers good swimming and windsurfing. Lew Grade turned the spa into a German prisoner-of-war camp for 'Escape to Athena'.

You can swim most of the way around the bay of Kallithea as far as Faliraki, which has a superb long stretch of sand beach and is fast growing from a small fishing village into the major beach resort of the island with a healthy strip of hotels and restaurants. Many people now stay here as an easy, quiet alternative to Rhodes town since it is only 15 kilometres down the coast, is slightly cheaper, and boasts calmer, clearer waters. It too has all the watersports.

You can swim too in the bay of Afantou as far as the promontory of Kolimbia, though it is better known as the island's golf and tennis centre. You can find 18 pearly green holes, tennis courts and professional coaching in an away-from-it-all setting just 22 kilometres from Rhodes town and about 7 from Faliraki.

It is the first real get-away-from-it-all beach near to Rhodes town. Development is strictly restricted by the golf course and there is little shade. But there are places to eat and drink on the road and at the Kolimbia end of the beach.

Kolimbia, a couple of kilometres off the main road – turn by the hospital – is special. A promontory with sandy beaches on both sides that opens up into a sandstone crater into which the sea floods at high tide. It offers a choice of swimming and windsurfing in a spectacular setting about 30 kilometres from town.

Kolimbia has grown like Topsy in the past ten years, with villas and hotels, and is now a sizeable resort for German tour companies. But it retains some coastal village atmosphere and the beaches cannot be classed as crowded.

Tsambika is different again – a broad stretch of brown sand with big cone-shaped rocks – and Stegena has a tiny toy-like harbour with a beach beside it, then comes Haraki. It is a pretty fishing village which has two or three separate beaches like Kolimbia, though not so grand, one doubling up as a harbour, a reed-fringed stretch to the right and another to the left of the village. The third beach is overlooked by Feraklos castle, which was a stronghold of the Knights of St John, and the skeletal remains of a Typaldos holiday village started when the cruise line was at its zenith in the mid-sixties, then abandoned to the elements like a modern monument.

The beach to the right of Haraki runs on and widens out to become the big sweep of Vliha Bay with a couple of beach hotels and restaurants at the far end between the pretty villages of Kalathos and Lindos.

Lindos is a jewel – the single most spectacular place on the island and the second biggest town after Rhodes, thanks to its dazzling white houses, winding streets and magnificent acropolis, but it lacks for nothing by way of beach. Again there is a three-way choice; the main sandy sweep of Lindos Bay with beach umbrellas, windsurfing, water-skiing and pedaloes below the town; the tiny enclosed bay of St Paul on the back side of the town and its rocky acropolis, which looks like a lake with two small strips of sand until you descend and see the break in the rock wall where the sea floods in; and a fair walk beyond the bay of St Paul, there is a long swimmable stretch of sand between the villages of Pefki and Lardos.

Pefki itself is remote and rocky, with surprisingly tarted-up bars and restaurants, but it has good hotels and a couple of patches of sand.

The first coastal village south of Lardos is Kiotari, which is founded on two seaside restaurants on the old coast road and is developing into a tasteful, quiet little resort of apartments, restaurants and shops on a long stretch of beach.

Despite two or three big hotels north of the village by a sandy beach, Kiotari retains its peaceful atmosphere and is an ideal place to spend a few days to tour the south of the island.

Between Lardos Bay and the southern tip of the island the coast road offers an expanse of almost continuous beach, interrupted only by exotic rocks, which split it into coves all the way down to Plimmiri. Genadion is developing into a sizeable resort with some good restaurants and a wide stretch of beach with more restaurants lies just 5 minutes walk away. Plimmiri itself has a modest taverna with a few rooms and a beautiful curving sandy bay beneath an abandoned Italian village. Beyond Plimmiri the tarred ring road becomes dirt track, but the beaches don't end. Intrepid travellers who penetrate as far as Cape Prasonisi ('green island') will find the cape itself rocky and wild, relieved only by a lighthouse, but a short walk away the dirt track runs into a narrow neck of sand with long, lagoon-like beaches on both sides, and two restaurants.

Between Plimmiri and Prasonisi are the best sand beaches of Rhodes, but they have little shade and no restaurants. Take the dirt road from Agios Pavlos and you will find Caribbean-style coves and sand dunes about 6 or 7 kilometers off the ring road. The dirt road leading down to them is marked only by the church of Agios Georgios on maps.

The west coast does not match the east, but it has some respectable beaches by the standards of most Greek islands. You can swim off shingley stretches the whole way along from the main Rhodes hotel strip to Kamiros, at Trianda, Ixia, Tholos, Kremasti, Paradissi, Soroni and Kamiros itself, where there are pretty restaurants close to the sea.

Skala Kamiros is a tiny fishing port backed by a cliff where the ships sail to the offshire islands of Halki and Alimia, but it has a fair beach with some sand and restaurants and a few rooms to match.

Beyond Skala the coast road runs inland and it is hard to get to the sea, but off the road near Siana a new little resort is emerging at Glyfada. The beaches are pebble, but they lie in a spectacular setting between high cliffs and there are rooms and restaurants to reward those who venture down the dirt road.

The road from Monolithos now reaches down to beaches at Frounion opposite the islet of Strongilo. There are three idyllic shingley coves and one barely accessible sandy cove in the middle surrounded by smooth sandstone rocks.

The south-east coast beyond Apolakia is as spectacular as any beach of the east coast. The whole 17 kilometre stretch that is known as the Bay of Apolakia is wide yellow sand dunes dotted with bushes and cactus constantly pounded by a foaming surf. It only runs out when the coast road turns east towards Katavia and it is possible to find accommodation either there or in Apolakia.

The southern end of the island is remote, rarely visited by package tours and only seen by a handful of people who do the standard tours from Rhodes to Lindos on the east coast and Kamiros on the west coast, so water-sports are rare down there, as are swimming pools and tennis courts. Those who want sailing and tennis should seek in and around Rhodes town as far as Lindos in the east and Trianda in the west. The Rhodes Yacht Club will advise on sailing and most of the big beach hotels around the town and as far down the coast as Afantou have tennis courts which can be hired by visitors.

People staying in Rhodes town who want to swim down the coast can easily travel halfway down each coast by bus, but need a car or a scooter for further ventures unless they are prepared to rise at the crack of dawn for buses penetrating the deep south. Good alternative transport for an easy passage to the east coast beaches like Kallithea, Kolimbia, Tsambika and Lindos is a boat from Mandraki Harbour.

Nightlife

Rhodes is one of the few islands in Greece that has nightlife on a West European scale, adapted to its hot climate, and Rhodes town is as lively by night as any port in the Mediterranean.

It has a casino in the Grand Hotel, open-air cinemas and discos, hundreds of cafés, bars and restaurants, dozens of nightclubs and cellar discos mostly in the big hotels, a sound and light display in the Old Town, a folk dance theatre, and a nightly wine festival at Rodini Park. There is music on every other street and you are hard pushed to do the same thing on two evenings in a fortnight.

For the casino in the Grand Hotel you need a suit and tie, passport and enough drachmas to match the minimum table stake for roulette, baccarat and black jack. For the 'Son et Lumiere' sound and light show at the Palace of the Grand Masters you need only a vivid imagination to conjure up scenes from the days of the Knights and the noisy siege by Suleiman the Magnificent, which are described in several languages two or three times a night throughout the summer.

Those who like a spot of tradition can also see folk dances performed in local costume at the Folklore Theatre in the Old City Theatre and can sample a large range of local wines – mainly CAIR or Compagne Agricole et Industrielle de Rhodes – at Rodini Park on the outskirts of town beneath Monte Smith. It is a pleasant garden setting with wine barrels and glasses set beneath spreading trees between ornamental ponds on which swans glide to and fro. Slightly surrealistic, especially after the first three or four glasses of different wines.

Any of these activities – and especially the wine festival – should be combined with a meal at an open-air restaurant. Rhodes town is one of the few places in Greece where trad Greek fare like kebabs and moussaka is offered cheek by jowl with a range of international dishes like pizzas from Italy,

smorgasbord from Denmark, gravalax from Sweden, roast beef in the English style and pepper steak in the French. There are many international restaurants and bars or 'pubs' that cater for customers from colder climates in a way that could make them feel at home if they could forget the heat and the cicadas buzzing away in the undergrowth.

There are floating restaurants in Mandraki harbour with Norwegian names competing with the Greek fish restaurants across on the quayside nearer the town and Danish pastry parlours vying with the Greek pastry shops around the market and bus station.

Dining out in the Old Town is a magical experience. Greek food with an occasional Turkish influence, tables set beneath trees or in alleyways, and lights reflecting off the high walls and cobblestones of a Medieval city. It tends to be cheaper than the new town too. Finish off with ice-cream or a sticky Turkish pastry and a cup of thick Greek (or is it Turkish?) coffee that looks as though it has been stewing from the time of Suleiman.

The best places to eat, I find, are in garden restaurants off narrow alleyways high up town close to the minarets.

If you have started off the evening eating out, you may like to follow it up with a foreign film shown with Greek subtitles or a Greek film dubbed with English. Or a disco/nightclub with an exotic name like the Sultana, the Sphinx, the Aquarius, Vikings, the Zig Zag, Kastro, the Can Can or Elli. Or join in traditional Greek dancing in a backstreet restaurant. Many of the big hotels have such nightspots.

You can find the same kind of scene,

but on a much smaller scale elsewhere on the island in places like Faliraki, Kallithea and Lindos, where there are a number of smart bars, pubs, cinemas and discos. But elsewhere nightlife is the more Greek mixture of eating out in a moonlit taverna and taking an ouzo by the harbourside watching the late fishing boats departing or coming home. Discos are not common in the villages where peace and quiet is the order of the day and night.

Rhodians are, in fact, becoming more image-conscious and are starting to put curbs on areas thick with discos after complaints from visitors that they cannot sleep with their windows open while two or three bars and discos are advertising their presence with loud music.

Not to be missed on Rhodes

Rhodes is a great island for sightseeing. There are delights all over which are guaranteed to raise the eyebrows of the most jaded world-travellers. If you set aside a day or two out of your holiday to see the sights, you will not regret it and can always take in a beach or two on the way.

Most people will make first for Rhodes and Lindos and rightly so, but where should they start in Rhodes, which boasts two towns in one plus the ancient city of Rodos on Monte Smith hill on the outskirts of town and three harbours to match? It is a good idea to start walking from the promontory of the new town along the harbourside and to go from there to the Old Town.

On the promontory itself is an aquarium, where you can check up on a number of the fish you can see snorkelling in the clear waters around the island, and a few big ones that you

won't want to encounter. The same building houses a museum with freaks of nature like a five-legged goat or two-headed calf.

You will soon reach Mandraki, the first of the three harbours. Its entrance is no longer guarded by the colossus, but by statues of a tiny stag and doe on high plinths, said to protect Rhodes against snakes since the time when deer were brought to the island at the behest of the Delphic oracle for that purpose. The far harbour wall supports the fort of St Nicholas built by the Knights to help defend the town against Turkish assaults and the remains of three windmills, which once worked in the corn trade alongside the wooden ships that moored in the harbour to load up.

Nowadays Mandraki is filled with yachts, fishing boats and small cruise ships that ply along the coast and do day trips to nearby islands and to Turkey.

The town side of the harbour is a tribute to the Italian occupation with a square of striking civic buildings constructed of smooth fawn bricks, which house the Governor's palace, the town hall, the post office, the National Theatre and other offices. Beside the palace is the new town's Mosque of Mourad Reis, called after a Turkish pirate.

The National Tourist office is beyond this square and Makariou Street, but there are signs pointing the way and it is clearly worth a visit to arm yourself with maps, tourist leaflets and programmes of local theatres, cinemas, sound and light displays, wine festival and casino.

You will soon reach the market square and the outskirts of the Old Town, which is flanked by two more harbours, Emborio or the commercial harbour and Acandia, which is used by the big cruise and ferry boats. You can enter the Old Town by one of three gates strung around the harbour.

The Old Town is fresh from the Crusades and the best memorial anywhere to those bloody plundering expeditions and holy wars masquerading as a quest for the holy grail and a free Jerusalem. The Medieval walls of the town, like those of Babylon, are high enough to withstand a fierce attack, thick enough to drive a chariot around and still failed to hold out invaders in the end. They have a number of grand gates and are surrounded by a moat where tiny deer now graze.

To get some idea of the scale of Medieval building, try walking around the moat surrounding the great walls. Allow an hour.

Along with the walled harbour, the Palace of the Grand Masters and the street of the Knights with their inns and hospitals, have all been beautifully restored to the point where they look like a gigantic film set. And they have been used many times in the filming of epics like 'The Guns of Navarone' and 'The Dark Side of the Sun'.

The pebble-paved street of the Knights is straight out of the 14th century except for the glass in the windows and crowds of camera-hung tourists on the pavements. It is lined with the eight inns of the old orders, including the magnificent Inn of France and the more modest Inn of England, which broke with the Order in the 16th Century, but was restored as a building during the brief post-war British occupation from 1945 to 1947.

The Street leads to the Palace of the Grand Masters, which dominates the whole of Rhodes town and contains magnificent halls, windows, furniture and mosaics. It was restored by the Italians after being used as a prison by the Turks and nearly destroyed in a gunpowder explosion in 1856. The upper rooms give great views over Rhodes and its harbours. Nearby is the archaeological museum housed in the 15th century Knight's hospital, an impressive two-storey building which contains the island's most famous statue, the Aphrodite of Rhodes or Marine Venus, statues of other gods and a collection of coins, vases and tombstones.

Walk deeper into the Old Town and you quickly enter the Turkish quarter. It has three mosques dominated by the Mosque of Suleiman, built by the conqueror of Rhodes, which still holds services. In this area you can also see the Old Turkish baths, library, bazaar and many houses with old Turkish-style wooden balconies.

Closer to the harbour is the Jewish quarter, much reduced since the German occupation during the war, but commemorated in a pretty way by the fountain in the Square of the Jewish Martyrs. It is a round structure inlaid with coloured tiles and topped by three bronze sea horses.

After this walk you will have missed few of the sights of Rhodes Town, other than a little zoo with more tiny deer, which you pass on the way out of town.

Most visitors who leave Rhodes town to tour the island head for the Valley of the Butterflies and the four ancient cities of Kamiros, Ialyssos, Rodos and Lindos. The Valley of the Butterflies, or Petaloudes, is inland from the airport on the west coast and is a green valley of streams, bridges and waterfalls where thousands of orange moths come in summer to cling to the underside of rocks and bushes and feed on the resin of the thorax trees. They fill the air at the sound of footsteps or clapped hands.

Petaloudes is on the road to Kamiros and Ialyssos, two old cities on completely contrasting sites. Kamiros is set in a cool pine glade close to the shore about 33 kilometres along the west coast and offers the impressive layout of a 3rd century BC city with a Temple of Apollo, market, streets and houses rather in the style of Pompei or Ephesus.

Ialyssos has less ancient remains to show, but is sited nearly 1,000 feet above sea level a few kilometres from the airport road. It has the remains of a Doric temple of Athena and a 4th century fountain set in a glade of cypress trees and also the 14th century church and monastery of Our Lady of Filermos with pretty gardens and an underground chapel. Ancient Rodos, set on Monte Smith hill on the immediate outskirts of Rhodes, and within walking distance of the centre, boasts a stadium, a theatre and another Temple of Apollo. It has few of the splendours of its proud past, but is curious for its name. It is called after the British Admiral Sydney Smith who used it as a lookout post during the Napoleonic Wars. The theatre has been restored to the point where it sports perfect rows of white marble seats.

Lindos is the place for superlatives. It was the most prosperous of the three old cities from around 2000 BC to 408 BC and today is the outstanding site as well as the unchallenged second town of Rhodes.

A dazzling white town of cubist houses and villas – but, mercifully, no hotels – clings to a hillside above a broad sandy bay which once harboured the biggest fleet in the Mediterranean. It is surmounted by the most spectacular acropolis in Greece.

The temple ruins may not quite match those in Athens, but the setting more than makes up for it. It gives a bird's eye view of the Bay of Lindos and the Bay of St Paul on the other side of the rock, where the Apostle is said to have landed on Rhodes. It looks like an enclosed lake from that vantage point.

The cliff face of Lindos was used to house the big guns in 'The Guns of Navarone' and the film kept the donkey drivers of Lindos happily employed for months carrying equipment up the steep steps of the town to the acropolis. Now their sole traffic is tired tourists, who don't fancy a climb of 400 feet in the heat of the day and succumb to the overtures of the donkey drivers in the little donkey park just beyond the main square of the town.

The best time to visit the acropolis is not at noon when tour buses pour down by the dozen from Rhodes Town, but early in the morning or late in the evening when there is a rising or setting sun to light up the scene and it is not uncomfortably hot to hike up the steps.

Pause on the way to look at the 15th century Church of Panagia, with its rich frescoes and pebble-dash floors inlaid with black designs, the old theatre of Lindos at the base of the town, and also the 2nd century BC trireme carved in the rock face at the entrance to the acropolis. You then enter the great gate of the Castle of the Knights, with its stairs, grand palace, dungeons and battlements. Today it guards a complex of portico, stairs and propylea leading to the holy of holies, the 4th century Temple of Athena perched on the edge of the cliff.

Many visitors staying in Rhodes and visiting by cruise ship make the bus trip to Lindos. The pity is that they see so little of the rest of the island. You really need to hire a car or motorbike for a day or two to do the whole circuit, perhaps using Lindos as a base. There are plenty of good quality rooms in the town and a little out of season it is easy to rent a villa with bathroom, kitchen and walled garden. The first notes for this book were made in such a place in a windy week in October when it was hard to keep paper straight in a typewriter and the view was too distracting for proper concentration.

From Lindos it is a short drive to the lovely white inland village of Archangelos with its two fine churches, 15th century castle and the monastery of Tsambika close by, to Efta Piges (or 'seven springs') where there is a café, a waterfall and a small lake in a cool glade with frogs and peacocks, and to the pretty harbour of Haraki with the castle of Feraklos nearby.

It is a quiet harbour with swimming and the best fish restaurant on Rhodes (the Argo) sandwiched between the Bay of Malona and the long sweep of Vliha Bay.

A few kilometres inland from Lindos lies another pretty cool spot, the village of Lardos, which boasts pleasant rooms and some superb restaurants in garden settings.

Lardos has grown well with tourism and is as friendly as it is sophisticated. Well worth the half mile hike to the seashore.

The deep south beyond Lindos and Lardos is beach country, but also worth visiting for wild unspoilt stretches of countryside stretching all the way to the lighthouse of Cape Prasonisi ('Green island'). It is possible to motor as far as the narrow neck of sand that separates the lighthouse rock from the main island, but usually best to complete the last part of the journey on foot. This area is not penetrated by the orange buses that run around the ring road of the island and usually depart at dawn and dusk.

The villages of the south like Genardion, Plimmiri, Katavia and Apolakia are all pretty and not much visited. All have rooms and restaurants in picture postcard settings, by the seashore in the first two villages and around village squares in the other two.

The road along the west coast offers quite different scenery, but no less spectacular, between Kamiros and Apolakia. The oustanding sight of this area is the castle of the Knights at Monolithos ('lone rock'), perched above a deep 800 foot gorge, looking totally unassailable and offering amazing views for those who make the crossing by narrow path without suffering a case of vertigo.

The village nearby has restaurants and a hotel with good views down to the Bay of Apolakia.

There is another spectacular castle below Kritinia near Kamiros Skala, a pretty port with boats to the offshore isles of Halki and Alimia. In this area

Apollona and Siana are pretty inland villages with great views of the coast.

Between the two there is some good walking from Embonas up and around Mount Ataviros, which has a temple of Zeus near the summit. The pine-covered slopes around Mount Profitis Ilias also offer good walking country.

Embonas is the wine capital of Rhodes surrounded by fertile vineyards. Anyone can drop in on the Emery wine factory to taste the best wines of the island and see the process. Leave time for a meal in the village square to sample more wines. You need a car or scooter to get there. Two other scenic drives across the island are from Apolakia to Genardion and from Kolimbia to Efta Piges and on to Soroni. Both routes are lined with pinetrees, oleander bushes and herbs.

Yet another great drive is up from Kiotari to Laerma, taking in the frescoes of 10th century church of Asklipion and the isolated little monastery of Thari.

But always leave plenty of time for inland trips and take a good map of the Clyde Surveys type. The roads are poor and wind through thick pinewoods. Signposts are few and it always takes twice the time you expect to drive between two remote villages. It can also be cold on a scooter outside the summer months.

Worth visiting off Rhodes

Rhodes is the main gateway to the Dodecanese, thanks to its international airport; Kos is the only other island in the group with that facility and inbound flights are nothing like so frequent as to Rhodes. You can easily travel by island steamer to any other island in the chain and there are regular day boats to Symi, Halki, Kos and Marmaris in Turkey.

There are also local flights to Kos, Karpathos and Crete and summer hydrofoils to Kos, Kalymnos and Patmos. So it is easy and tempting to take a day or overnight trip to another island for a change of scene if you have a week or more on Rhodes.

Craggy Symi, with its seaside monastery, quiet Halki, Kos, looking like a miniature Rhodes with its grand harbour and towering Castle of the Knights, Patmos with its imposing monastery and cave of St John, and Nissiros with its steaming volcano, all beckon alluringly for day trips. Karpathos and Crete are both easy steps on a touring holiday with a view to seeing another island offering a complete contrast to Rhodes, while Marmaris offers a glimpse of a different country and continent.

Be chary, though, of trying an excursion to more remote islands like Astypalea, Kastelorizo and Tilos, unless you have time to spare, since they can involve long sea voyages and don't enjoy the luxury of daily steamers.

6. The Ionian Islands

A chain of seven green islands, known in Greek as the 'Eptanisa', straggles down the west coast of Greece and halfway around the Peloponnese. They are called the Ionian isles after the sea between Greece and Italy, and have a common history that dates back to the days of Odysseus. Their history has been extended by successive occupations by the Venetians, the French and even the British, who ruled the islands as a 'protectorate' through the middle years of the last century.

They are all fertile, floral isles and are prone to earthquakes, like the one that wrecked many villages on Cephalonia and Zakinthos in 1953. Here you see red tiled or even corrugated roofs and high buildings rather than the whitewashed squat cubist style of the Aegean.

Kythera is the odd island out; barer, southerly and served by ships that run down the east coast of the Peloponnese and the Saronic Gulf. But, there is never any easy logic to Greek island groupings.

Corfu, Paxos, Lefkas, Cephalonia and Ithaca are linked by island steamers. Lefkas can also be reached by a road causeway. Zakinthos, Cephalonia and Kythera are served by regular ferry services from the Peloponnese coast, as well as being on the domestic air routes.

The Wine Isle – Kefalonia

Kefalonia has opened up to tourism in recent years, thanks to direct flights from Britain, but it is such a big island – bigger, for example, than its famous neighbour, Corfu – that it can easily absorb new visitors.

It has a dozen sandy beaches along the south coast. It is also green, hilly and fertile with scores of red-roofed villages peeping through its pine, cypress and olive trees, three big sprawling ports in Argostoli, Lixourion and Sami in the south and two extremely photogenic ones at Fiskardo and Assos in the north. The three big ports have never quite recovered from the 1950s earthquake which struck hard at the central Ionian isles, but most people stay at the beach hotels down the coast from Argostoli, the capital, or at Poros, a beach resort in the south-east, or Skala to the south.

Sami was the old capital of Kefalonia, or Keffallinia, or Cephalonia – there are half a dozen ways to spell it in English – and was ruled by nearby Ithaca in the days of Odysseus. It is still the main port for steamers from the other Ionian islands like Ithaca and Lefkas, and Patras on the Peloponnese, though some call at Fiskardo. Motor boats from Kyllini on the Peloponnese run to Poros and Agostoli has the airport.

The patron saint is Saint Gerasimos and a third of the boys on Kefalonia are called after him. His body rests in the old church of Agios Gerasimos in the south of the island, which is

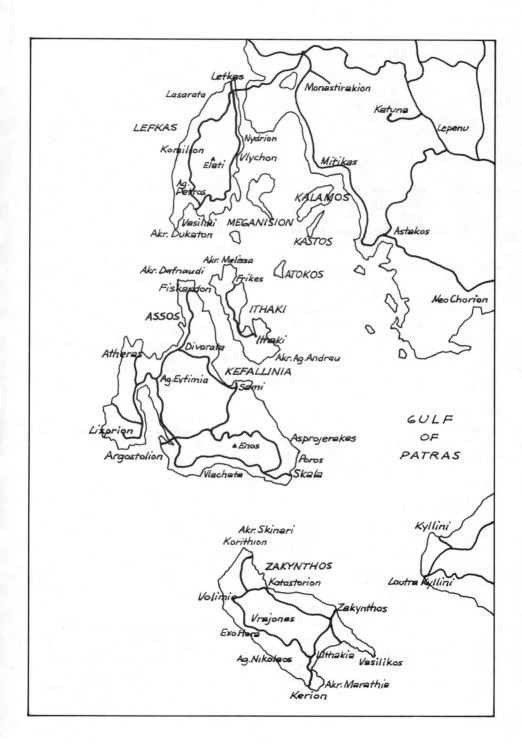

dominated by Kefalonia's highest mountain, the 5,000 foot Mount Ainos.

Kefalonia's vines and blossoms are reminiscent of Zakynthos and its greenness and grandeur of Corfu. It is not so neat as the other two islands, nor so rich in history, but it beats both, and most other Greek islands, with its wines which are premium brands over Greece. The best-known are flinty-white Rombola and lusty red Manzavino and Calliga, but local wine served by the carafe is usually of high quality and a lot cheaper than the big brands.

Argostoli is an honest, though dull, town with numerous hotels, a good fruit market on the quayside and a road on a causeway across its narrow gulf. Ferries run from the harbour to Lixourion half an hour away across the Gulf of Argostoli, there are regular buses to other parts of the island from the market, and cars and scooters can be hired from shops in town.

The west coast boasts spectacular scenery north of Argostoli where the road is cut into the side of a mountain high above the sea. South of Argostoli is a seemingly endless series of sandy beaches.

Beaches

Planes from Britain and Athens fly in over some of the island's best beaches along the coast down to the airport 7 kilometres south of Argostoli. Half a dozen sandy coves explain why the island's big beach hotels like the White Rocks and the Mediterranee are sited on this coast on the beaches of Plati Yialos, Makri Yialos, Livadi and Irina. They also have all the watersports. But there are good beaches in most parts of the island for those prepared to travel.

Along the south coast Gallini and Afrata have pretty beaches with sand and rocks. So do Spartia, Lourdas, Katelios and Skala. On the east coast both Poros and Sami have long pebble and shingle bays, of which Poros is unquestionably the prettier and ringed with good restaurants. Agios Ephimia north of Sami has another passable beach and so does Fiskardo.

But the most spectacular beaches lie on the west coast of Kefalonia. Apart from those below Argostoli, there is a pebble beach at Assos, the prettiest coastal village on the island, and just a few kilometres south are the island's two most spectacular beaches, Myrtou and Agios Kyriaki, which are both long, dazzling white strands backed by high cliffs and approached by the high coast road between Assos and Argostoli. The western peninsular also has a gentle sand beach with first-class taverna at Variko, which is a much better place to stay than Lixourion, and another on its southern tip at Agios Georgios.

There are plenty of other remote coves along the southern coast of the Lixourion peninsular.

Nightlife

Argostoli has lively nightlife, which extends along the coast to the beach hotels and includes two discotheques as well as dozens of restaurants on the edge of town. Poros also has restaurants that put on bouzouki music in season and Fiskardo caters well for diners from the rich yachts that call there.

Not to be missed on Kefalonia

It is a spectacular island to travel around by car or scooter. The road from Argostoli to Poros is well-tarmaced and runs through the hillside stronghold of Kastro with a well-preserved castle of Saint George,

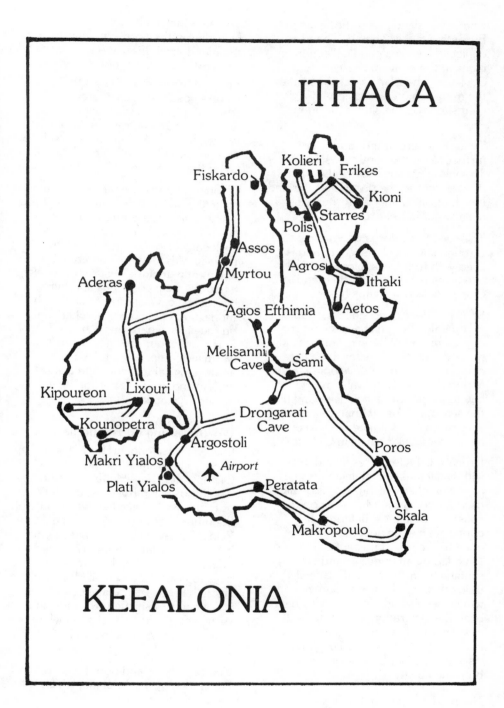

ITHACA

Kolieri

Frikes

Fiskardo

Kioni

Starres

Polis

Assos

Agros

Myrtou

Aderas

Ithaki

Agios Efthimia

Aetos

Melisanni
Cave

Sami

Kipoureon

Lixouri

Kounopetra

Drongarati
Cave

Poros

Argostoli

Makri Yialos

Airport

Plati Yialos

Peratata

Skala

Makropoulo

KEFALONIA

where the island's governor lived in Byzantine times. Then you have a choice of seeing a good collection of ikons at the convent of Agios Andreas or viewing the island's patron saint at the more remote monastery of Agios Gerasimos on the slopes of Mount Ainos.

There is a third grand monastery further along the south coast, called Theotikon Sission, before the road divides right to the pretty harbour and beach of Skala and left through a narrow gorge to Poros.

The road from Poros to Sami passes through spectacular scenery and is lined with fruit trees, blossoms and bee-hives that produce the island's crop of delicious thyme-honey.

Sami has developed since the 1950s earthquake, but still has its neat rows of prefabs where people were quickly housed after the disaster. It has a colourful harbour, a developing town and there is a pretty walk around the bay to a café with a goldfish pond by the seashore. Also within walking or easy motoring distance are two of the most spectacular caves in Greece.

Drogarati, 4 kilometres inland, bristles with stalactites and stalagmites in a huge chamber which is occasionally used for concerts. Melissani, on the coast, is completely different. It contains an eerie aquamarine lake open to the sky at its centre and said to be fed by an underground stream running from Argostoli. Strange lights strike through the water illuminating wriggling eels and it could easily have been the inspiration for Homer's description of the entry to the underworld in the Odyssey. You can visit all parts of Melissani in a flat-bottomed boat.

The road north from Sami is good

asphalt and it leads along spectacular high cliffs in the northern peninsular of the island. Both Fiskardo and Assos are worth seeing for themselves since they are the kind of villages that picture postcards and posters are made of. Fiskardo is a classic port, while Assos lies out on a spur of land leading to a peninsular topped off by a well-preserved Venetian castle. Plan to linger there a while.

Lixourion on the western spur is a place you want to get out of, but it is a gateway to some pretty rocky landscapes. The south coast has a rock called Kounopetra, which is said to sway with the tide – and did apparently until the 1950s earthquake – and the west coast has another interesting cave at Drakondi plus the monastery of Kipourio perched high on the cliffs, where there are now only four monks, but they give visitors a warm welcome. Argostoli has an archaeological museum and a short walk inland are the appropriately named Cyclopean Walls.

Worth visiting off Kefalonia

Ithaca is close enough for a day trip by boat. So is Kyllini for a day visit to Olympia. It is possible to island-hop to Zakynthos using Kyllini as a junction, or to use Kyllini as a gateway to any of the other sites of the Peloponnese like Pylos, Epidavros or Mycenae, if you have a car or fancy a mainland bus ride. But it would be best to allow two days to visit Epidavros or Mycenae, since they are a fair distance away and it is a pity to visit such treasures in a rush. You could also take in Delphi by taking a ferry across the Gulf of Corinth.

You can also island-hop to Corfu and Zakynthos by a light plane, which links the three Ionian islands.

CRETE
Walking the Samarian Gorge.

RHODES TOWN

Shopping in the old quarter.

Kefalonia —
High, mighty and scenic

MYKONOS

One of the island's four hundred
wedding cake churches.

The Flower Isle – Zakynthos

Zakynthos is a stylish green island with an Italian flavour off the western tip of the Peloponnese and south of Kefalonia, which has sprung to fame in recent years thanks to a number of good beaches and a direct air link with Britain as well as Athens.

It was known to the Venetians, who ruled the island for 350 years and called it Zante, as the 'Flower of the Levant' or 'Venice of the East'. It suffered, along with the other central Ionian islands, from the 1953 earthquake, but unlike the big towns on Kefalonia, the main port of Zakynthos was carefully rebuilt on the former Venetian plan with green squares, palm trees and stately buildings in pink and beige.

Zakynthos port is a bustling place, with ferries shooting off to Patras and Kyllini two or three hours away on the Peloponnese. It also has buses to all main villages along the three main coast roads, going south, east and north, and bikes and scooters can be hired. The hill above the town supports the ruins of a fort in which a British force was garrisoned during the Ionian mandate in the 19th century.

The impression of style and fertility sticks on a trip along the south and east coasts – the only ones really accessible by road as the west is high and rocky. The roadsides are often hedged with pomegranate and quince bushes giving way to pine-cloaked hillsides and pale yellow beaches.

The countryside produces some of the best wines in the Ionians, going under names like Verdea, Laganas and Byzantia.

In the springtime and early summer the countryside is a riot of flowers, especially the road north from the port to Alikes and the Argassi peninsular, which yields a fresh picture postcard scene around every bend of the road south to Porto Roma.

Zakynthos also boasts an unusually rich marine life, including turtles, seals and dolphins. Gerakas Beach, which is one of the island's two big breeding grounds for turtles, appeared in David Attenborough's wild-life documentary, 'First Eden'.

The four main resorts of the island are Alikes and Tsivili north of the main town and Argassi and Laganas to the south. They all have a selection of watersports.

Smaller developing resorts are Alikanas near Alikes and Crystal Bay, called after its natural outcrops of crystal at the northern end of Laganas Bay.

Argassi has the twin merits of being within walking distance of town and the gateway to the beautiful Argassi peninsular. It is a miniature Garden of Eden with low hills, pinewoods and olive groves fringed with yellow sandy beaches.

Beaches

Beaches line the south coast and south-east peninsular and also occur intermittently along the east coast north of Zakynthos town. The town itself has a small pay beach but Laganas beyond the airport on the south coast is the island's premier beach resort with a broad sweep of golden sand stretching for four miles surrounded by hotels, restaurants and pine trees. It has all the watersports on offer.

Porto Roma and Gerakas at the tip of

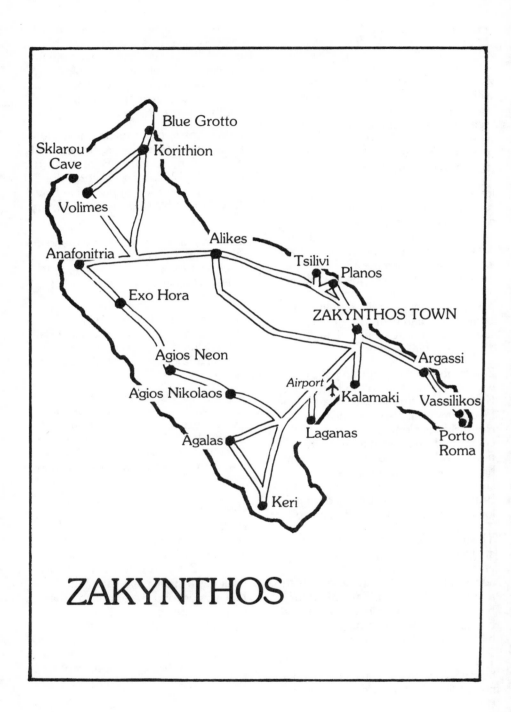

ZAKYNTHOS

the south-east peninsular below Vassiliki also have good sand and are more remote from civilisation, yet they have restaurants and an access road from Zakynthos.

Agios Nikolaos has a series of attractive sandy coves, plus one long stretch, which is the single most spectacular beach on the island, while Porto Zoro further north is a tiny developing resort with hotel and restaurant. But the most exotic beach on the island is a long stretch at Dafni, sometimes called Mela, reached by a dirt road running south from the Porto Roma road just past Xirokastelo. It has two restaurants and is backed by high cliffs as it winds around the bay. It is also popular with the logger-head turtles, who beach on the broad sweep of the Bay of Laganas.

There are other slightly less accessible strands in the lee of the south-east cape beyond Vassiliki and nearer town at Argassi and Kalamaki, while Keri in the far south-west corner of the island has a swimmable beach at its small harbour reached 3 miles before the village itself.

Beaches are not so easy to find on the east coast of the island, but Alikes 11 miles north of Zakynthos has a magnificent stretch backed by a salt lake with two or three beach tavernas. Tsivili, halfway between Zakynthos and Alikes, also has a good beach.

Nightlife

Zakynthos town boasts a dozen good restaurants on picturesque squares and terraces where strolling musicians revive the Venetian occupation at its best with local cantades or folk-songs accompanied by guitar or mandolin. This is a particular delight of Zakynthos which is found on no other

Greek island. Try the two restaurants up by the fort for spectacular views of the town, and the beach restaurants along the coast towards Akrotiri for sunsets.

The Panorama restaurant below the fort serves some of the best food on the island in a pleasant garden setting and has superb views of the harbour and town, which looks like an illuminated toy model at night.

The Arekia restaurant along the promenade towards Akrotiri has live music and good cooking. And a restaurant bar on the rocky tip of Akrotiri gives stunning views of the sea and Tsilivi hundreds of feet below.

All the main beach resorts have developed a good choice of bars and tavernas and are alive with music and discos at night in the summer.

There is also a discotheque in Zakynthos and three or four cinemas.

Not to be missed on Zakynthos

Zakynthos town has four grand churches which survived the earthquake, including the 15th century Agios Nikolaos just off the harbour, and two museums which house other religious relics salvaged after the quake, paintings of the Ionian School and writings of the island's most famous poet, Dionysus Solomos. He popularised demotic Greek, and wrote the National Anthem during the War of Independence. The Venetian castle is a pleasant evening's walk away from town and gives amazing views of the island and the Peloponnese.

Visitors staying in the town should take buses or rent their own transport to see the rest of the island. The road along the south coast leads through pinewoods.

Gerakas and Crystal beaches at the north end of Laganas Bay are breeding grounds for loggerhead turtles measuring up to 4 feet. In fact, the Greek Government has had to limit building on a 500-metre strip of Crystal Bay where the turtles lay their eggs to prevent them being harassed by building, visitors and disco-music. Keri in the south-west has pitch springs which have been famous since the time of Herodotus and is also the centre of a hunting area, which adds spicy rabbit stew and game birds to the menus of the village restaurants.

The island is renowned for its healing sulphur springs and picturesque caves, which are found mainly along the inaccessible west coast and are most easily reached by boat from the quayside at Zakynthos or from Alikes. The three big sea caves are Agios Gerasimos and Sklavou on the west coast and Kianoun or the 'Blue Grotto' just north of Korithi on the northern tip of the island. There is also the big Megali cave between Kampi and Kallithea in the middle of the island.

A boat ride along the high west coast passes something like 100 caves and also the famous Smugglers Cove. It is often pictured on postcards thanks to the sail boat half-buried in its sands.

A short boat ride from Keri harbour takes visitors to the tiny islet of Marathonissi, where turtles breed in relative peace and quiet. The harbour itself has a quota of wildlife like frogs and baby turtles in a limpid stream and also boasts two good restaurants, so it is worth a visit.

Anyone with a car or motor-bike should make a trip to the north west end of the island. Take in the island's best-known monastery of Anafronitria, the rug-making village of Volimes and the tiny fishing harbour of Korithi. It is short on beach, but long on restaurants in a pretty setting and one of them has a surprisingly good swimming pool overlooking the sea for a pre-lunch dip. Allow plenty of time for this trip as the road is longer than it looks and Zakynthos has more than its quota of pot-holes where drivers least expect them.

Another worthwhile excursion, and a much shorter one, is up to the fort overlooking the town, taking in the pretty, spread-out suburb of Akrotiri where you can find many of the island's finest mansions sited along country roads in a cool hilly setting.

Worth visiting off Zakynthos

There is a regular ferry to Kyllini on the Peloponnese, which makes it easy to visit Olympia or to island-hop to Kefalonia and Ithaca.

There is also an extremely useful island-hopping Olympic plane, which flies to and fro from Corfu via Kefalonia. It is an extremely scenic route with surprisingly modest fares.

Kyllini can also be used as a gateway to all the other attractions of the Peloponnese if you have time and a car or fancy a mainland bus ride. But allow two days to visit the likes of Epidavros and Mycenae since they are some distance away and it is a pity to see them in a rush.

Delphi could also be taken in by ferry across the Gulf of Corinth.

Paxos

Paxos, or Paxi, is a tiny jewel of an island, around 10 kilometres long by 3 or 4 kilometres wide, which is about three hours' sailing time south of

Corfu and lies opposite Parga on the mainland, which is 1–1½ hours away by caique. It is a quiet place beside its famous neighbour to the north, its development limited by its size and a shortage of water.

It is the smallest of the seven main Ionian islands and everything seems miniaturised. Gaios, the capital and main port, with a former British residency, clusters around a small square facing two small offshore islands, Kastro and Panagia, which make a natural little harbour. It has a Lilliputian feel when a big ship goes down the channel between them.

An easy bus ride takes you from Gaios to Lakka, the second village of the island which lies on a big bay in the north, via lush olive groves and close to the pretty harbour of Longos on the east coast, which also seems small-scale. Alternatively, there are bikes and scooters for hire and the island is so small that it is possible for the energetic to walk everywhere.

Gaios only seems to teem with life when boatloads of day trippers descend from Corfu and when yacht flotillas arrive. Paxos has become a favourite base for yachting and sailing holidays, thanks to the clear, calm coastal waters around the island and around Antipaxos to the south, and many good anchorages around tiny islets and across on the Epirot mainland. Gaios and Lakka are the two main centres for dinghy sailing, yachting and also windsurfing.

Beaches

Paxos is not blessed with much sand, but it is easy to walk along the coast to find an uninhabited shingley cove with good swimming from pebbles or rocks anywhere on the east coast. There is a small sand strip near Gaios

and Lakka has sand in the water. Mongonissi also has sand in the south of the island and Longos has a pretty shingley beach. The west coast is mainly high cliffs with sea caves plunging deep into the water, but nearby Antipaxos has two superb beaches reached by boat from Gaios.

Nightlife

Gaios has most of the action in the evening, when the square is filled with tables and diners. It has two discos and late bars. But Lakka also has a lively night-time dining scene and a disco in a nearby olive grove.

Not to be missed on Paxos

It is well worth taking a boat trip around the island to see the deep blue sea caves on the high west coast, where seals are said to live. Kastro, the nearest islet facing Gaios, has a well-preserved Venetian castle and two other islets, Panagia and Mongonissi, can both be reached by boat from Gaios. Inland villages like Mazazia and Boikatika have pretty churches.

Worth visiting off Paxos

There are regular island steamers to Corfu and to Fiskardo and Sami on Kefalonia. Caiques also run to Kavos on the southern tip of Corfu, to Parga on the mainland and to the satellite island of Antipaxos for those seeking a change of scene and good sandy beaches.

Antipaxos

Antipaxos, or Antipaxi, lies about 40 minutes caique ride south of Gaios and has two distinct villages, but is only just inhabited. Its main attractions are its red and white wines and two shining sandy beaches, Voutoumi and Vrika, around the coast from Agrapoia, the tiny port of the island.

Ithaca

Lying close to the eastern shore of Kefalonia – so close at places that you feel you could swim across – Ithaca is the island kingdom of Odysseus, the legendary Greek hero who was responsible for the successful siege of Troy and spent years wandering back to his island home. It doesn't quite fit Homer's description, but there is enough evidence for the legend to stick.

The evidence includes the name of the island, Homeric age pottery found there, the steep, narrow and rocky terrain, and the way it still supports vineyards, olive groves, herds of goats and the odd cornfield. A hill in the north near Stavros overlooking 'three seas' has been identified as the site of the palace of Odysseus, the tiny horseshoe harbour of Polis as his harbour, and signs in the south point to the Cave of the Nymphs and the Spring of Arethusa. All bear close enough resemblance to Homer's descriptions for the whole legend to come alive when you are on the island.

Ithaca's more recent claim to fame is that the Prince and Princess of Wales chose it as their first anchorage in Greece when they honeymooned aboard the Royal Yacht. It is usually approached by island steamers from Corfu, Paxos, Patras, Lefkas or Kefalonia, with the trip from the neighbouring island taking about an hour. A few call at Frikes on the north-east coast, but most put in at Vathi, the modern port and capital of Ithaca. A red-roofed town with tall houses, it curves around a horseshoe harbour at the heart of a deep fjord-like bay and has been well-rebuilt since the 1953 earthquake hit the Ionian islands.

Ithaca is only about 18 kilometres long by around 6 kilometres wide and narrows to half a kilometre in the middle when the road linking north and south runs close to both shores. Buses run the length of the island, to Stavros and Frikes, there are bikes and scooters for hire, and caiques ply from Vathi to beaches around the coast, but it is also great walking country and many trips can be made on foot.

Beaches

The beaches are mostly shingle and white pebble set in pretty coves. Two can be found by walking across the headlands to the bays of Pisaetos and Sarakiniko across the headlands from Vathi and there are more by the coast road north at Agios Ioannis and Polis.

There are more beaches in the north in Asphales Bay and near Frikes and Kioni, which attracts both artists and yacht flotillas to its pretty harbour.

Nightlife and Dining Out

The quayside at Vathi is ringed by restaurants, kebab stalls and bars, which are lively at night. A few have music which can lead to energetic Greek dancing in the summer.

Not to be missed on Ithaca

You can find signposts in Vathi pointing to the 'Cave of the Nymphs' where Odysseus hid his going-away presents from the Phaecians, and it is an easy short evening walk. If you are feeling more energetic, push on to 'Arethusa's Fountain', which is about 4 kilometres south of Vathi over some lovely walking country. What is known as 'Odysseus' Castle' is a good walk or bus ride west of Vathi on the way to Pisaetos where there are the ruins of an ancient city.

A more likely site for Odysseus' castle is a hill beyond Stavros in the north, where Mycenean remains have been found within the walls of a Venetian castle, and Polis Bay makes a convincing 'Harbour of Odysseus'. Both can be reached by bus from Vathi, but a more spectacular trip is by boat via Vathi harbour and Frikes.

Vathi has a small museum with finds from the Homeric age to complete this Odysseus pilgrimage.

Worth visiting off Ithaca

A day trip to nearby Kefalonia, a huge green island, is a must for anyone staying in Ithaca for more than a few days. Most ships run to Sami, which has a passable pebble beach and two caves nearby dating back to ancient times to further supplement the Odysseus legend. If there are boats running in the other direction, Lefkas also presents a fascinating contrast to Ithaca.

It is possible to take a ship to Patras and bus on to big mainland sites like Olympia and Delphi – reached by ferry across the Gulf of Corinth – but you need more than a day for such journeys.

Kythera

Kythera is a sizeable island and a spectacular one but it is surprisingly neglected by tourists. It may be because it nominally belongs to the Ionian group, the seventh member of the Eptanissa 2 but is stuck out on its own south of Cape Maleas on the south-east tip of the Peloponnese.

It must be partly because it does not have the feel of a particularly friendly or welcoming island. It is decidedly short on good accommodation and eating.

It looks more like it should belong to the Cyclades because the landscape is burnt brown and the villages are white, while it has ferry and hydrofoil links with the Saronic isles, the Peloponnese and Crete. But the Venetian castle on the hill above Chora speaks of a common history with the Ionian group west of the Peloponnese, and Kythera was part of Britain's Ionian protectorate during the 19th century. The accents of many of the locals indicate strong modern links with Australia.

The island's bus service is intermittent, especially from Agia Pelagia, but access to the island is relatively good thanks to regular hydrofoils from Monemvassia and Gythion, ships from Neapolis and Gythion, calling at both main ports of Kapsali and Agia Pelagia, and a plane service from Athens, which lands at the little airport near Potamos.

Chora, the capital, stands high above Kapsali with its lofty Venetian castle and breathtaking views of two bays and the road snaking back to the port below. It is a tough walk uphill, but buses leave Kapsali for most villages on the island once a day and more frequently to Chora.

Beaches

Both the main ports on opposite sides of the islands have good sandy beaches in adjoining bays and there are better, more remote beaches north of Agia Pelagia at Platia Ammos and east of Kapsali on the track to Vroulaia, which itself has a pebble beach. There are more shingley beaches on the west coast. But the prettiest beaches are on the east coast below Avlemonas.

Nightlife and Dining Out

The big eating out scenes are at Agia Pelagia and Kapsali, though there are charming tavernas inland at both Chora and Potamos.

Not to be missed on Kythera

Helen of Troy chose Kythera for her honeymoon isle and it is pleasing to the eye. Chora has the most impressive buildings on the island, the Venetian fortress and stately mansions from the same period bearing coats of arms. It also has a small museum dating back to the ancient times and an amazing view.

But there is plenty to see if you are prepared to be patient with the buses and do some hill-walking. Get off the bus at Dokana and walk the road to the pretty village of Milopotamos, then down to the Agia Sophia cave near the sea, which boasts some of the best stalactites and stalagmites in Greece. The spectacular Nereides waterfall fills a small pool where the old people of Kythera take medicinal baths once a year. Kato Chora near Milopotamos has the walls of a Venetian castle and some fascinating ruined houses and old churches.

Plan to linger a while in Milopotamos. It is the Venice of Kythera with its main streets criss-crossed by a network of canals with attractive cafés on the side.

There are more Venetian remains at Avlemonas and a Byzantine castle at Palio Chora near the airport looking over a deep gorge where it is said many Greek mothers threw themselves and their children to death to avoid a worse fate at the hands of the Turks. The monastery of Myrtidiou is a stiff walk from Kapsali or Livadio, but has a magnificent setting high on the west coast and can be combined with a visit to Milopotamos.

Worth visiting off Kythera

Those who fly down to the island from Athens should take advantage of the good sea links to visit the mainland wonder of Monemvassia with its big Byzantine fortress and old town perched on a rock offshore. Boats go north and south to the small islands of Elafonissos and Antikythera. The latter is only for the birds or a quick visit en route for Crete, but Elafonissos is well worth a visit.

Elafonissos

Don't be put off by the name. Elafonissos is a sandy island with half a dozen great beaches that can be reached in just ten minutes by small boat from a tiny port 5 kilometres north of Neapolis. The straits are so narrow at that point you feel you could swim across and both the mainland and the island boast good yellow sandy beaches at that point.

The island has only one village with a strip of restaurants around the port and some good rooms along the beach that stretches away beyond the promontory. But there are short walks of an hour or so to some delightful desert island beaches across the island.

Elafonissos does not have the spectacular scenery of Kythera, but it feels more friendly, is more accessible and offers better beaches and eating. If you get bored with the island, there are good places to eat and stay just ten minutes away on the Peloponnese mainland.

Antikythera

Antikythera is a few hours from both Kythera and Crete, and isn't worth staying on unless you want real solitude off the tourist track. It has two villages and a few trees, but is mostly rocky and populated by goats.

Lefkas

Lefkas, or Lefkada, is only just an island. A tarmac road stretches across the limpid lagoon that surrounds its main port and links it with the mainland, of which it was once part. So it is not surprising that it resembles the Epirot countryside with wooded hills and high cliffs reaching down to the sea and more wildlife than most of the other Ionian islands. It is called Lefkas ('white') after the sheer chalk cliffs on the west coast.

The main port, which is also called Lefkas or Lefkada, lies directly across the lagoon on the northern tip of the island facing the Medieval castle of Santa Maura across the straits. There are flat-bottomed fishing boats on the lagoon and seagulls perch on the remains of an old Turkish aquaduct.

It is an exotic scene and it continues in the town, which has stone Venetian churches and tall houses with Turkish-style wooden balconies separated by thin alleyways. It suffered earthquake damage in 1948, but has now been substantially restored and has a colourful pedestrian walkway and square lined with restaurants, shops and cafes running right through it from just right of where the lagoon road reaches the island.

Nidri halfway down the east coast is a sprawling village with numerous tavernas which a German archaeologist once pronounced to be the capital of Odysseus when he found traces of a 1st millennium BC town there. It looks out on a cluster of rocky islets, Meganisi, Scorpios, Sparti

and Mandouri, between Lefkas and the mainland, which have an endless supply of sheltered anchorages and have helped to put Nidri on the map as a major sailing and yacht flotilla centre.

South-east Lefkas has half a dozen other sheltered harbours such as Vliho, Roda, Sivota and Vassiliki, which are almost landlocked by high wooded cliffs and are popular ports for yachts. The peninsular in the far south around Cape Lefkada is of different character because the lush landscape changes to a barren rocky promontory with sheer white cliffs and a lighthouse stands at the highest point, called Sappho's Leap, where the poetess is believed to have taken her last bow when spurned in love. The west coast of the island also has sheer cliffs until you reach Agios Nikitas 10 kilometres south of Lefkas town.

Lefkas is easily accessible from Athens and the mainland, due to the drive-on road from Epirus and also the airport of Preveza, which is only half an hour's drive from Lefkas port.

Beaches

Lefkas has some extremely scenic beaches, though they tend to be shingle rather than sand. The best ones are on the west coast.

There is a sandspit called Yiro just outside Lefkas town and another magnificent stretch of beach just 2 kilometres away called Agios Ioannis. Agios Nikitas is favoured with three beaches, a sparkling little cove next to the harbour, a long stretch to the north with two tavernas and a third at Kathisma 2 kilometres south with taverns and rooms.

The most famous beach on the west coast is the much-photographed Porto

Katsiki, backed by high cliffs, but there are plenty of other good stretches below the pretty hill villages of Athani, Komilio and Kalamitsi.

The east coast beaches facing the mainland enjoy calmer seas, but are thin and pebbly. Nidri has a passable strip, but it is crowded. The best are around Nidiana.

The best pebble beaches on the south coast are the sparkling harbour of Poros and the big bay of Vassiliki.

Nightlife and dining out

Nidri has a busy eating out scene with occasional music, and Vassiliki has a bar and two discos in season, but nightlife on the island is what you make it and largely confined to outdoor restaurants.

Not to be missed on Lefkas

There is a ring road around the island, making it easy to drive to the scenic wonder of Sappho's Leap.

There are regular caiques and buses to Nidri, and some go from there to the offshore islets so you can catch a glimpse of the yachts and armed guards on Scorpios, the private island of Aristotle Onassis, the Greek shipping tycoon, now owned by his grand-daughter.

Nidri is also the place to see Derpfeld's 1st Millennium town, but it is too busy for a relaxing place to stay. Much better is the pretty compact village of Agios Nikitas. Nidiana is the pick of the east coast resorts and Vassiliki, with its pretty harbour and dining scene, wins out on the south coast.

Worth visiting off Lefkas

Boats go most days from Nidri across to Vathi, the main port of Meganisi island, the biggest in the offshore group. There are some huge sea caves around its rocky shores.

Lefkas also has occasional connections by ferry to Ithaca and Kefalonia, which are only a few miles to the south of Cape Lefkas.

Since Lefkas is almost attached to the mainland, it is easy to drive or bus to some of the big mainland sights like Meteora and Delphi.

Meganisi

Meganisi is one of the quiet gems of the Ionians. It has two ports at Spilia and Vathi that link to the nearby hill villages of Spartochori and Katomeri. All are linked by a good tarmac road and you can walk the four in just over an hour and scarcely pass a car.

Yet all four have good restaurants and rooms, and access to pretty shingle beaches by passable side roads. The island is just struggling on to the package tour track and sees a fair number of foreign visitors during the day, thanks to boat excursions.

In summer there are around four ferries a day from Nidri that make the crossing to both Spilia and Vathi in around half an hour. Spilia and neighbouring Spartochori have most of the action, thanks to the excursion boats, the yacht flotillas and a long beach running along from the harbour. But Katomeri is the best place to stay for a few days.

It is a friendly, floral village with spectacular views in all directions and an amazing wealth of restaurants and cafes.

Katomeri also has the island's only year-round accommodation at the lovely little Hotel Meganisi and access to five isolated beaches in nearby bays. The best are Limonari and Athineros near the east cape light facing the mainland.

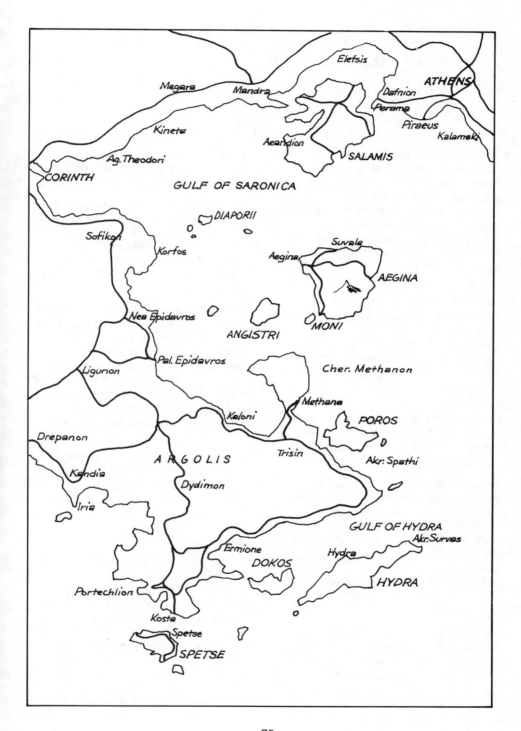

ATHENS

Elefsis

Megara   Mandra   Dafnion

Kineta   Perama

Piraeus

Aeandion   Kalamaki

Ag. Theodori   SALAMIS

CORINTH   GULF OF SARONICA

DIAPORII

Sofikon   Suvala

Korfos   Aegina

AEGINA

Nea Epidavros   MONI

ANGISTRI

Pal. Epidavros   Cher. Methanon

Ligurion   Methana

Keloni   POROS

Drepanon   Trisin   Akr. Spathi

A R G O L I S

Kandia   Dydimon

Iria

GULF OF HYDRA

Akr. Survas

Ermione   Hydra

DOKOS

Portechlion   HYDRA

Kosta

Spetse

SPETSE

75

7. Isles of Saronic Gulf

You can take a mini-cruise all the way down the Saronic Gulf as far as Spetse island and return the same day, calling at three other islands and the Peloponnese on the way and passing five other islands. You can do it even quicker by hydrofoil from Zea Marina, which halves the trip to Spetse to two hours.

But the isles of the Gulf are all different and it is worth lingering a while on each if you have the time. The ships and hydrofoils are so frequent and turnrounds in port so fast that it is easy to island hop and cover the whole chain in a few days.

Aegina

First port of call for most of the ferries that ply the Saronic Gulf islands is Aegina. It takes about 1½ hours by ferry and 30 minutes by hydrofoil.

Aegina is close enough to Athens for many city workers to commute each day, and is the busiest island in the Gulf. Yet it is well clear of the cloud of pollution that hangs over Athens and the Piraeus and has a great away-from-it-all atmosphere, absorbing the thousands of people disgorged by the ferries without ever looking over-crowded.

The main port is grand, bustling and colourful. Island buses, bicycle hire shops and painted carriages drawn by plumed horses compete for attention with sponge and pistachio nut sellers and the most exotic fruit and

vegetable market in Greece – operated by dozens of wide-bottomed caiques moored around the harbour.

On the jetty around the harbour is a little white wedding cake of a church dedicated to Saint Nicholas, the patron of Greek sailors and a grand view of the town, which is full of high mansions and church domes hinting at a rich past.

Aegina was one of the most powerful seafaring states in ancient Greece and minted coins as early as the 7th century BC. It sent a large fleet of ships to the neighbouring island of Salamis to help defeat the Persian fleet in 480 BC, but a few years later fell foul of the imperial ambitions of Athens and was absorbed into the Athenian confederacy.

It was one of the first places in Greece to be liberated from the Turks and in 1828 briefly became the capital of Greece and the residence of John Capodistra.

Beaches

Aegina town has a swimmable sandy beach to the left of the harbour, but for a day on the beach it is worth taking a bus or bicycle to the village of Perdika opposite the islet of Moni, to Souvala on the north coast or to the long beach of Aegina Marina a 20 minute bus ride across the island, where a string of hotels, restaurants and tourist shops look over a curving bay dotted with yachts, windsurfers and water-skiers. There are even better beaches on the satellite islets of Moni and Angistri, which are reached by daily caique from the harbour near to Saint Nicholas' chapel.

Nightlife and Dining Out

Aegina town's waterfront is crammed with places to eat out in the evening, but you might find better fish in Perdika and Aegina Marina. The latter's restaurants know how to charge, but it is often worth it to sit on a balcony high above the sea and watch the sun set.

Not to be missed on Aegina

The island's main site is the beautiful little temple of Athena Aphaia, which dates from the 5th century BC and has two concentric rectangles of Doric columns in a superb state of preservation. It stands on a pine-clad hill a short walk or donkey ride from Aegina Marina and is served by buses that run between there and Aegina town. It is dedicated to the goddess Aphaia, a sister or rival of Artemis, who was a huntress and was herself pursued by an amorous beast. She threw herself into the sea to escape and would have drowned, but was rescued by friendly fishermen.

The main bus route across the island also takes pilgrims to the shrine of Saint Nectarios in the middle of the island. The church is modern, but a short walk uphill there is a fascinating glimpse of the past in the ruined medieval capital of Paleochora. It flourished from the 9th to the 19th century and has the remains of over 20 Byzantine churches and monasteries.

Worth visiting off Aegina

Visitors staying on Aegina should certainly take a day trip to Athens to see the city's ancient sites and catch the mood of a modern Greek city. It is easily accomplished by ferry or hydrofoil.

Aegina's own interior is peaceful, but it is worth taking a boat to Angistri or Moni for a glimpse of a more away-from-it-all island, though neither has anything to offer beyond good beaches, peaceful walks through the interior and seaside restaurants.

The other islands in the Saronic chain, Poros, Hydra and Spetse, can also be reached in a day trip by boat or hydrofoil from Aegina and it is also possible to cross to the mainland via either Poros or Athens to visit the sites of the Argolid peninsular.

Poros

Second port of call for ships that run down the Saronic Gulf, Poros is a little over two hours from Piraeus by ship and an hour by hydrofoil. It is smaller than its northern neighbour, Aegina, and so close to the Peloponnese coast that you feel you could swim across the straits – a trip that is usually made by benzina or water taxi.

Poros has a stunning port that rises like a white pyramid above its bustling harbour. Its quayside teems with cafés, restaurants, hotels and tourist shops. The benzinas skip across the straits to Galata on the mainland and to the beaches of Poros island, adding a Venetian flavour to the scene.

The port is the only town and it stands on a tiny peninsular of the main island called Sferia, which you can walk around easily in an hour. The Bay of Neorion on one side contains a naval school and an old battleship, the 'Averoff', which was flagship of the Greek navy until 1945.

The atmosphere of Sferia is not that of

a peaceful Greek island, but there are delights on Kalavria, the main island, which is green and quiet surrounded by rocky coves and occasional shingle beaches. It also contains most of the hotels that have drawn package tours to Poros in recent years.

Like Aegina with Aphaia, Poros has its own special god, Poseidon, and he was worshipped on a sanctuary in the heart of Kalavria. Demosthenes fled there from the wrath of the Macedonians and took the hemlock in the sanctuary. In the 19th century, after an allied force of European nations threw out the Turks, the Russians had a naval base on Poros beyond the present naval school. It is still known as Russian Bay.

Beaches

There are beaches on both Neorion and Askeli Bays with windsurfing and water-skiing, including Kanali which is more organised than most and is by a canal.

The beaches of Kalavria are not the stuff that dreams are made of and are mostly shingle, but you can find attractive little coves with amazingly clear waters.

Nightlife and Dining Out

If you eat in the port, which has a string of restaurants along the quayside, you will be entertained by regular ship arrivals and departures, punctuated by bells, loud speakers and much churning of water as well as a scene of constant to-ings and fro-ings by small boats and benzinas. There is never a dull moment. There are also two discotheques on the Sferia peninsular.

Not to be missed on Poros

There are two pleasant walks inland on Kalavria to the monastery of Zoodochos Pigi (the 'spring of life') and to the remains of a temple on Poseidon in the ancient sanctuary.

Worth visiting off Poros

Poros is a good island base for visiting the wonders of the Peloponnese across the straits. Galata has a pleasant beach and there are more along the coast from there. A short bus ride away is the famous amphitheatre of Epidavros, the colourful port of Methana, ancient Troezene with a Frankish castle, Lemonodassos (the 'lemon forest') and the waterfall of Devil's Gorge.

Hydra

Hydra is a bare, brown rock of an island, with virtually no roads or cars. Most goods are transported around the island either by boat around the coast or by mule train up the steep hillsides. But its port is one of the smartest in the Aegean, rivalling Mykonos for beautiful people, boutiques, discotheques and restaurants overflowing with lobster.

It is a galaxy of colour in an amphitheatre setting of a bay between two cliffs with stately mansions in white, blues and reds with red roofs rising from a harbour full of boats. Cannons stand at the harbour mouth testifying to Hydra's proud seafaring past and its vital role, along with neighbouring Spetse, in the Greek War of Independence.

It is not surprising that it has become a haunt of artists, film-makers and fashion-conscious sun-worshippers. Hydra starred in the film, 'Boy on a Dolphin' and also featured in 'Phaedra'.

The waterfront usually seethes with

people and is an expensive place to eat, drink and shop, but there is normal Greek life a few yards beyond to be seen by visitors who wander through the town's labyrinth of alleyways. It takes over too in the early morning when most foreign visitors are still abed. Women shop for fruit and vegetables from wide-bottomed caiques and sleepy-looking mules wait for their daily burdens on the quayside.

Hydra is three hours from Athens by ferry and about half that by hydrofoil.

Hydra's mansions were built in the 18th century by rich sea captains when the town had a merchant fleet of nearly 200 vessels trading all over the Mediterranean. It was a natural place for the flag of Greek independence to be raised as early as 1821.

The Hydriots under admirals Miaoulis and Tombazis harried the Turkish fleets in a most effective way. The famous leaders are remembered today in the names of ships and there is a Tombazis' school of fine arts on Hydra.

Beaches

The beaches are not great and many sun-worshippers spread themselves on rocks on either side of the port, which reek of sun oil in summer and reflect big sheet mirrors used by dedicated worshippers seeking a quick all-over tan.

The best beach within easy reach of the port is Mandraki, a sandy strip in a bay half an hour by foot to the east. There are two or three pretty pebbly coves about the same distance away to the west of the port, but nowadays more people go for a longer walk or a boat trip to the pine-fringed Molos Bay further west, or take a boat to the Hydra Beach on the mainland or to a big bay on Dokos island just off the mainland.

Nightlife and Dining Out

Hydra port throbs with life at night when the tables around the quayside get crowded with diners. It also throbs to the music of two or three discotheques. Open-air cinemas add to the general bustle.

Not to be missed on Hydra

Anyone who likes walking can find a totally different world in the bare hills above the port. An hour uphill takes you to the monastery of Profitis Ilias and the convent of Agia Evpraxia where the nuns are keen to sell their handicrafts. There are some splendid open views from there and also from the monasteries of Agia Triada and of Zourvas in the far east of the island and from the villages of Zougeri and Episkopi in the hills above Molos Bay.

Worth visiting off Hydra

There are frequent ferry connections to Spetse, Poros and Aegina, to Athens and also to Ermioni on the Peloponnese. From there it is possible to visit Epidavros.

Spetse

Spetse is the most southerly island of the Saronic Gulf, hugging the southern tip of the Argolid peninsular and so close to the mainland you feel you could swim across on a fine day. In fact, it takes about half an hour by small boat to the mainland and Spetse is less accessible than the other islands of the Gulf. It takes four hours by ferry from Piraeus, two hours by hydrofoil and about five hours by bus.

The island has a lively port and gently undulating pine-covered hills where tortoises roam across the paths. It also has a ring road, which gives easy access to dozens of little coves containing shingle beaches. The island is so small that you can walk round it in a day, but transport is usually by boat or horse-drawn carriages which clatter along the narrow streets around the port with a haunting rhythm. There are also bikes and mopeds for hire.

The absence of cars gives Spetse a relaxed air and the island was immortalised as 'Phraxos' by John Fowles in 'The Magus' in quieter days. Nowadays it draws a high quota of tourists, many young, who are attracted by its lively night life. That takes place around the main port, which now spreads a long way along the waterfront either side of the harbour or Dappia.

Like Hydra, Spetse was one of the first islands to rebel against the Turks and spark off the War of Independence in 1821. It sent 100 ships to war and destroyed almost as many Turkish ships in its own straits with fire boats.

The local museum, housed in one of the 18th century mansions in the port, contains relics of the War and Spetse's Joan of Arc, a fierce amazon of a woman called Bouboulina who helped lead the struggle against the Turks. A bust of Bouboulina and two cannons stand in the port as a reminder of the fight.

Beaches

There seems to be a shingley cove around every headland of the island, all within walking distance. Three of them, Paraskevi and Anagyri on the west coast, and Zogeria in the north, are established favourites with beach tavernas, windsurfing and water-skiing, and boats from the harbour. If you don't want to travel that far, you can swim from a small spit called Agia Marina at one end of the town or from another strip at the other end next to Anagyros College.

The best sandy beach is not on the island, but across at Costa on the mainland where there is a string of hotels and restaurants and a bus service to the Peloponnese.

Nightlife and Dining Out

Spetse has a lively nightlife with pubs, discotheques and music in tavernas rocking the heart of the town around the harbour every night. The port stays awake until early morning and sleeps late, and so do some of the beaches in summer when parties go on well into the night.

Not to be missed on Spetse

It is easy to walk everywhere around the island and in its wooded interior. A short walk around the south of the island beyond the port brings you to the shore opposite Spetsapoula, a private island owned by the Niarchos family of shipping fame. A short walk to the west is Anagyros College and the pine coast that inspired John Fowles to write 'The Magus'.

Worth visiting off Spetse

There are good boat connections with Costa, Porto Heli and Ermioni for a quick visit to the mainland and buses from the three ports to the nearby sites of the Argolid peninsular such as Epidavros. There are also ferries and hydrofoils to Piraeus, which make it possible to do a quick tour of Athens and the other islands of the Gulf in a day, though anyone bent on seeing the sights of the capital would be well-advised to stay overnight there.

Angistri

Angistri is half an hour's sail by caique from Aegina and developed as a satellite of the bigger island, but thanks to its beaches and its closeness to Athens is now flourishing as a resort island in its own right with boats direct from Piraeus.

Two simple little resorts have grown up around two sandy beaches at Skala and Milos, which are 30 minutes apart by foot, around 10 minutes by hired bicycle and 5 minutes by bus if it is running. The beaches have clear waters, windsurfing, water-skiing and restaurants, and both have caiques to Aegina. Angistri is strictly for people who like to laze on the beach and walk the hills among herds of goats.

Salamis

Salamis is the site of the famous sea battle of 480 BC that ended the Persian invasions of Greece, and is the nearest island of the Saronic Gulf to the mainland. It can be reached in only 10 minutes from Perama where flat-bottomed ferries depart for Salamis every quarter of an hour. But, alas, it is not a particularly inviting island.

The ferries from Perama land at Paloukia on the east coast and others from Piraeus dock at Selinia. The villages on this coast are white, but not pretty and there is an air of abandon in both the villages and dockyards that occupy the bays on the east coast, while the north faces the industrial mainland of Elefsis and Megara.

The west coast is served by frequent bus services from Paloukia to Salamis or Koulouri and has a number of small shingley beaches at places like Psili Ammos and Moulki, but they are not somehow as appealing as they should be. The best beaches are found in the south where pinewoods stretch down to the sea.

8. The Sporades and Evia

North of Evia and east of Mount Pelion lies a group of a dozen pine-clad islands called the Sporades or 'scattered isles'. Four are inhabited and have developed as tourist islands, thanks to good ship connections from Agios Constantinos and Volos on the mainland and Kimi on Evia, an airport on the most developed, Skiathos, which has direct flights from Britain as well as Athens, and an airstrip on Skiros with Athens flights.

They have no ancient civilisation and not much history, but they are great holiday isles. They are a bit remote from Athens by ship, but easy to island-hop once you are there.

Alonissos

Alonissos is the most unlikely holiday island of the Sporades. Most of it is bare of habitation and it suffered bad earthquake damage in the mid-sixties, but it swept on to the tourist track in the early 1970's when a French architect built the Club Marpounta on its southern tip. A bustling new port has developed at Patitiri on the coast an hour's walk below the original Chora of the island, which was earthquaked. Parts of that are now being restored with the help of foreign residents, many of them artists.

The island is the biggest in a group of half a dozen, most of them uninhabited, which can be reached by caique from Patitiri harbour. The same form of transport has opened up a number of good pebble and sand beaches around the long shoreline of Alonissos.

Beaches

When they built the Club Marpounta, the French had to import sand to give it a beach fit to match the tennis court and dance floor. Most of the beaches around Patitiri and the nearby village of Votsi in the south of the island are of the pebble variety, although the best like Kokkino Kastro ('red castle'), Chryssi Milia ('golden apple') and Agios Dimitrios on the east coast and Yiala on the west are big and glitter in the sunshine. Peristera, the satellite island to the east of Alonissos, has an abundance of sandy coves and can be reached by caique from Patitiri.

Not to be missed on Alonissos

The old capital of Chora is well-worth a stiff walk of 2 kilometres or about half an hour uphill to see old houses, some of them now restored, which are much prettier than the concrete slab style of Patitiri and Votsi.

Worth visiting off Alonissos

Alonissos has an easy half hour ferry connection around two spectacular capes to Skopelos and then on to Skiathos, while a ferry in the opposite direction takes 2–3 hours to reach Skiros or Kimi on Evia. It is possible to visit all the small satellite isles by caique, but the only easy, regular runs are to Peristera. Panangia Kyra to the

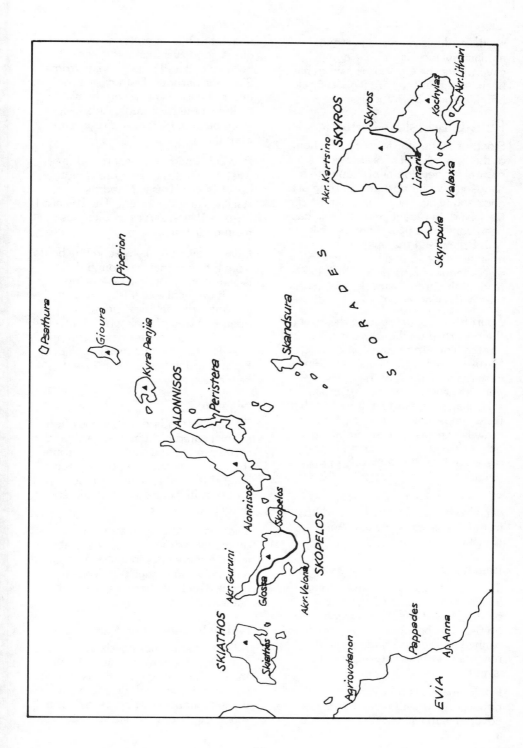

north of Alonissos has a pretty old monastery and Gioura has a huge cave where the Cyclops is said to have been born, but they are a good three hours by boat from Alonissos.

Pine-Clad Isle – Skiathos

Skiathos is the star tourist attraction of the Sporades. It was always a natural for development thanks to a handsome white port and a string of good sandy beaches which almost ring the island. In recent years its role has been confirmed by a direct air link with Britain and the opening of a host of smart restaurants, boutiques and discotheques in the port, which have made it the premier tourist island of the north Aegean.

Apart from a short road to the airport, the only road on the island is a 7-mile stretch along the south coast, which features a regular bus and is within easy reach of most of the island's popular beaches, hotels, water-ski school and windsurfing. It means that those who want to get away from the crowds can easily do so by taking a boat or walking to the north of the island, or by hiring a bicycle in the town.

Skiathos is easy to get to by air, but can also be reached by bus and boat from Athens via Volos and Agios Konstantinos.

Beaches

The long sandy curve of pine-fringed Koukounaries must be the most photographed beach in Greece, but on Skiathos beaches come, like Heinz canned foods, in 57 varieties and reach most of the way around the island.

Koukounaries is now flanked by hotels, dotted with restaurants, and covered with windsurfers and hired boats, but it is as pretty as ever and offers good swimming. It is served both by bus and regular boats from Skiathos harbour. Both pass a number of other good beaches on the way, including Megaliammos, Akladias, Vromolimno, Platanias, Troulos and Maratha.

Beyond Koukounaries, around the western headland, lie more remote beaches like Krassi, Mandraki, Aselinos and Agia Eleni. The so-called Banana Beach serves as Skiathos' main nudist beach.

Lalaria cove, usually reached by boats, from the port that go around the island, is the most exotic-looking beach on Skiathos. It is a curve of shining white pebbles ending in an open archway of rock which looks like a prehistoric monster rising from the sea. The same boats usually call at Kastro, which has another lovely beach.

Nightlife

By Greek standards, Skiathos offers sophisticated nightlife in smart bars, restaurants and discotheques around the main port and the pretty green peninsular that juts out into the harbour. Its peninsular sometimes doubles as a disco.

There is a great open-air eating scene on the waterfront and on steps above it and a number of 'pubs' can be found offering a wide range of European beers. The town has cinemas and occasional theatre.

Not to be missed on Skiathos

A boat trip around the island to Lalaria and Kastro is a must. Kastro is the fortified old town of the island on a high cliff in the north where most of the inhabitants lived up to 1825 as a safe refuge from the Turks and

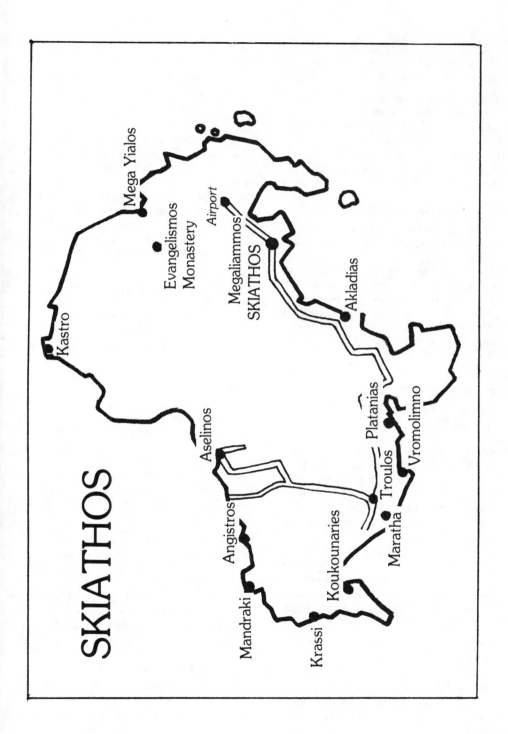

marauding pirates. It has a Byzantine monastery, a church with frescoes and the remains of a castle and old houses.

Those who want to escape the crowds can walk across the island through pine-covered hills to Kastro. It takes around two hours either by the Evangelismos monastery or via Agios Apostolos church and the fountain of Agios Dimitrios.

Worth visiting off Skiathos

Skiathos has easy ship connections with Glossa on Skopelos and on to the other Sporades. In the other direction ships go to the mainland at Volos and Agios Konstantinos, but the most rewarding trip is by ferry to Platanias on the tip of Pelion for a glimpse of an extraordinarily fertile peninsular with early 18th century villages poking out of wooded hillsides.

Skiros

Skiros is remote from the rest of the Sporades and from Evia, the ships in both directions taking around three hours, and it is bursting with its own individual character. It is famed for miniature ponies and miniature furniture and for local peasant dress. The women wear black dresses, embroidered blouses and patterned scarves and the men baggy pants and flat leather shoes. The islanders are also curiously addicted to copperware and ceramic plates and the houses in Skiros town usually open their doors for public viewing of these treasures in the evenings.

The main town is one of the most spectacular in Greece. It is white in colour and sprinkled like salt down a hillside high above the coast. It was built up there to protect the islanders from pirates and marauding Turks and has gained great style from its position

and unusual houses. They are white cubes topped with grey gravel roofs, strangely similar to Moorish dwellings in Almeria province of Spain, and are linked by pathways that are more terraced steps than roads.

Skiros is where Rupert Brooke, the First World War poet is buried and it was the setting of the film, 'Cry in the Wind'. There is also a psychotherapeutic community in the town teaching people a new way of life, and a Holistic centre in Atsitsa Bay teaching windsurfing, aerobics, massage, painting, pottery and writing.

The island's main road connects Skiros town to the port of Linaria, where the island steamers call, and is served by buses that meet the ships. There is now a daily flight from Athens to the airstrip in the north of the island.

Beaches

Both sides of the island are blessed with good sandy beaches. In Skiros you don't have to walk further than the coast below the town to Magazia beach and that runs almost uninterrupted around the wide bay, but there are less crowded coves both north beyond the headland and south in Achilli Bay.

There are equally convenient and less crowded beaches on the west coast flanking Linaria harbour, notably the broad sweep of Kalamitsa Bay, at Pefka and pine-fringed Atsitsa, which is a stiff walk from either Linaria or Skiros town. All have beach tavernas operating in the summer.

Nightlife and Dining Out

The main town rocks with music and carousing in summer when restaurants along the main street seem to spread upwards from the pavements to balconies and rooftops. There is also a lively scene below the town above Magazia beach where two discos make intermittent appearances and send music booming along the coast.

Not to be missed on Skiros

Visitors staying in Skiros should take the bus for a day out in Linaria and vice-versa since the two places are so different in character. In the main town it is worth climbing to the acropolis to see the remains of a Venetian castle and the 10th century monastery of Agios Georgios. Below it lies a memorial ground to Rupert Brooke set high above the coast and close by are two lovely little museums, one devoted to folk art and one to archaeological finds.

Rupert Brooke's grave is in the big bay of Tris Boukes in the south and is best visited by caique from Linaria or Skiros. He died offshore on route to the Gallipoli landings.

Worth a visit off Skiros

It is a long way to both the northern Sporades and to Evia, so both trips are worth combining with an overnight stay. Alonissos, the first port of call in the north, is a much rockier island, while Evia is fertile and heavily wooded around Kimi, the port of the east side of the island, which is connected to the pretty hill village of the same name by a long serpentine road. Skiros is a long haul by road and ferry across Evia and there is a case for staying en route in one of the big Evian resorts like Eretria.

Skopelos

Skopelos means 'the reef' in Greek and the second port of call for the Sporades steamers after Skiathos is more rocky and less developed than its famous neighbour to the west. It is also more wooded and fertile, producing olives, nectarines, almonds and plums. It does not have the great sandy beaches of Skiathos, but it appeals to visitors who value nature above beaches.

It has one main road, which runs the lengths of the island from its hospitable white pyramid of a port, Skopelos, to Glossa on the northern tip, which also serves as a port for many ships. A good bus service runs between the two and Loutraki, which acts as the port of Glossa. Bicycles may also be hired to make the journey.

Both villages tumble down hillsides, their houses connected by paved steps. The roofs of Skopelos are tiled with attractive grey slates, and the town is crammed with churches and tavernas where strong drink seems to flow more freely than it does on most islands.

Beaches

Sand is rare around the coast, but there is no lack of swimmable beaches. You can swim from the broad sweep of bay around from Skopelos harbour, walk straight across the island to shingley coves at Staphylos and Agontas, which has a sand beach reached by small boat or a wooded walk at Limonari. Further west are more pebbly stretches at Panormos, Milia, Elia and Klima.

There are few windsurfers or water-skiers to be seen on these beaches, just tavernas in the trees, and another isolated strand can be found in the north of the island by walking across from Glossa to the east coast at Perivoli.

Nightlife and Dining Out

Nightlife in both Skopelos and Glossa revolves around eating out in the open air and drinking at the many bars in Skopelos town. Discos are thin on the ground.

Not to be missed on Skopelos

It is a great island for walking. There are short walks from Skopelos town to the Venetian castle above, to Ambeliki where there are the ruins of an ancient asklepion or hospital, and to Agios Konstantinos around the bay, which has a watchtower above a shingle beach. A good long walk from the town goes across the spine of the island around Mount Dhelfi to the west coast at Elios passing the churches of Agios Alexandros and Agios Riginos.

You can walk across the island from Glossa to the monastery of Agios Ioannis Kastri as well as Perivoli beach.

Worth visiting off Skopelos

Take the island steamers to Skiathos one way, and close to Glossa, and the other way to Alonissos to see completely different islands, the first touristy and sandy, while the second is barer. The steamers can be taken on to Platanias on the wooded peninsular of Pelion or to Kimi on the big island of Evia.

Evia

Evia is the second biggest island in Greece after Crete and is strangely neglected by foreign tourists, though much appreciated by mainland Greeks. It is sad that it is not better known abroad because the island has a lot going for it and is tailor-made for a motoring holiday.

It has grand fertile countryside with magnificent scenery and a wealth of good sandy beaches, far superior to those of the mainland, mostly in the north and south rather than the middle, and is unbelievably easy to reach from Athens. There are no less than six ferry connections from the mainland – from Rafina to Karistos, Rafina to Marmaris, Agia Marina to Nea Stira, Oropos to Eretria, Arkitsa to Aedipsos and Glifa to Agiokambos – taking between half an hour and two hours. There is also a regular bus service to Chalkis.

It means that you can reach Evia in 1½–2 hours from Athens or its airport by car, bus or taxi, and delightful beach resorts like Nea Stira, Marmaris and Karistos are just 45 kilometres from the capital including the ferry crossing.

Evia touches the mainland at Chalkis, where it is connected by a swing bridge. It looks as though it was attached in bygone days and could have been separated by an earthquake. It has been volcanic in the past and you can see traces of green marble and lignite in the interior on the fringes of Mount Dirfis (5,500 feet).

Chalkis is the natural gateway to the island, and saves motorists a ferry fare, but it is a big, bustling port and is the centre of Evia's industrial coast in the middle of the island. It is worth visiting to see the museum or to marvel at the tides, which change in an inexplicable way six or seven times a day, but there are greater delights elsewhere for visitors seeking relaxation.

The island's two big towns have always been Chalkis and Eretria. In ancient times Halkis established many colonies abroad, notably in Halkidiki, and was for long the home of the philosopher, Aristotle, who drove

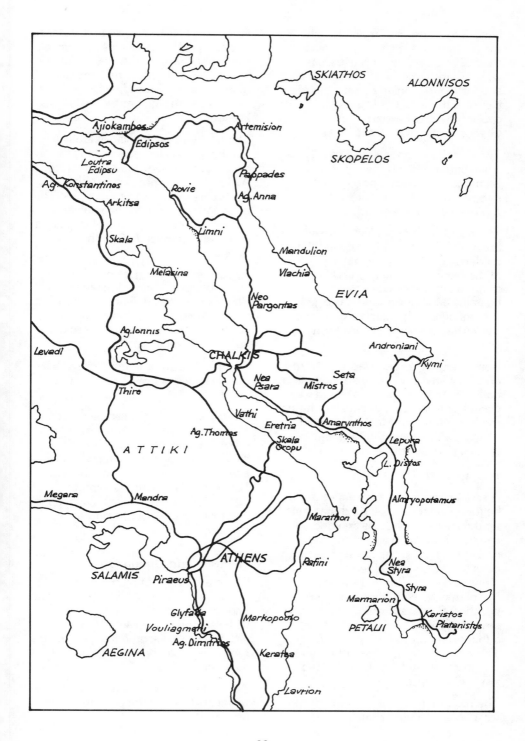

SKIATHOS

ALONNISOS

Ajiokambos

Artemision

Edipsos

SKOPELOS

Loutra
Edipsu

Pappades

Ag. Konstantinos

Rovie

Ag. Anna

Arkitsa

Skala

Limni

Mandulion

Melasina

Vlachia

EVIA

Neo
Pargontas

Ag. Ionnis

Androniani

Levadi

CHALKIS

Kymi

Seta

Nea
Psara

Mistros

Thire

Vathi

Eretria

Amarynthos

Ag. Thomas

Lepura

ATTIKI

Skala
Oropu

L. Distos

Megara

Mandra

Almyropotamus

Marathon

SALAMIS

ATHENS

Rafini

Nea
Styra

Piraeus

Styra

Glyfada

Marmarion

Vouliagmeni

Markopoulo

Karistos

Ag. Dimitrios

PETALII

Platanistos

AEGINA

Keratea

Lavrion

himself to distraction trying to solve the mystery of the changing tides in the Euripus Channel. Eretria shared with Athens the doubtful privilege of supporting the Ionian revolt which incurred the wrath of Darius and caused the first Persian invasion of Greece in 490 BC.

The Greeks fought a series of big naval battles just off the coast of the island during the second Persian invasion of 480 BC, weakening Xerxes' fleet at every turn.

The best traces of ancient civilisation are at Eretria in the hills beyond the modern port, where there are remains of the once-imposing city walls, temples and a well-worn amphitheatre boasting an underground passage through which the demon kings of old made their dramatic entries to the stage.

Roman emperors like Hadrian, Nero and Augustus came to take mineral baths at Aedipsos and the island was clearly prosperous and coveted during the Byzantine and Medieval periods because almost every hilltop and coastal port is crowned by a castle.

Beaches

A score of good sandy beaches are to be found alongside the road that runs up the east side of the island and you can never go far wrong heading for one of the ferry ports since all seem to be in big bays surrounded by sandy strips and calm waters. Karistos, Marmaris and Nea Stira all have good beaches. So does Eretria, which has a strip alongside the town and others on a thin promontory jutting into the gulf. There are more beaches at Limni, Gregolimano and Agiakambos and north of Aedipsos.

The road that runs around the north-west coast to Pefki, Kimassi, Artemissi, Peleki, Kotsiki and Vassilika also has good wide open stretches of sand to the right of the road. Kimi, the port on the east coast that serves Skiros and the Sporades, has a swimmable stretch next to its long harbour.

The northern peninsular of Lihas has a number of isolated beaches in little coves stretching around the bay from Aedipsos to the north coast beyond the tiny resort of Agios Georgios. This coast looks across to the mainland and gives a close-up view of ships and hydrofoils skimming off to the Sporades.

Anyone seeking a quiet beach resort close to Chalkis should make for Politika, around 20 kilometres north of the big town, where there is a long stretch of shingle beach flanked by hotels and restaurants.

Another charming little resort with a pebble beach is Rovies just north of Limni.

But if you are choosing a beach resort at which to stay for a week or more it is hard to beat Marmaris. It has two sandy beaches of its own and there is a wealth of sandy coves on the nearby Petali islands around 40 minutes offshore, which are easily reached in summer by small boat from the harbour.

Nightlife and Dining Out

There are lively eating out scenes at all the main towns, including Eretria, Kimi and Chalkis, whose ports are lined with seafood restaurants. There are also traces of discotheques, but they rarely seem to operate outside high summer.

Aedipsos has some superb eating at restaurants along the quay from the ferry-port.

Not to be missed on Evia

It is worth visiting the site of the old city of Eretria and the archaeological museum at Chalkis for a glimpse of the island's proud ancient past. But there are more traces of its Byzantine and Frankish periods.

There is a Medieval museum in Chalkis, there are forts at Karistos, Prokopi, Orei, Nea Stira and Kimi, and old churches and monasteries near Amarinthos, Galataki and Rovies. Aedipsos is one of the biggest spas in Greece for those who like to take the waters.

Walkers can find some magnificent scenery around Mount Dirfis in the middle of the island and Mount Ohi (4,800 feet) in the south.

The northern peninsular of Lihas offers spectacular scenery. So does the pass of Pagondas through which the road snakes from Chalkis to north Evia.

Worth visiting off Evia

Athens and the Attic coastline are easily accessible from all parts of Evia for visitors staying on the island, thanks to its many ferry routes. A long serpentine road across the central spine of Evia leads down to the port of Kimi, which offers ships to Skiros and the other Sporades. There are occasional ferries to Volos and Pelion from the north coast, so that visitors with a car could take in a tour of the wooded Pelion peninsular.

9. North East Aegean Islands

There are a dozen or more islands scattered around the north east Aegean east of the Sporades and north of the Dodecanese group, hugging first the northern coast of Greece and then the Turkish mainland. Turkey makes occasional claims to them, which accounts for the heavy Greek military presence on some islands.

They are much more sporadic than the Sporades. But they tend to be more fertile and wooded than the Cyclades islands in the central Aegean and some are bigger with large bustling ports. Although they are remote from Athens, most are easily accessible. There are airports on all the big four, Samos, Lesvos, Limnos and Chios, the first two boasting direct flights from London, while the most northerly isles of Thassos and Amouliani have quick, regular ferry connections with the mainland.

The Blessed Isle – Samos

It is easy to see why the ancients called Samos 'The Isle of the Blessed'. It has an abundance of good things – green, tree-covered hills, orchards, colourful towns, a great range of wines and some of the most spectacular beaches in Greece.

It is the closest of all the big islands to Turkey, separated by only a 3 kilometre strait, and has the most dependable boat connections to that country. It also boasts a good ring road, making all parts of the island easily accessible by bus, car or scooter, and has some of the best outside connections of all Greek islands.

Regular flights from Athens and charter flights from Britain land on the flat coastal strip near Pythagorion, regular ships ply between Samos and Piraeus, calling at one or more of the Cyclades, and the island acts as a junction for shipping routes from the north-east Aegean islands and the Dodocannese. As if that weren't enough, it sometimes has hydrofoil links with Pamos and on to Kos and Rhodes.

The two main ports, and biggest towns on the island, are Samos or Vathi and Karlovassi, both on the north coast. Samos is a lively town with white houses and red roofs, merging into Vathi higher up the hill, but Karlovassi is a dull, sprawling place best visited as a bus halt en route for the great beaches in the west of the island.

Prettier places to stay are Kokkari on the north coast, the old capital of Pythagorion on the south-east coast or in the beach area of Marathokambos in the south-west. Kokkari is a bustling, young resort just 10 minutes from Samos town, while Pythagorion is more up-market with sophisticated restaurants and fancy yachts in its colourful harbour.

All over the island hills and pinewoods

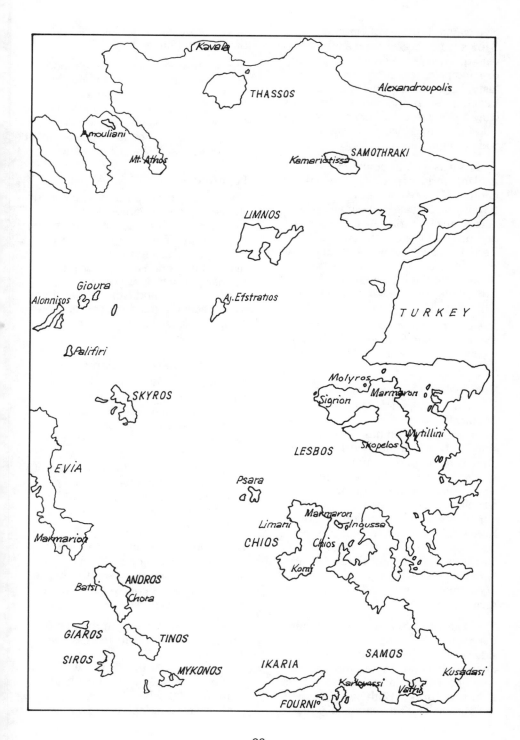

give way to terraces of vines and Samos wines are as good as they are varied. They come sweet and brown, dry and pale, resinated yellow, and lusty. Legend has it that the god Bacchus taught the Samians to make wine as a reward for helping him to get rid of the Amazons, who had been rude to him.

Samos was a great power in the ancient world, especially in the 6th century BC when it was ruled by the tyrant Polycrates. He built an empire across neighbouring Aegean islands and ordered the construction of the Temple of Hera, which was ranked as one of the Seven Wonders of the World, and the Efpalinion tunnel to bring water over half a mile to the old capital of Pythagorion.

It was named more recently after the mathematician, Pythagoras, who was a native of Samos in the 6th century BC.

Beaches

There are swimmable beaches practically everywhere but not all are sandy. Samos town has its own shingley beach at Gangou 1 kilometre around the bay. Kokkari has a spectacular big pebble beach with windsurfing and there are pretty shingley coves all the way along the north coast around Kokkari, Agios Konstantinos and Kondakeila. But the best beach on the north coast is in the far north-west beyond Karlovassi at Iamatike Pige, which is a huge crescent of golden sand with a taverna.

The south coast has more sand than the north. There are beaches on both sides of Pythagorion and at Possidonion and Psili Ammos on the south-east shore facing across the straits to Turkey. Both have beach restaurants and are within easy reach

by car or bus, or even foot, of both Samos and Pythagorion.

The south-west corner of the island around Marathokambo is almost a continuous strip of sandy bays, the three best-known being Votsalakia, Ormos Marathokambos and Psili Ammos – called like its namesake in the south-east after its 'high sand'.

Nightlife

There is a lively night-time scene along the waterfront of Samos where the tables of every restaurant seem to touch those of another on both sides. Pythagorion also has a great deal of dining out at open-air restaurants by the harbour which are on the expensive side, and Kokkari has a similar scene around the main square. All three places have discotheques and cinemas.

Not to be missed on Samos

A circular tour of the island is a good idea to take in its beautiful shorescapes, pine-clad hills and monasteries. Pythagorion has the history with the surviving stones and one column of the huge Heraion, or temple of Hera, plus the open jaws of the Efpalinion aquaduct, which speak volumes for their 6th century BC builders. There are a few remains of an old theatre nearby.

Both Pythagorion and Samos have museums containing archaeological finds, statues, coins, vases and reliefs from the island'a golden age. Samos also has a Byzantine museum.

The oldest monastery on the island, Vrondiani, dating from 1560, is a stiff walk uphill from Kokkari or Agios Konstantinos via Vourliotes, while the Evangelistria is a short walk inland from Votsalakia beach towards Mount Kerkis. The Zoodochos Pigi

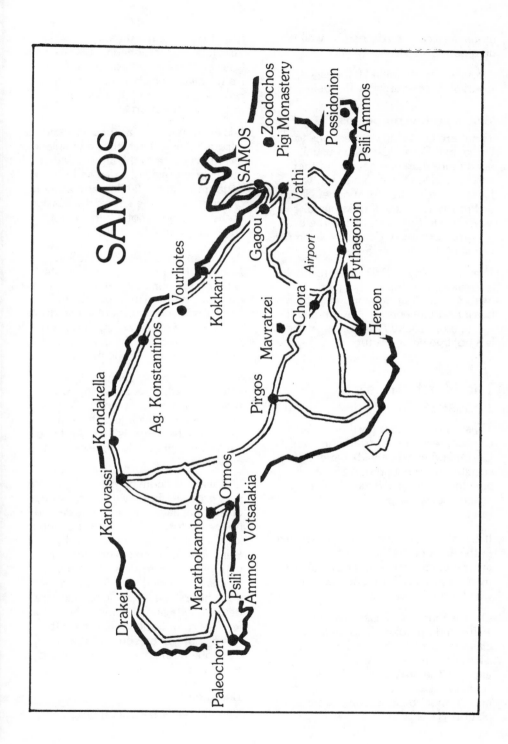

SAMOS

Zoodochos
Pigi Monastery

Possidonion

Psili Ammos

SAMOS

Vathi

Gagou

Vourliotes

Pythagorion

Airport

Kokkari

Chora

Hereon

Ag. Konstantinos

Mavratzei

Kondakella

Pirgos

Karlovassi

Ormos

Marathokambos

Votsalakia

Drakei

Psili
Ammos

Paleochori

monastery can be reached by walking up a path from Samos town.

If you like pretty inland hill villages, try Vourliotes, Mavratzei or Pirgos.

Worth visiting off Samos

There are easy ship connections to Ikaria, and Patmos, but you usually need more than one day to get there and back. Don't miss a day trip to Kusadasi in Turkey from either Samos or Pythagorion, and if possible take in a bus trip to Ephesus, one of the best preserved classical Greek towns in the whole of the Mediterranean.

Visitors staying in Pythagorion should also take a day trip to the gentle offshore island of Samiopoula, which has a pretty beach with taverna, and to the more rocky Agathonissi, if there is a boat going and returning the same day.

The Northern Isle – Thassos

Thassos is the most northerly island in Greece, reaching far to the north of Corfu, and boasts a wide variety of scenery, from high mountains and pine forests to broad, gently-sloping beaches of white pebbles and yellow sand.

It lies off the shore of northern Greece at the apex of the Aegean Sea. Its greenery, pine trees and olive groves match those of Corfu and Halkidiki, which both lie west of it.

Oil was found off Thassos in the early 1970s and provoked Turkey to lay claim to some of the north Aegean isles and their offshore waters. This explains the presence of Greek soldiers on apparent war footing, dug in on remote beaches, and illuminated platforms out to sea.

It is also one of the most accessible Greek islands, reached in just over an hour by regular, flat-bottomed ferries from Kavala, which is a spectacular provincial town and port with an international airport.

It is even quicker – around 35 minutes – from Keramoti, which is a mainland ferry port close to the airport with a busy harbourside of cafes and restaurants and a 2-kilometre stretch of superb sandy beach on the seaside of the ferry port; not a bad place to linger on a hot afternoon.

As a result, it is well-populated in summer by campers and motorists with foreign number plates who drive down from Germany, Austria and Yugoslavia and pour across the straits to the island's twin ports, Prinos on the west coast and the capital, Limin or Thassos town on the north.

Yet Thassos never seems overcrowded. Its coastal ring road, regular bus service, plentiful flatland by the sea and thick forests combine to absorb its many visitors. And you can always hire a bike to escape the crowds.

It is also a welcoming place. The main port greets visitors with a long string of national flags on the dockside and notices in foreign languages covering local hotels and shipping schedules. But it can be noisy in summer when young tourists arrive and the town's discos boom loud and clear into the early hours. Those seeking quiet are better-off staying at Prinos, the second ferry port, or Limenaria, the pretty fishing port in the south of the island, or in one of the many resorts of the east or south coasts.

Beaches

You are never far from a beach on

THASSOS

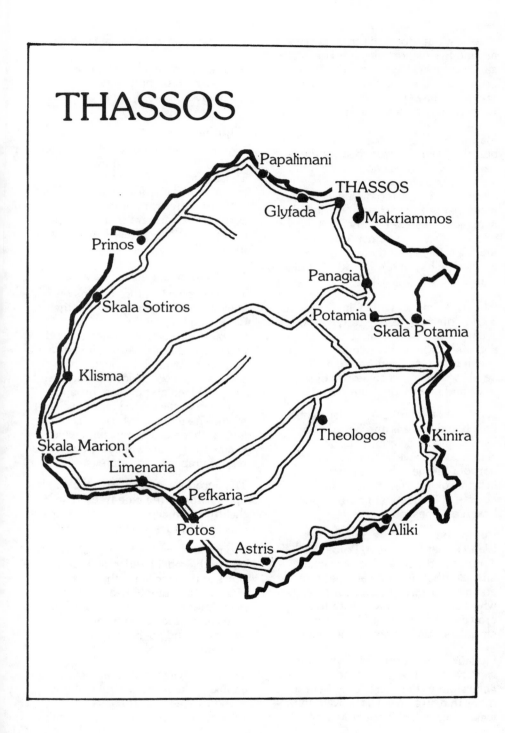

Papalimani

THASSOS

Glyfada

Makriammos

Prinos

Panagia

Skala Sotiros

Potamia

Skala Potamia

Klisma

Skala Marion

Theologos

Kinira

Limenaria

Pefkaria

Potos

Aliki

Astris

Thassos, but those on the west coast around Prinos are shingley. The best sand beaches stretch round the east coast from Thassos town to Limenaria and many have water-sports such as windsurfing and water-skiing.

Makriammos, a few kilometres walk or bus ride from Thassos town, is the best-known and has good sand, but for most of its long stretch is a pay beach and a trifle too organised for most tastes. Further south, below the spectacular village of Panagia is a good stretch of sand at Chrisi Amoudia ('Golden Bay') and there is another across the bay at Chrisi Akti ('Golden shore').

Chrisis Ammoudia and Chrisi Akti, or Skala Potamias, as its pretty harbour is called, almost run into one another and offer 2–3 miles of gently-shelving beach with restaurants and small hotels set against a backdrop of plane trees and pine-clad mountains.

Kinira has a long, spectacular pebble beach and there is another of fine sand a mile or so south opposite Kinira island. Aliki is another pretty harbour village, which has attracted an artists' colony to its slate-roofed houses. It is the most photographed beach on Thassos.

But the best sand beaches of the island are at Limenaria, Potos, Psili Ammos and Astris. They come one after another around each headland and allow plenty of space for those who do not like to swim with the crowds. The beach at Limenaria stretches west for about 3 kilometres.

Skala Marion, south of Prinos on the west coast, has a good sand beach, at either end of the village and there are other thin stretches all the way up the west coast, which are easily accessible from the road as far as Skala Rachoni.

Thassos port also has strips of good sandy beach on both sides of the harbour.

Nightlife

Nightlife is eating out on the seafront most of the way around the island, but Thassos town has more than its fair quota of discotheques and bars. They rock the waterfront of the port most evenings. An ancient theatre plays host to a festival of classical pieces in the summer.

Not to be missed on Thassos

Thassos town has the remains of ancient Thassos, including the theatre, Roman agora and three or four temples. You can also trace the old city walls on a pleasant 4-kilometre stroll right around the port, which affords some good views of the island and mainland and passes through a Venetian castle on the hill above the town. The town also boasts a cute little archaeological museum, which seems to specialise in lions, but also has a number of fine statues.

The acropolis is well worth the climb uphill through the pine trees. The theatre is 5th century and still showing classical dramas today.

From the summit you look out over one of the most handsome island ports in the Aegean with red roofs enclosed in a amphitheatre of green hills. After the climb visit one of the cafes along the harbour for a lemonade and yoghurt with walnuts and honey.

Visitors staying in the main town should make a circular tour of the island to see its pretty bays and villages. It is easy by bus, car or bike, though cyclists need more than a day since the ring road is around 80 kilometres long.

The east coast is high and mighty, and gives a spectacular drive along the cliffs between Thassos port and Aliki.

Limenaria has something of the feel of a German lakeside town, due no doubt to its occupation by a German company at the turn of the century. It is comfortable and has good eating.

Despite two or three skyscraper hotels, it is a good place to stay and a good centre for a beach holiday.

Inland Thassos has an abundance of pretty mountain villages, like Panagia, Theologos and Potamia, which have running streams and an Alpine flavour.

Don't miss Theologos, a handsome old hill village 10 kilometres from the coast, which was the capital of the island under the Turks. It has a number of good restaurants, traditional houses and churches and grand views across the hillsides.

Aliki is a cute place with village houses to rent and 5th century remains. Just along the coast perched on a high rock is the island's most spectacular monastery, Archangelos, which welcomes visitors.

Worth visiting off Thassos

Regular ferries make it easy to visit the colourful mainland port of Kavala, the Roman remains at nearby Phillipi and even the eastern shores of Halkidiki. There are also ferry connections with the neighbouring islands of Samothraki and Limnos but plan to stay overnight if visiting either since they are about four hours journey.

Samothraki

Samothraki is remote and mysterious, as befits an island dedicated in the ancient world to Thracian fertility rites. It is not distinguished for its beaches, is easiest reached by a 2½-hour ship journey via the ugly frontier town of Alexandroupolis, and is closer to the Turkish island of Imbros than any Greek island. It also has the dubious distinction of being coveted by Turkey for traces of oil found between the two countries, so there is usually a strong garrison of Greek troops in the castle at Chora.

Yet Samothraki is bounding with beauty and romance. The scenery inland is green and lush dominated by Mount Fengari, the highest point in the Aegean at 5,500 feet, which looks down on the Sanctuary of the Great Gods where the statue of the Winged Victory, now in the Louvre in Paris, was discovered. The coastal plains are open and grazed by flocks of goats and the port of Kamariotissa is pretty and welcoming.

Beaches

You can swim along the coast in either direction from Kamariotissa, below Xeropotamos and Lakkoma in the west or Paleopolis and Loutra on the north coast, but the beaches are of the stone and pebble variety. The best beach on the island is the appropriately-named Ammos ('Sand') on the south-west coast, which is a fabulous strand, but can only be reached by a boat trip from Kamariotissa.

Nightlife and Dining Out

Samothraki is no island for people who like a boisterous nightlife. It is restricted to eating out in the port and drinking around the garrison at Chora.

Not to be missed on Samothraki

There are regular bus connections along the north coast to Loutra or Therma, which has curative baths and a pretty monastery in a wooded setting, and to Paleopolis, which is the point to alight for the Sanctuary of the Great Gods. It is one of the great archaeological sites of the Aegean with Doric columns protruding from a green glade to mark the spot where the Winged Victory was found and where some of the ancient world's most elusive mysteries were practised.

The columns are all that remain of the hall of initiation or Hieron. Next door is the Arsinoe rotunda, the biggest circular building in ancient Greece which is called curiously after an Egyptian queen whose name spread to the furthest corners of ancient Greece and Cyprus.

There are also the Nike fountain, which used to support the Winged Victory, and a little museum above the site.

Chora has a medieval fortress and is an easy walk uphill from the port in the cool of the evening.

Worth visiting off Samothraki

The mainland port of Alexandroupolis is a good place to miss, but it is worth taking a ship to either Thassos or Limnos, which are both pretty islands and are about 4 hours sail from Samothraki.

Agios Efstratios

You won't find Agios Efstratios on any package tour schedules, and it is not mentioned by the classical writers, but it is on the ferry route between Evia and Limnos and makes a rewarding stop for anyone searching for solitude, sandy beaches and hill walks.

The main village has more connotations with World War Two prefab estates than pretty Greek island ports. It lacks whitewash and the higgeldy-piggeldy look that comes with age. Not surprising, because Agios Efstratios suffered an earthquake in the 1960's and was rebuilt in double-quick time with neat rows of single storey bungalows. It was then used in the 1970's as a place of exile for political offenders.

Even so, there are a few rooms and bungalows to let and you can have a happy exile on the island today, so long as you are not bent on fleshpots and nightlife. The village is welcoming and has a couple of shops, and there is a taverna along the beach that runs around the bay.

If you walk from there across the headlands in either direction you will find good sandy beaches in every bay. They have no restaurants, but are usually within an hour or two of the main port, so they are easy to visit with a picnic lunch or walk back at mid-day.

Agios Efstratios has no ancient civilisation to show, but you can find the ruins of a Medieval settlement on the north coast facing Limnos and there are many old buildings on the outskirts of the modern town from the pre-earthquake era, including an old hospital and a church on the promontory overlooking the port with an old graveyard which is worth a second glance for a glimpse of Orthodox church burial customs with open coffins and small coffins for people who died a few years ago.

Lemnos

Limnos, or Lemnos, is a big island in the north Aegean with regular flights from Athens and good ferry connections with Kimi, Kavala, Thassos, Lesvos and Samothraki. It also has one of the prettiest ports in the Aegean at Mirina with a Medieval castle above it and a tiny enclosed harbour crammed with boats below.

Yet the island is not on the main tourist track and has little development away from its main port, other than at the huge enclosed Moudros Bay in the south below the airport. The bay appears to be a land-locked lagoon and gave safe anchorage to the British fleet before the ill-fated Dardanelles landing in World War One. Now it is being used by the Greek military as a base because Lemnos is one of the most vulnerable islands to Turkish ambitions for expansion over this part of the Aegean.

Beaches

There are good sandy beaches on both sides of the castle promontory dominating Mirina and other sandy coves can be found along the coast below Platis and Thanos. There is another good beach at Kotsinas on the north coast. Moudros Bay has beaches of a kind with tavernas, but they are not particularly attractive. Transport is usually by taxi, though there are occasional buses to Moudros Bay.

Nightlife and Dining Out

Mirina has lively restaurants along the main harbour and there are others along the beach across the headland, which curves around to a beach hotel. There are also restaurants in Moudros Bay, but they are mostly frequented by the military.

Not to be missed on Limnos

Mirina is without doubt the prettiest place on the island and it is well worth

walking up to its acropolis for a good view of the surrounding countryside and a Medieval castle in a fair state of preservation. The eastern part of the island has two ancient settlements at Hephaestia, where there are the remains of an amphitheatre and an agora, and Paliochni, where you can see the walls of an old town, wells and baths dating back to 4,000 BC. There are finds from Paliochni in a tiny archaeological museum.

Worth visiting off Limnos

Frequent ferry connections make it possible to visit Thassos, Samothraki, Lesvos and Agios Efstratios, though it would be wise to plan to stay a day or two when visiting the last-named as boats do not call there every day.

Chios

Chios – not to be confused with the Cycladean island of Ios – is a big island with spectacular countryside and a proud history, which hugs the Turkish coast as though it once belonged to it, which it did for nearly 300 years. It has air flights from Athens and regular ships from the mainland, Lesvos and Samos, which dock in its grand harbour boasting one of the longest waterfronts in Greece.

If you are looking for a big island that is blissfully unmarked by tourism, try Chios. Although one of the Big Seven Greek islands and roughly the size of Corfu, it is remote from Athens, has no direct flights from Britain and hardly any package tours.

It is hard to find a hotel outside the main port or the main resort of Karfas 8 kilometres south of there. Tourist development seems to be actively opposed by rich shipowners and landowners, who rely on the island for labour and have plush villas in coastal villages and along the main road that runs south from Chios town.

They have recently been mounting a strong lobby to oppose the extension of the island's airport, which would allow in regular charter flights from Western Europe.

But this does not mean Chios is unfriendly or short of attractions for any away-from-it-all holiday.

It has dozens of deserted beaches, with rooms and apartments to let, an amazing variety of landscape and two remote satellite islands in Inoussa and Psara close by. It is also rich in new roads, including one that cuts across the middle of the island from the main port to the west coast via the monastery of Nea Moni and gives easy access to a string of good beaches.

It is a prosperous island, thanks to a number of ship-owning families and the mastic plantations in the south, producing a dull grey gum which was once much prized by the Turkish court and still finds its way into chewing gum and local liquors. The island's port or Chios town, from which all roads and buses run, sprawls below a Genoese castle and is a heavily-built bustling place crammed with bars, restaurants and shops selling Turkish delight, ouzo and mastic products.

Its architecture and sweet shops in the old bazaar district reflect the centuries of Turkish occupation. So does a strong Greek military presence which extends down the rocky east coast of the island facing the Turkish coast.

The island has the best claim to being the birthplace of Homer, the author of The Odyssey and Iliad, in the 9th Century BC and is near enough to Troy for the poet to have visited the great walled city and the scene of the

10-year siege by the Greeks.

Chios was one of the few islands to remain independent of Athens and was respected for its government, arts and navy in the 5th and 6th centuries BC. It was also more of an ally than a subject of the Romans, but it was conquered by the Byzantines and given to the Genoese in 1261.

It came under the Turkish yoke in the 16th century and was ruled from the nearby mainland until 1822 when it rebelled with the rest of Greece and fought with such enthusiasm that the Turks wrought a terrible vengeance on the island. They massacred 30,000 Chiots and took another 45,000 into slavery. The Greek fleet took revenge on the Turkish admiral who had ordered the massacre, but Chios stayed part of Turkey until 1912.

Beaches
Chios is not known for its beaches, but they are many and varied. They stretch almost continuously from the main port to the southern tip of the island on the east coast, along the south coast and up gloriously remote stretches of the west coast as far as the monastery of Agios Markelas. They are harder to find on the north-east coast, but Vrontados has a pebble beach, Marmaro has a shingle stretch to the east of the harbour and Nagos a divine little pebble cove with a welcoming restaurant.

The most accessible beach from town is Karfas a few kilometres south. It has good sand, restaurants and hotels, but tends to be crowded. There is another in the next bay at Agia Fotinis.

There is a better sandy beach at Komi further south, which also has restaurants and rooms and is less crowded. A little further south from there is Emborios, which has two magnificent stretches of black pebble beach known as Mavra Volia, backed by high cliffs, rooms and restaurants. Dolia on the southern tip of the peninsular has a spectacular little sand beach backed by cliffs.

The south coast has two more passable beaches at Kato Fana and Karindas reached by dirt track roads from the mastic villages of Pirgi and Olymbi.

But the biggest collection of remote deserted beaches are up the west coast. Lithi is the most popular with perfect sand and a string of half a dozen restaurants, but anyone with their own transport should explore northwards to Elinda and as far as Agios Markelas and Volissos.

This area has half a dozen pretty stretches of shingle, including one with a restaurant below the monastery and another over the hill from the attractive little harbour of Limnia, which has rooms, restaurants and an occasional ship to Psara.

Nightlife

Chios town seethes with life at night when the waterfront almost becomes one long bar-restaurant. It also boasts a number of cinemas.

Not to be missed on Chios

Chios has plenty to offer visitors who get tired of lying on the beach. It is worth taking a bus to Pirgi 15 miles from Chios in the heart of the mastic country, which is said to be the only place in Greece where the plant will grow – even attempts to grow it in the north of the island have failed. The mastic plantations are worth seeing for their colourful old buildings and serried ranks of lentisk bushes, while Pirgi itself is a most unusual town. Its entire centre is decorated with a grey-white geometric design set in plaster, a technique copied originally from Italy and now celebrated on many Greek postcards. The town is dominated by a Genoese tower and also contains the pretty 13th century church of Peter and Paul.

Another worthy place of pilgrimage on the island is Nea Moni, an 11th century monastery set high in rugged hills just eight kilometres west of Chios town and now maintained by a handful of nuns. It has beautiful medieval mosaics and a clock that stubbornly keeps Byzantine time, like many on Mount Athos. A chapel on the side contains the bones of the victims of the 1822 massacre by the Turks.

A few kilometres deeper into the mountains is the village of Anavatos, now almost deserted where thousands of Chiot women and children jumped from the walls rather than surrender to the Turks.

Anavatos is well worth the trip. It is a gaunt grey village of castle-like houses typical of inland Chios, built on one side of a high gorge, with the remains of a castle on top of the village. Peering down the gorge from the walls, you can recapture some sense of the mass suicide.

Most of the villages in the south of the island have similar houses and Mesta and Olymbi are just as atmospheric as Pirgi with narrow roads, archways and pretty floral squares. Anyone staying in the area should visit all three. Komi or Emborios are good places to stay.

Another good area to linger is around Volissos in the north east. It is one of the villages that claims to be the birthplace of Homer, and is strung across a ridge that rises to a castle higher up. The top part of the village above the square is semi-deserted and you can explore houses from the last century similar to those in Anavatos.

The monastery of Agios Markelas has a huge festival every July attended by thousands of exiled Chiots.

The most famous sights near to Chios town are three windmills on a promontory and Homer's Stone at Vrontados 4 kilometres north where the writer leant to address his audience on history and poetry.

Further north is the pretty U-shaped harbour of Langada, which is not a great place to swim, but a good one to pause for a meal or a drink.

If you have transport, do drive down the middle of the island from Chios town to the mastic country beyond Armolia – recognised by small plantations of bushes that look like small olives with twisted trunks and bright green leaves. It is an extremely fertile area boasting some grand villas.

Then for contrast drive across the barren grey mountainous part of the island between Vrontados and Volissos or around the hilly north of the island between Kardamila and Volissos.

Worth visiting off Chios

No-one staying on Chios should miss out on boat trips to its two satellite islands of Psara and Inoussa. They have the quintessential Greek island ports and beaches which are somehow lacking on Chios.

Chios also has good sea links with Lesvos to the north and Samos to the south and occasional boats to Turkey, though the latter is an intermittent service which may owe something to the sufferings of the island in the War of Independence.

Psara

Psara to the west is linked by boats from Chios town and also occasional caiques from its west coast ports. The islet is most celebrated for its part in the Greek War of Independence as a result of a sea action fought off the island in 1824 and its massive contribution to the Greek fleet along with Hydra and Spetse. Like Chios it suffered a dreadful massacre by the Turks for its part in the war and today has only 500 islanders compared with the 30,000 or so who once lived there.

It has a great get-away-from-it-all atmosphere, a gem of a main harbour – all white with red roofs – and two passable beaches. It also has Paliocastro, a monument to Greeks who fled the Turkish yoke to the isolated islet.

Inoussa

Inoussa is the best place for beaches. It vies with Samos for the title of the Greek island closest to Turkey, but is very Greek in atmosphere with a pretty main port, no military presence and good sandy coves around almost every headland along its coast. It is a lovely quiet place to stay for a few days and soak up sea and sand.

Lesvos

Lesvos is the island of Sappho, the poetess ranked by the ancients alongside Homer. It is also the third largest island in the Aegean after Crete and Evia. Like them, it is grand, tall and fertile with flower-decked hillsides, olive plantations and pine forests around the 3,000 foot bald peak of Mount Olympos in the south. It also has two big sandy bays, the Gulfs of Kaloni and Yera cutting into its land mass from the south coast, and coastal plains supporting herds of goats, pigs and horses.

Sometimes called Lesbos or Mytilini, Lesvos is served by regular ships from Lemnos in the north, Chios in the south and Piraeus. It also has a regular air link with Athens and for the past few years its airport south of Mytilini, the main port, has enjoyed charter flights from Britain.

Lesvos was under Turkish occupation for nearly five centuries until 1912 and many of its villages have tall stone-built houses with red roofs and balconies like those in Turkey and northern Greece. The island supports big populations in its main villages like Plomari, Agassos, Moria, Kaloni and Polihnitos, and even more so in Mytilini in the south and Mithimna in the north. Both are called after the daughters of the first settler of the island, Macar, and both have Genoese castles dominating their skylines.

Mytilini, which forms a horseshoe around a huge natural harbour, is not a town to spend a holiday week in. It is big and bustling and has only a passable beach below the castle. But it has buses to all the outlying parts of the island, which are often a fair distance away, as well as cars and scooters for hire.

Molyvos, or Mithimna, just over 60 kilometres away, is a more obvious place to holiday. It is one of the prettiest villages in Greece, rivalling the likes of Hydra, Lindos on Rhodes, and Paleocastritsa on Corfu, with stately houses of many colours tumbling down a hillside beneath a Medieval fortress and ending in a pretty miniature harbour from which small fishing boats with big lamps on their sterns regularly set sail on convoys. Molyvos has featured on the sleeves of record covers and is a haunt for painters.

Beaches

There are beaches at Neapolis and Kalimari near to Mytilini and prettier ones further down the peninsular below the airport at Kratigos and Agios Ermogenis. But there are even better beaches for those prepared to travel.

On the north coast Molyvos has a long stretch of pebble with some sand curving around the bay beneath the castle and there is a good stretch of sand just 5 kilometres away along the coast at Petra.

There are even more spectacular beaches along the south coast at Agios Isidoros, a few kilometres out of the bustling port of Plomari, and at Vatera, south of Polihnitos where there is a long pine-fringed bay 7 or 8 kilometres long with a little fishing port at one end and rooms and restaurants dotted along the coast road. The bus goes as far as Vrisa 4 kilometres inland.

There are other sandy beaches on the Gulf of Yera south of Skala Polihnitos and at Skala Kaloni and north of Achladeri. Going west, Skala Eressos is emerging as a beach resort, with a fine sandy strand and windsurfing, and Sigri, a remote little village on three bays beneath a castle, has a series of silver sand coves.

Nightlife and Dining Out

Mytilini's bustling waterfront is crammed with diners and drinkers at night, and has cinemas and discos, though they are hard to track down. Plomari also has a lively eating and drinking scene with vast quantities of local ouzo consumed at every table on the seafront and pretty restaurants by a stream behind. But Molyvos is the most appealing, with a cobbled street that seems solely dedicated to eating out and two discotheques which operate intermittently through the season.

Not to be missed on Lesvos

Both the castles at Mytilini and Molyvos are in a surprisingly good state of preservation and the one towering over the main port has clearly been rebuilt many times using materials from Roman and Hellenic times. Mytilini also has an archaeological museum in a mansion along the harbour with ancient vases. The town has other features.

One is the Lesbos Statue of Liberty, which is a small copy of the one in New York harbour, and the other a statue of Sappho, the first known poetess, who gave the word 'lesbian' to the world by composing love poems to her students.

But Molyvos and nearby Petra are more picturesque. Molyvos is a beautiful village to walk in and around and Petra boasts a pretty little 18th century church with a golden altar on a high rock, which gives the village its name and great character.

Agiassos is a pretty inland village 20 kilometres inland from Mytilini, which has tall mansions, cobbled narrow streets, a 12th century church and a Medieval castle all nestling below the peak of Mount Olympos.

Sigri has a famous 'petrified forest' nearly 1 million years old, which is hard to find, but well worth looking for. The biggest cluster of stone trees is in the village square, but there are others in a rocky cove on the far side of Megalonisi island in the bay, reached by small excursion boat with a guide, and there are one or two more standing proud on the hillside beneath the Ipsilou Monastery a few kilometres inland from Sigri.

The Mytilini–Sigri road is a good one for students of religious history. It passes two other big, spectacular monasteries, Limonas beyond Kaloni and Pythagorion near to Eressos, while Skala Skaminias on the north coast has a pretty chapel perched on a rock in the sea. The coast road north also passes through Thermi, where there are warm natural springs.

Worth visiting off Lesvos

The two nearest islands, Limnos and Chios, are both about three hours from Lesvos and both of completely different character. There are also occasional trips to Ayvalik on the Turkish mainland.

Ikaria

Ikaria is a bleak, rocky island, despite an abundance of wooded hills in the interior, and not so much visited as its big neighbours, Samos, Chios and Lesvos. Unlike them, it has no airport, even though it is called after Ikarus, the first flyer whose wax and feather wings melted in the hot sun above the island plunging him to earth there.

Yet Ikaria's main port of Agios Kirikos on the south coast is a regular stop on the sea route from Piraeus to Samos and also on the Rhodes–Samos route, and it can be a dramatic one when the wind blows because the seas around Ikaria are often turbulent and the biggest ships sometimes have problems docking. Evdilos, the main port on the north coast is also an occasional ferry stop and the best one for visitors seeking a beach holiday.

The island has its own character, deriving from the big flocks of goats, hot springs and pretty inland villages. It manufactures goat skin products and is famed for its honey, raki and canned sweets. It also boasts the most radioactive springs in Greece and their main centre, Therma on the south coast, is served by a regular benzina taxi service taking ten minutes from the quayside at Agios Kirikos.

Agios Kirikos is a grand port backed by high hills and has a number of small hotels, but they can be hard to find. Therma seems more welcoming on the south coast and Evdilos and Arministis on the north coast.

Beaches

Agios Kirikos and Therma both have pebble beaches and there are others at Faros and Keramos reached by small boat from Agios Kirikos, but the best beaches are unquestionably a series of pine-fringed sandy stretches on the north coast of the island around Arministis and Yialisea, Rakis and Nas.

Nightlife and Dining Out

This is not an island for people who like lively nightlife. Despite evidence of one or two bombed-out discotheques, it is usually restricted to dining out in restaurants in Agios Kirikos, Evdilos and Armenistis, which occasionally have live music in summer.

Not to be missed on Ikaria

Therma's springs can cure arthritis, rheumatism, gout and even lack of fertility quicker than any others in Greece and have been visited since ancient times. There are many tales of the sick taking up their beds and walking and the village is so close to Agios Kirikos that it has to be worth a visit for anyone staying in the main port.

Faros on the eastern tip of the island has the remains of an ancient tower, which might have been a lighthouse,

and is close to the acropolis and ruins of Drakanon, which dates back to the 5th century BC. Kambos, a short walk inland from Evlidos, has the remains of a Byzantine palace and Agios Liskaris has a church on a tiny offshore islet.

Worth visiting off Ikaria

Samos, 3–4 hours east of Ikaria, depending on which port you choose on the island, is a great contrast to its neighbour. It is bigger, greener and more developed. Fourni, is much closer – around 1½ hours by small boat, which runs every day in summer from Agios Kirikos weather permitting. It is a gentle contrast to Ikaria and offers much better swimming than its south coast villages.

Fourni

Fourni is two islands, but only the main one has many rooms and restaurants. The daily boats from Ikaria, and occasionally from Karlovassi on Samos dock at the tree-lined harbour of Chora or Fourni, which is linked to Chryssomilia around the bay by the island's only road.

It is an island that deserves more visitors because it has a great air of peace and there are both pebble and sand beaches across the headlands on both sides of the port. The best one is Kambi, which has a taverna and good sand.

There are two other good beaches on Thimena island, which can be reached by boat from Fourni.

Amouliani

Amouliani is the biggest of a cluster of islets lying offshore from the Athos peninsular opposite Tripitj and north of Ouranoupolis. It is a little jewel of an island for anyone who wants a lazy beach holiday and walking among low hills away from the crowds without the hassle of a long sea voyage. It is blessed with eight spectacular long sandy beaches.

Regular ferries run from Tripiti, which is connected to Thessalonika and Ouranoupolis by bus, and take only 20 minutes. There are others running from Ouranoupolis taking half an hour. It is also possible to visit Amouliani by small hired motor boat from Ouranoupolis.

The port, and only village, is in traditional white-walled and red-roofed Halkidiki style, spoilt just a bit by the building of high concrete summer houses behind, but they do supply rooms to rent and there is a hotel on the headland to the right of the port. There are also four restaurants, two pastry shops and two discos, but the latter are in the hills well away from the port and serve more as landmarks than as places of entertainment.

Life on Amouliani is simple. One of the best beaches, Aliki, has two restaurants, a campsite and transport from the port by horse and cart, but you can as easily walk across the island to the south coast by the salt lake in less than half an hour. It takes about the same time to walk along the coast to Agios Georgios and Megali Ammos beaches opposite Ouranoupolis. The long south coast has two other beaches and the short north coast has three interconnecting beaches about 45 minutes walk from the port, which have fine sand and are usually deserted.

Amouliani offers fine views of the Halkidiki mainland and craggy Mount Athos, and there is no need to get bored staying a week on the island because it is so easy to take a boat to Ouranoupolis for a day or more and to view the monasteries of Mount Athos. You can also reach Ierissos by ferry and bus or taxi in just over half an hour.

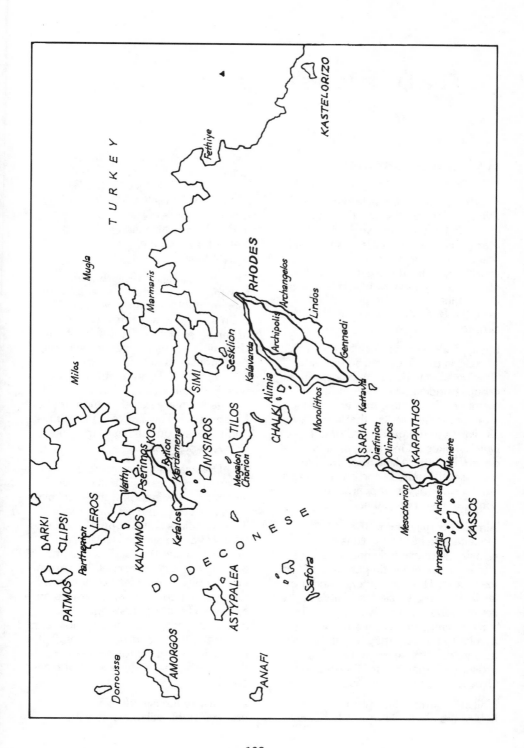

10. The Dodecanese

A Greek dozen makes fourteen

Fourteen lovely islands known as the Dodecanese curl around the Aegean coast of Turkey from Kushadasi to Marmaris, linking up with Samos and Ikaria in the north and Crete in the south. They are the biggest of a chain of over 200 islands, of which less than 20 are inhabited and their name dates from the Byzantine empire in the 8th century AD.

It is typically Greek to call a chain of 14 islands the Dodecanese (literally 'Twelve Islands') and the biggest in the group, Rhodes, was not originally a member. To confuse matters even more some people say that there are 13 islands in the group and omit Lipsi, which makes a Greek dozen a baker's dozen. It matters less, though, than the essential unity of the group, which have a similarity in appearance and common historical links.

Almost every island in the Dodecanese has some Classical remains, modern Italianate buildings and a Crusader castle perched over its main port. They are greener and more fertile than the Cyclades islands of the central Aegean, and less buffeted by the meltemmi wind and strong tides thanks to the way they hug the Asian mainland. They seem more prosperous than most other islands in Greece, and more religious.

It all stems from their position at the hub of the old trade routes between Asia and Europe, their distance and independence from Athens in the early days, and their links with the Bible story. St Paul visited Rhodes and other members of the Dodecanese and St John was exiled to Patmos where he wrote the book of Revelations.

The Dodecanese were grouped together by the Byzantine empire and then by the Crusader Knights of St John after they were thrown first out of Jerusalem by the Turks and then Cyprus. They were later thrown out of the Dodecanese by Suleiman the Magnificent of Turkey, but not before they had built strong thick walls and castles on every island as monuments to their stay. The Turks left mosques and minarets on the big islands like Rhodes and Kos.

The Dodecanese were grouped together again early in this century when the Italians took the islands over from the Turks in trust for Greece. The occupiers stayed until the Second World War, to symbolise Mussolini's dream of ruling the Mediterranean, and they tried to suppress the natural Greek culture and ideas of union with Greece, but compensated for it to an extent by building handsome civic buildings, ports and roads. Union with Greece in the late forties brought with it a customs-free status for many of the Dodecanese and the start of mass tourism.

Even today the islands have an uncomfortable relationship with

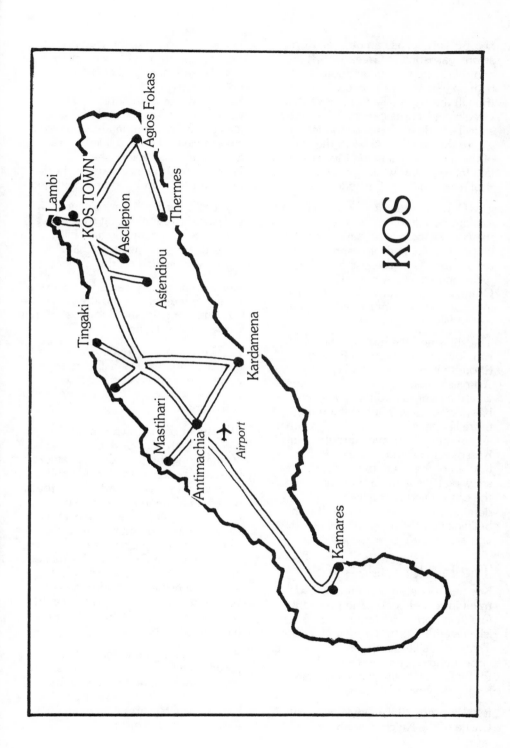

KOS

nearby Turkey, as can be seen from strong garrisons of Greek troops here and there and the surreptitious way boats ply between the two countries, though they give a lie to the idea that Greeks and Turks cannot live side by side. They do in Kos and Rhodes where the minarets echo to the sound of the mullahs calling the Moslem faithful to prayer while church bells peal from a nearby Orthodox church.

The Dodecanese are a great chain to explore by island-hopping because they are all exotic and have good links by plane, ship, hydrofoil and catamaran. They are also linked by plane and ship to Athens, Cyprus and Crete, and both Rhodes and Kos have frequent flights from Britain and the rest of Western Europe.

The ships and the hydrofoils mostly run down the chain from Patmos to Rhodes via Kalymnos and Kos Astipalea is out on a limb to the west, where it nudges into the Cyclades, Kastelorizo is way out east looking more like an offshore Turkish isle than any of the others, and Karpathos and Kassos hang a little loosely off the bottom of the chain to the south showing links with Cretan culture. But the castles and windmills that dominate their ports and the Italian buildings on the quayside tell you that you are in the Dodecanese.

The Healer's Isle – Kos

Kos has rocketed on to the tourist track in recent years, and now ranks fourth in popularity among Greek islands after Corfu, Crete and Rhodes. This has resulted from an international airport and a range and appeal similar to, though on a smaller scale, than, its bigger neighbour Rhodes.

It has a pretty, Italian-style port with a Castle of the Knights, sophisticated

eating and drinking at cheap prices, easy access to other Dodecanese islands, and long sandy beaches, notably along the east coast at Kardamena and Kamares and on the west coast at Tingaki and Mastihari. It also boasts fascinating archaeological sites in Kos Town and a few miles away at the Asclepion where Hippocrates, the most famous healer of the ancient world, taught medicine.

Kos has a verdant interior which supports a wealth of fruit trees, olives and vines, protected by high hills. It helps to support the story that Kos lettuces originated on the island.

Kos town is neat, clean and cheap – a legacy of the Italians and the special customs status granted to most of the Dodecanese islands.

Local wines and spirits come in big bottles at agreeably small prices, which may explain why the town seems so vibrant with atmosphere and activity at night.

The layout of the town is most pleasant with cool gardens and cafés strung along the promenade, flanked by sandy beaches on one side and a magnificent curve of harbour on the other. It has a mosque dating back from the days of Turkish rule, and a small Turkish community, which is a reminder that the island is one of the most eastern in Greece and is tucked in the lee of the Turkish mainland. It also has a plane tree hundreds of years old of enormous girth beneath which Hippocrates is supposed to have taught medicine.

Kardamena has emerged as the island's main resort over the past ten years, thanks to an endless sandy beach and its close proximity to the airport, which is about 15 minutes away by car, bus or taxi. It was an

112

abandoned fishing village with boat trips to the nearby island of Nissiros, but now it is a long strip of hotels, bars, discotheques and restaurants. It lacks the squares and trees of most Greek villages, but still has charm.

Kos is superbly served by transport – air links with Athens, Rhodes and overseas, ship connections with Rhodes and the other Dodecanese, summer hydrofoil links with Rhodes and Patmos and local boat trips to Nissiros, Pserimos and across the narrow straits to Bodrum in Turkey, though that trip is costly and the boat sometimes hard to find.

Kos flourished in the ancient world as a school of medicine, under Hippocrates from 460 BC. He taught mainly under an enormous plane tree in the town – probably an ancestor of the one that marks the spot today – and also 4 kilometres away in the countryside where you can see the ruins of the most famous Asclepion in Greece. The Asclepion was built after his death in 357 BC when Kos was becoming a rich trading nation and used by the Asclipiades, an order of priests who practised medicine by his method using herbs from the hillsides and healing waters.

Beaches

There is an abundance of sandy beaches on both sides of Kos town, stretching towards Lambi in the north and Agios Fokas in the south. In fact, the strip that fronts the town to the right of the castle is as good a beach as you can see on many Greek islands and it has all the watersports – windsurfing, water-skiing and paragliding. But the setting becomes wilder and more secluded the further you travel from town and there are some pretty spots within easy cycling distance in both directions.

Go past Agios Fokas, which is a mushrooming resort complex, as far as Thermes and you will find a hot pebble beach washed by thermal waters, which are reputed to be good for aches and pains, along with a spa and café.

There are other sandy beaches within cycling distance of town on the north coast at Tingaki and Marmari if you don't mind the heavy seas that often wash this side of the island. There is a third beach on the north shore at Masthari, but that is more of a car, scooter or bus ride than a gentle morning's cycle. All are surrounded by pleasant little resorts with restaurants and hotels.

But the best beaches on Kos are on the south coast where the sand is finer and the seas usually calmer. This is one big reason why Kardamena has developed into a thriving beach resort in recent years. Its beach boasts fine sand and runs for many kilometres in each direction, giving a good choice of watersports for those who want them and more isolated spots for those who want peace and quiet with only the waves for company. The village also has a wealth of restaurants and bicycles, cars and scooters for hire.

One of the best beaches on the island is further west at Kamares – which is also called Agios Stefanos after an ancient church on the seashore – 6 kilometres from the hill village of Kefalos. There are sand dunes to laze in, pine trees to take shade under, and a fishing port for local life and lunch. The only threat to this idyllic scene comes from a huge Club Mediterranee complex close by the church.

Another lovely little beach is the 'Bubble Beach' just south of Kardamena, which can be reached by regular caiques from the harbour. It too has fine sand, dunes and a bit of shade for those who don't want to roast in the sun.

Nightlife

Kos town has a heavier concentration of nightlife than its neighbour Rhodes. A string of tavernas fronting the harbourside compete with an array of dishes and music against a number of smart outdoor bars along the same strip, and there are more restaurants flanking the seashore both north and south of the harbour for those who prefer a quieter scene.

The best fish restaurants are to the north of the harbour and they are unique in the whole of Greece in the way they display their dishes, or plastic replicas, in glass cases outside their front doors. In some of them you can dangle your feet in the sand and watch the big ships to-ing and fro-ing at the entrance to the harbour.

The town centre scene is lively, especially around the square, but it does go quiet around midnight. Then late revellers have to make for the edge of town where nightclubs and discos like the Kahlua and Heaven have bouzouki and dance music into the early hours.

Kardamena is quieter than Kos town and relies more on the traditional Greek nightlife of dining out and drinking under the stars. But there are now two discos at each end of the village, which offer western and Greek music in summer, as well as a number of lively bars with music. The best restaurants also tend to be a short way away from the centre of the village.

Other resorts like Tingaki rely on friendly restaurants and bars for nightlife.

Not to be missed on Kos

Kos town is a delight to look at and walk around. In an hour or two — or even less for those in a hurry – you can see a well-preserved Castle of the Knights, a colourful harbour dating from the same era, a Turkish mosque, a British-style tearoom, a covered market overflowing with fruits and vegetables, a small museum, the plane tree where Hippocrates is reputed to have taught medicine, and the remains of a major Graeco-Roman town. All are linked by handsome tree-shaded streets.

The old town is in two parts and contains an odeon, an ancient gymnasium, a big marketplace and many temples. Yet it is left casually in the middle of the town for visitors to wander over. Anywhere else the town council would quickly have fenced it off and charged an entrance fee, so see it now while it is so attractively open and casual. It looks more like a public park than an archaeological site.

The Castle of the Knights is set in magnificent gardens ablaze with blossom and shaded with tall trees, and contains marble statues, pottery and old cannons. It is only a short step to the legendary plane tree of Hippocrates, which is supported by stones and wooden props, and looks suitably gnarled but can only be 300 or 400 years old.

Bicycles and scooters can easily be rented in town and the island has good roads. Many places are within a day's cycle ride and the Asclepion within half an hour's pedalling distance. The ancient healing centre, built after the death of Hippocrates, is in a cool green setting in the hills 4 kilometres from town and has a good view of the Turkish mainland. It is a remarkably well-preserved terraced building at the end of an avenue of cypress trees, which has the remains of Roman baths, a hospital and a fountain where healing waters have been flowing for at least two millenniums. It is surmounted by thin pillars and temples, mostly dedicated to Ascelpios, the God of Healing.

Kardamena, around 36 kilometres from Kos Town, is a little far for cycling, but is itself a good centre to cycle to the nearby castle of Antimachia towering above the hills inland as another monument to the builders of the Middle Ages. There is a third castle at Palio Pili between Kos town and Kardamena and it is also worth visiting the old hill village of Kefalos in the south of the island. The nearby beach resort of Kamares has the church of Agios Stefanos on the seashore.

Worth visiting off Kos

Kos is an ideal centre for visiting other islands. There are regular ships to Rhodes, Kalymnos and Astipalea and regular day excursion boats visiting Pserimos and Nissiros. From Kardamena is the easiest passage to Nissiros. And there is now a de luxe catamaran plying between Kos and Nissiros.

An even easier way to travel is by hydrofoil when it is running. From the beach beside the Castle of the Knights in Kos town it takes just 1½ hours to Rhodes in one direction and Patmos in the other with a flying view of other islands on the way.

Several boats ply for hire in the harbour for trips to Bodrum in Turkey, but they charge a lot for such a short trip.

The Isle of Revelations – Patmos

Patmos is a divine little island, which offers a rare blend of sightseeing, beaches and good eating coupled with great peace and quiet, except on the occasions when the cruise ships call and camera-hung tourists throng the port of Skala and the big fortified monastery in Chora.

It is the northernmost island of the Dodecanese and the first port of call coming from Samos or one of the Cyclades islands like Mykonos and in appearance Patmos seems like a close relative of the Cyclades rather than the eastern Aegean isles. It has a brown landscape dotted with outcrops of neat white villages and enclosed sandy bays.

It does, though, have the typical trade marks of the Dodecanese – an arched Italianate harbour authority building at Skala – which has one of the most reliable daily shipping reports to be found anywhere in the Aegean – and a castle rising grandly over the main town of Chora on the hill behind the port. In the case of Patmos the castle is unique. It is the monastery of St John the Divine, built to commemorate the memory of St John and his two-year exile on the island in which he wrote the Book of Revelations, the last and most lyrical book in the Bible.

But Patmos is much more than a memorial to St John. The village of Chora surrounding the monastery is one of the oldest and prettiest in the Aegean with winding streets and little squares surrounded by white buildings which trace their foundations back to Medieval times.

Like most of the Dodecanese, Patmos has easy connections to other islands in the chain, including daily steamers from Samos, Kalymnos, Kos and Leros and a summer hydrofoil that links with either Kos or Samos in about 1½ hours. It also has regular boats making the short journey to Lipsi, including excursion caiques in the tourist season. Others run around the island to remote beaches, offering views of weird rock formations and fascinating inlets on the way. A shop in Skala offers an alternative way of travel by renting bikes and scooters.

Although Patmos has a lot to offer and is much visited, it is mainly patronised by a quiet group of tourists, as if they are conscious of the island's religious past and want to preserve the holy atmosphere in the frenzied world of the twentieth century.

Patmos seems to have been considered an unimportant, inhospitable island in the ancient world. Its fame dated from 95 AD when St John was exiled from Ephesus to Patmos and received revelations from God through three cracks in his cave of refuge behind the port of Skala. He dictated them to his pupil Prohoros and they became the final and most intriguing book in the Bible.

The island was then uninhabited during the Dark Ages and only returned to the path of history in 1088 when a Christian monk called Christodoulos settled on the island and built the monastery in Chora in memory of St John. As a reward for prophesying his ascent to the throne, the Byzantine Emperor, Alexis Commenus, gifted the whole island to Christodoulos and paid for the building.

The monastery ruled the island as a monastic state for centuries and the village of Chora grew up in its shadow

from the 13th century onwards.

Beaches

Patmos is rich in beaches and most of them are sand. Skala, the main port, itself has several beaches, on both sides of the narrow neck that links the island at this point, but two of them are stony and the others get crowded in high summer. However, there are better beaches within half an hour's walk or a five minute bus or taxi ride at Meli and Agriolivado north of the port and at Grikou to the south.

Grikou is a lovely little village with two hotels, three restaurants and no less than five beaches to choose from if you include a sandspit on the island of Traonisi in the bay, which is easily reached by hired boat from the landing stage at Grikou, or even by swimming if you feel energetic.

The best beach on the island for sand is Psili Ammos, a dune beach with a taverna on the southern peninsular of Patmos, which can be reached either by boat from the port or by a spectacular 1½ hours walk from Chora or Grikou. But there are many others, including Kambos in the north, which has a regular bus from Skala, Lambi, which has multi-coloured pebbles, Netia, Livadi and Stavrou.

Nightlife and Dining Out

There is little by way of discos on Patmos, but there are plenty of good tavernas in the port of Skala, up in Chora and in Grikou. The best are in the main square of Chora and on the fringe of the village off the stepped walkway from Grikou.

Not to be missed on Patmos

All roads on Patmos lead up the Chora and the Monastery of St John, which lie about 2 kilometres above

Skala by road. The village itself merits a tour since it is one of the prettiest in the Aegean and has splendid views, squares and two convents, but the monastery towers head and shoulders above everything else and it is well worth the effort of donning long trousers or a long skirt to avoid affronting the canons of the Orthodox church.

It is a fascinating mini-village of winding streets, stairways and chapels plastered with icons showing St John's sufferings at the hands of the Romans. The monastery contains the remains of Christodoulos, its founder, and the edict from the Emperor gifting Patmos to him. It also boasts a rich collection of religious treasures, including bibles, silver altar ornaments, bishop's robes and staffs, jewelled crosses, icons and ancient manuscripts.

It has a version of St Mark's Gospel written in the 5th century and an ancient manuscript of Aristophanes' Comedies.

The road up to the monastery runs past one of the most precious and authentic shrines of Christianity – the cave where St John received the Revelations from God through cracks in the roof and spent two years putting them on manuscript with his pupil Prohoros. It is on the left of the road on a bend not far from Skala, and is now surrounded by a religious school and topped by a small church, so it is not exactly obvious or advertised to passing tourists. But it is well worth the trouble of rousing one of the monks to unlock the church door for a view of the cave and the silver plates that indicate where St John lay to hear the word of God. Although it is depicted on many postcards, many cruise ship passengers visiting the monastery rush past the cave, which

seems a pity. They also, through sheer lack of time, often miss the rest of the island and which certainly deserves a tour by either boat, car or foot. If time is limited and no transport available, it is worth walking to Grikou to see its enclosed bay and island, and to take a cup of coffee at one of its welcoming restaurants.

If time is plentiful, it pays to walk through the whole island, which is tranquil and scenic, and dotted with churches and monasteries.

Worth visiting off Patmos

Lipsi makes a good day's outing from Patmos for a change of scene and a swim on a different beach. So does Fourni if a boat is going there.

Anyone staying a week or two on the island should certainly take a ship to Samos, Leros, Kalymnos or Kos. It is easy to visit Samos and Kos for the day if the hydrofoils are running.

Lipsi

Lipsi is a small, sleepy island between Patmos and Leros, which is visited about twice a week in summer by ships of the line that ply the Dodecanese islands and by caiques that make day trips from Skala on Patmos and Agia Marina on Leros. It can be a welcome refuge from the other two islands when they become crowded in mid-summer.

The journey takes an hour from Patmos and two hours from Leros, and Lipsi is often treated as a satellite isle of one or both of the bigger islands, but it was listed as one of the original twelve Dodecanese islands and has a character all of its own. First sight of Lipsi's pretty port suggests that it has more blue-domed churches than houses or hotels, but it has a busy little fishing harbour surrounded by a number of good restaurants serving fish and sweet dark local wine and clean, if simple, pensions. It also has some of the most delightful, polite island folk in the Dodecanese, and its lack of roads make it blissfully quiet.

There is not much to do on Lipsi other than eat, sleep, walk and swim, but it is a good place for all of those. Like all the Dodecanese, it has a castle on the hill overlooking the port, which does not compare with the wonders to be seen on Patmos, Kos and Rhodes, but makes a healthy walk. There are other good walks along goat tracks across the island to sandy beaches on the east shore, one of which has a simple beach restaurant.

If you don't want to walk so far, there are two or three perfectly good curves of sand for swimming around the bay containing the port.

Lipsi is a rocky, brown island for most of the year and has been suggested as one of the places that inspired the isle of Calypso in the Odyssey. It is not far from Troy and its name has the same root as Calypso, but is too distant from the Ionian islands that feature in the tale to put much faith in the legend.

Agathonissi and Arki

Two other rocky little islands that fan out from Patmos towards the Turkish coast are Agathonissi and Arki, reached like Lipsi, by occasional Dodecanese steamers that sometimes go on to Samos. Agathonissi has two separate villages, Megalo Horio and Mikro Horio, linked by a poor road. Mikro Horio is almost uninhabited and could soon be a ghost village.

The beaches are pebbly, but pretty. There is one by the port and another two just over the cliff beside the port. A fourth lies in a tiny inlet on the north coast.

Leros

Leros is the first port of call for many Dodecanese steamers making the long voyage from Athens and yet few tourists alight. Most are bound for the delights of Kalymnos, Kos or Rhodes. Leros has no great sites or beaches, so it remains little known, little recommended, and host to few package tours.

Yet the island has its own charm, and part of it is the absence of high-rise hotels and other foreigners. It also has a dramatic landscape with a high brown interior fanning out towards fertile valleys in six huge bays and it is often easy to walk from one to another. In shape and size, it is not unlike Patmos and it has friendly natives who welcome visitors, most of whom are mainland Greeks.

Although mentioned by Homer and Herodotus, Leros does not have a great history dating back to an ancient civilisation, but it has had an important military role in this century, thanks to its sheltered bays and harbours, which some say are the best in the Aegean. It was a naval base for the Italians, then taken over briefly by the British, and two huge guns on the island inspired Alastair Maclean to write 'The Guns of Navarone'. A British cemetery, immaculately kept, commemorates a battle on the island in 1943.

The Castle of the Knights at Platanos, which maintains the island's links with the Dodecanese, still houses a garrison of Greek troops, who are now keeping a wary eye on the Turkish mainland, and it has other army camps. It also has a mental hospital and the remnants of a prison camp used to house political offenders during the military dictatorship of the colonels from 1967 to 1973.

Leros shares with its bigger neighbour, Kalymnos, the practice of sending ships annually to North Africa to fish for sponges, and its closest sea links are with Kalymnos. It also has regular ferry connections with Kos and Rhodes to the south and Patmos and Samos to the north, though it usually seems to miss out on the hydrofoil that links Kos and Patmos.

Beaches

There are no wonderful beaches on the island, but every bay has one or more shingle stretch, so there is always a beach within easy reach. Alinda, which is a thriving little resort, has a long beach around the bay from Platanos and Agia Marina, Gourna Bay a kilometre away across the island has another, and Pantele 2 kilometres across the peninsular has a third. It also has three tavernas lying beneath the four windmills on the hill and a rival beach with a taverna at the southern end of Pentele bay.

There is another beach at Koulouki a short walk around Lakki bay from the port of Lakki on the west side of the island. There are other more remote beaches in Partheni bay in the north and Xirokambo bay in the south.

Nightlife and Dining Out

Lakki has a lively dining out scene around its quayside and seashore. Platanos, Agia Marina and Pentele, which are almost a continuous strip of houses, between them support a good selection of restaurants plus a cinema and two discotheques in season. A taverna in Pentele has a resident bouzouki player.

Not to be missed on Leros

Nowhere on the island is more than a mile from the sea, so it is appealing to walk from one place to another. Lakki has the Italian architecture, broad avenues, squares with statues, and a colourful giant harbour with palm trees along the quayside. Platanos has the Castle of the Knights and from there to Lakki is only 3 kilometres, so it is easily walkable. The Castle is uphill and it's worth knowing that there is an occasional bus that goes everywhere on the island, there are plenty of taxis and there are scooters and bikes for hire.

It is worth walking the 350 steps uphill to see one of the best preserved Medieval castles in Greece. It has frescoes and a miraculous icon in the chapel and often a garrison of the Greek army in the keep.

It is not far either to the British cemetery on Alinda Bay, which is an unusual memorial in Greece.

Worth visiting off Leros

Kalymnos is an obvious trip for anyone staying on Leros wanting a different scene since there are daily ships, while Patmos and Lipsi beckon with their beaches, and Patmos should certainly be visited for its monastery and the cave of St John.

Kalymnos

The home of the Greek sponge-fishing fleet, Kalymnos is a bustling island of great character. The main port of Pothia or Kalymnos Town is colourful and seems to hum and rustle with activity 20 hours a day.

It is an amphitheatre of houses painted in patriotic white and blue – a legacy of protest during the Italian occupation – and the waterfront shops are hung with brown and yellow sponges, but it is not a peaceful place to spend time.

However, Pothia is only the gateway

to the delights of the island which lie along its east and west coasts, and can be reached by a public (collective) taxi system adopted from Turkey and the Middle East. You can jump in a taxi with other passengers in one of the squares in Pothia and be in one of the main coastal resorts in ten minutes. It is much quicker than travelling by one of the island's occasional buses and you may share a taxi with a family of friendly chattering island Greeks.

Vathy is one of the few places to which a regular bus service seems to run and it is worth the trip to see the little fishing harbour village tucked away at the apex of a Norwegian-style fiord and backed by a fertile valley. A good road up the west coast leads to a series of beach resorts like Linaria, Panormos, Myrties, Massouri, Aginonta and Emborio.

There are few traces of the sponge-fishermen in mid-summer since they are away working the coasts of north Africa for four to six months. Their departure just after Easter is an occasion for great feasting and religious ceremony, and their return in the autumn is another excuse for parties. But you can see plenty of sponges on sale on the island and also get the feel of the grimmer side of this colourful-sounding activity practised by the islanders for many centuries.

You can buy postcards of men in ancient diving kit and note the number of women in black in Pothia and the number of men with prematurely aged faces who testify to the risks of this ancient trade.

Kalymnos is more easily accessible than many of the Dodecanese islands since it is one of the main calls on the ferry routes from Piraeus to Rhodes, and has regular crossings by both boat

and hydrofoil from Kos, which go on to Leros, Astipalea and Patmos.

A new airport is under construction on Kalymnos, which will make the island even more accessible.

Beaches

There is a tiny strip of sand in the harbour at Pothia, but don't consider it while the beaches and sparkling waters of the west coast are so close. Pamormos, Linaria and Kantouni just 5 kilometres from town have curves of pretty shingle around the Bay of Linaria and there is more sand further up the coast at Myrties and Massouri, two white cubist villages ablaze with flowers sited opposite the islet of Telendos. If these beaches are too crowded, take a bus or taxi further north to Aginonta or Emborios, or a boat across to Telendos. Eborios, isolated on the northern peninsular, is a good get-away-from-it-all spot with a calm enclosed bay and reasonable beach. It is hard to imagine it was once the main port of the island.

Nightlife and Dining Out

Pothia is a scene of seething activity after dark with restaurants, bars and cinemas, and resorts along the west coast like Myrties also have lively bars and tavernas, plus the occasional discotheque.

Not to be missed on Kalymnos

Don't miss a drive up the dramatic west coast and try to get to Vathy too for a completely contrasting scene. Horio on the road to the west coast, at a distance of 2½ kilometres and within walking distance of the town, is a place to stop to see the old walled city of Kastro with its nine churches standing below a Medieval castle. To the south lie two monasteries.

Another healthy walk from Pothia is the cave of the seven virgins, also called the Grotto of the Nymphs, where the luckless seven fled to escape pirates or the Turks and were supposedly lost in its deep passageways.

A boat trip along the south coast west from Pothia goes to the cave of Zeus, which has impressive stalactites and stalagmites, known as Spilia Kephalos.

Worth visiting off Kalymnos

There are regular boats from Pothia harbour to Pserimos for a day's swimming on a smaller island and regular boats from Myrties and Massouri to Telendos for the same purpose. When the hydrofoil is running it is easy to visit Kos or Patmos for a day or two, and regular island steamers bring Leros and Astipalea within reach, though the latter is a few hours by sea and the ships don't run every day.

Telendos

Telendos is a mountain islet half a mile off the west coast of Kalymnos, which can be reached in about 15 minutes by small boat from Myrties or Massouri. It has a small village called Telenda with restaurants, a series of small sandy coves along the shore which offer good swimming, and some wonderful local tales.

In the straits off the village an old town lies buried under the sea and you can see the outline of walls and houses on a calm day. Legend has it that Kalymnos and Telendos were once joined together and were separated by an earthquake in 595 AD, which launched the town into the sea and made the peninsular an island. The theory is supported by the mountain-like appearance of the islet and Roman remains on Telendos.

Locals will tell the tale with gusto, especially after a few ouzos and will also point out the sleeping princess rock on the mountain and her sleeping prince lying facing her across the straits on Kalymnos.

Pserimos

Pserimos is a small barren islet about halfway between Kos and Kalymnos, which has a smooth curve of sandy beach surrounded by its main village and restaurants. It makes an easy day's excursion from either of the two bigger islands and as a result sees regular day trip boats pouring into its tiny harbour in summer.

It is also possible to stay on Pserimos for a glimpse of a simpler life and to explore the island, which offers delightful walks across its spine to the shore opposite Turkey.

The trip takes about an hour from Kos or Kalymnos and makes a good retreat for those seeking a break from the bustle of Kos town or Pothia.

People who stay on the island – and there are a few package tours going there now – will see little activity beyond fishing and herding goats, and most supplies are brought over from Kos or Kalymnos, along with the daily tourist boats. But there are two good sandy beaches on the Turkish-facing shore.

Halki

Halki is one of nine small, brown, hilly islands clustered off the west coast of Rhodes which makes a handy retreat from the bigger island to sample small island life and lose the crowds.

Nearby Alimia has a better harbour beach, but Halki is the biggest island in the group and has a character all of its own, as befits one of the original members of the Dodecanese. Daily boats ply from Kamiros Skala on Rhodes to its port of Niborio and it is visited a couple of times a week by the Dodecanese steamers on their way between Rhodes and Karpathos.

It is closer to Rhodes than Simi, smaller and has better beaches, so it is surprising that it is visited less frequently. It has only one road, few cars and no buses, but is eminently walkable. In the same manner as Simi, it has a grand port of old mansions painted in white and pastel colours dominated by two high bell towers – one of which, on the church of Agios Nikolaos, is reputed to be the tallest in the Dodecanese.

Like Simi and Kalymnos, it once owned a rich sponge-fishing fleet and this wealth funded the island's single road, which ascends to the island's Castle of the Knights, the Monastery of Stavros and the best sandy beach on the island. But in recent years much of the population seems to have left for the cities and many of the houses in the port are empty of residents except when they return for the summer holidays.

Beaches

Beaches are few on the island, but there are enough for the few tourists who are prepared to walk a short way. There is a tiny sand strip near the port by the road up to the Castle, which has a restaurant and rooms, but it becomes crowded. Better is a pebble stretch about ten minutes walk away, which has sand in the sea. But the best sand beach is at Pontamos about 15 minutes walk to the south of the port towards the castle cliff. It can be reached by boat from the port.

There is another much quieter beach the other side of the castle cliff.

There are also a few small coves to the north of the port beyond the first bay you reach, which also have a mixture of pebble and sand in a lovely lonely coastal setting. The best is called Kania.

Nightlife and Dining Out

Halki is a little short on accommodation, with only three or four small pensions in the port, but it is long on restaurants. There are four in the port and one more along the coast towards the castle. However, this is a quiet Greek-style dining out scene rather than the kind of nightlife offered by Rhodes town and you have to concentrate on good food rather than music and dancing. The harbourside restaurant by the ferry serves excellent pasta dishes and the other restaurant by the harbour has good fish.

Not to be missed on Halki

Walks in both directions from the port are rewarding. The north leads only to open country and coast, but the road to the south leads to the old semi-deserted capital, the monastery and the Castle, which is well worth a hike to see its crumbling walls, frescoes in the church and the view down the coast.

Don't be alarmed if you see the odd snake when out walking in this region. There are a few around early in the summer, and they quickly take fright and seek refuge under walls or rocks. But it is worth taking a little care to avoid the fate of a Greek lady I met who was bitten. She was told with typical Greek fatalism: 'It's not snake-bite. There are no snakes on this island'.

Worth visiting off Halki

It is worth taking a boat to Alimia for a

122

day's swimming. There is a small café by the beach. Anyone staying on Halki for a week will also want a glimpse of civilisation on Rhodes and the journey to Kamiros Skala takes only a little more than an hour. Once there, you are within easy reach of Rhodes town or the fascinating ancient city of Kamiros.

Simi

Brown, barren Simi boasts one of the most stunning sights in the Aegean. The harbour of Egiali (or Simi or Yialos) is a magnificent amphitheatre of tall 19th century mansions rising in tiers from the port and linking it to the island's capital of Horio 15 minutes uphill as if they were one.

It testifies to a proud past. Simi was called after a beautiful princess of Rhodes, who was abducted to the island, and had enough wealth to send three ships to Troy led by King Nireus, one of the leading Greek heroes of the siege. In the last century it enjoyed free port status under the Turks and had thriving sponge-fishing and boat-building industries, importing its timber from the Turkish mainland.

Most of that ended under the Italian occupation and Simi has been cut off from the brooding mainland ever since. Its decline explains the many ruined mansions in the port. But today it is thriving again, thanks to tourism. Ships come over daily from Rhodes and even Kos, and there is a steady package tour trade in Egiali which has stimulated its reconstruction with small pensions and restaurants.

Dodecanese steamers also call at Simi, but can take a long time about it, so it can pay to ship over from Rhodes rather than from Piraeus.

Beaches

Simi has no sandy beaches, but its coastline is indented with small bays which contain adequate strips of shingle and pebble for swimming. The lack of sand does not seem to worry regular visitors, who enthuse about the clear waters around the island.

There are beaches across the bay from Egiali at Nos and Nimborio, where the local discotheque is also sited, and there is also one at Panormitis on the south coast where the Rhodes boats usually call. But there are better ones at Pethi and Agia Marina, about half an hour to an hour's walk across the island towards the Turkish coast or reached by boat from Egiali port.

A longish walk in a westerly direction will take you to a swimmable cove at Skoumissa Bay by the church of Agios Emilianos around 6 kilometres from Egiali and another track to the south goes to another swimmable bay at Agios Vasilios, a distance of about 4 kilometres.

The beach of Marathounda and the islet of Sesklia can be reached by a boat that leaves each morning from Egiali.

Nightlife and Dining Out

Egiali is a lively place in the evening with restaurants everywhere around the harbour and a discotheque often booming away as Nos across the bay. Horio also has restaurants and cafés.

Not to be missed on Simi

Horio has the remains of a castle and a small museum containing sculptures, icons and manuscripts. It is an easy walk from the port, via the island's biggest church, Agia Panagia, up winding streets paved with pebble mosaics of ships and mermaids. But the island's most exciting sight is the monastery of St Michael at Panormitis on the south coast, which is often a calling point for day excursions from Rhodes. It can be reached by boat from Egiali, or even by walking, but that can take a few hours each way.

It is a beautiful monastery dating mostly from the 18th century surrounded by fertile valleys and woods, which make a contrast to the bare north coast of the island. It has a spectacular carved wooden altar screen, a silver and gold icon, and many votive offerings from local sailors and fishermen.

Pethi makes a pleasant evening's walk along the island's best road, if you do not go there in the daytime for a swim.

Worth visiting off Simi

Anyone staying on Simi for a week should certainly make a day trip to Rhodes to enjoy the contrast of a much bigger, more touristy island. A 2-day trip would be even better to see that island's stunning port, old town and four ancient cities.

Karpathos

Karpathos is a long, narrow island about the same size as Kos with a wonderful variety of scenery and people. The south below the main port of Pigadia is fairly flat and sparse on vegetation, the inland hill villages above the port are set in wooded glades, then the middle spine of the island is bare and rocky, and the north around Diafani and Olympos is hilly and sports trees and exotic bushes beside streams.

The people in the south are normal island Greeks making regular contact with the outside world by the ferry service from Rhodes to Crete and the daily planes from Rhodes and two a week from Athens. Occasional charters from northern Europe also now land on the airstrip at the southern tip of the island. The people in the north of the island, although closer to sophisticated Rhodes, seem remote from the modern world. The women wear embroidered blouses and headscarves and the men make music on local bagpipes (tsabouna), lyre and guitar in ceremonies that often go on for days.

Karpathos has been opened up to tourism in recent years, thanks to the air link with Rhodes, the hotels and restaurants of Pigadia, and the pretty resort of Ammopi which has grown up a few kilometres south of Pigadia, as well as the attraction of seeing the past come alive in the north of the island. But it is not a touristy island and has many remote spots for visitors to walk, rest and swim.

Beaches

Karpathos has a good quota of sandy beaches, mainly in the south of the island. Pigadia is set on the bay of Vrontis, which is itself a curving stretch of sand with a restaurant and hotel above. Ammopi, which is little more than an hour's walk across the headland to the south, is a beautiful little spot with two sandy coves – one usually occupied by nudists and topless bathers – which have stimulated the development of a small resort with pensions and restaurants.

There is another more remote beach at Makri Yialos near the airstrip, which can be reached by bus from the port or by hired scooter, and there are others in the west coast at Arkassa, Finikes and Lefkos, approached by a road around the southern tip of the island or bus across the middle via

Aperi or Menetes. The west coast can be rough and the long beach at Arkassa then becomes more suitable for surfing than swimming.

North of Pigadia are three more beaches at Ahata, Kyria Panagia which boasts a monastery of the same name, and Agios Nikolaos, which has a church and simple food and lodging beside a pretty, though pebbly, little anchorage.

The beach at Diafani in the north is also pebbly, but it is long and spectacular. Well worth the trip for anyone staying in the south.

Nightlife and Dining Out

Pigadia has most of the nightlife in the south of the island, with restaurants ranged along the harbourside, occasional music and a discotheque which opens in mid-summer. Diafani in the north makes its own music, but needs few excuses to do so. Strolling players can often be seen doing the rounds of the tavernas on the pretext of a festival or wedding and such events can last for days and nights with alternate feasting and fast-stepping dances.

Not to be missed on Karpathos

Both ends of the island should be seen for their contrasts and it is worth hiring a scooter to tour the south. Apart from the beaches and fishing villages like Arkassa, Finikes and Lefkos, you can take a pretty road inland to the fertile little villages of Aperi, Volada, Othos and Piles, which are strung across the middle of the island as if sited for an early morning or evening drive. If it is hard to reach them all, go at least as far as Aperion, which clings to the side of a leafy gorge and can offer simple food and lodging. It has two tiny cafés with tables out of doors in a distinctly Alpine setting.

Arkassa is a pretty old fishing village and a few minutes' walk leads to ancient Arkassa by the sea where you can see the ruins of early Byzantine churches with mosaic floors. Lefkos has an isle in the bay called Sokastro, which as its name implies has a medieval castle. Some people take the occasional bus as far as Spoa and then walk along the spine of the island to Olympos in the north, but be warned – it can take four or five hours. Better to search out one of the island's taxis, which navigate the road along the island for a price or take a boat to Diafani.

Diafani and Olympos are certainly worth a visit, and the walk between them is pretty and not so arduous. It takes about two hours uphill along fertile valleys between brooding hillsides to Olympos, which is a majestic cubist village with windmills set high above the sea on one side and high above a valley on the other. Olympos has the feel of a village lost in time and you may be lucky enough to chance on a local orchestra which makes the setting even more surrealistic.

Worth visiting off Karpathos

Caiques run occasionally from Diafani to the islet of Saria off the north coast of Karpathos and it is worth taking the short trip to enjoy a swim off a different beach and to see the ancient town of Nissiros.

Rhodes is a long sea voyage from Diafani and should only be attempted for a stay of a few days to make the journey worthwhile. The same goes for Halki, though it is nearer.

The easiest way to Rhodes is by plane

from the airstrip in the south and it is only a short sea trip of a couple of hours to Kassos or Diafani from Pigadia, but still make sure of your return boat before making the trip, as they do not always run regular services.

Kassos

Tiny Kassos is the most southern island in the Dodecanese chain and one of the most remote. It has a barren brown landscape of volcanic rock, and is sparse on both trees, beaches and population, but the people are hospitable and there is a tiny airstrip served by Skyvans from Rhodes in addition to the regular Dodecanese steamers.

There is no good reason why Kassos should be so neglected when Simi is becoming so popular as the two islands are alike in many ways.

Kassos does not have an obviously scenic port at Agia Marina where the steamers call, but the old fishing port of Fri around the headland has accommodation, restaurants and much of the life of the island, and is a picture postcard scene. The inland villages of Polis and Avrantohori are also pretty, are within walking distance and offer good views of the coastline below.

The island has a glorious past that is not immediately evident today. Homer says that Kassos sent ships to aid the Greek cause in the Trojan War and it repeated the exercise when the Greek War of Independence against the Turks started in 1821. Its little ships covered themselves in glory in many sea actions and Kassos suffered for its loyalty to Greece in 1824 when the Turks invaded the island, massacring and enslaving most of its inhabitants.

Beaches

You have to look hard for a beach on Kassos and it is easiest to swim from short pebble stretches between the rocks along the coast from the port or at Amousa by the airport. There is a small stretch of sand in the harbour where the steamers dock, but the best real beaches around are a long stretch of yellow sand on the nearby islet of Armathia, which can be reached by small boat, and the Bay of Kelathros on the other side of the island.

Nightlife and Dining Out

It is a quiet island with most of the activity in the main port, but the islanders will use any excuse – a saint's day, family occasion or commemoration of history – for a festival in the main village and visitors are usually invited.

Not to be missed on Kassos

Kassos is a great place to walk because it has few trees and views are uninterrupted in all directions showing off flocks of goats and an occasional hawk. The obvious walk is up to Polis and the cave of Selai, which bristles with stalactites and stalagmites. Nearby you can also see some ancient walls, but they have no meaningful shape. A longer walk across the island leads to a monastery and the beach at Kelathros surrounded by cliffs.

Worth visiting off Kassos

The island is only three miles from Karpathos at the nearest point and steamers make the trip in under two hours, but ships are not so frequent, so you might have to visit Karpathos for a few days. The same goes for Crete in the other direction. The ships run around twice a week to Agios Nicolaos or Sitia in eastern Crete, from which you can easily reach the

Minoan sites of Malia, Knossos and Zakros and also the palm-fringed beach of Vai.

The easiest trip from Kassos is to the nearby islet of Armathia which has a small village and a lovely beach. That takes less than half an hour by caique.

Astipalea

Astipalea is remote from the other Dodecanese islands and acts as a bridge, geographically and architecturally, between them and the Cyclades. It is on the sea route between Kos and Amorgos and looks more like the latter with white villages peeping out from craggy rocks and hills burnt brown by the Mediterranean sun and the mid-Aegean winds.

But the island also has green fertile valleys which produce the local Kastellani wines, fruit and vegetables and has strong affinities to the rest of the Dodecanese through a well-preserved Castle of the Knights that towers over the port and Hora, the main town up the hill nestling into the walls of the castle. Half a dozen windmills also sit on the crest of the hill and line up with the castle to give Astipalea a most distinctive skyline, which is featured on many local postcards.

The island is shaped like a balloon that has been squeezed in the middle to make two bulging halves joined by a narrow strip, which is less than 100 yards wide at its narrowest point. Most of the inhabitants live along the squeezed middle strip with the action focused on the port, also known as Astipalea, and along the road that runs west to Livadi 2 kilometres away and east to Analipsi or Maltezana and Vathi. Analipsi is an easy ride of 12 kilometres by taxi or bus if it is

running, but Vathi is far more remote, reached either by a riverbed-style road or by sea when it is calm enough for the trip.

The port has an abundance of small hotels and restaurants, including the quaint Hotel de France, which is run by a French couple and twinned with a Gallic bakery next door. The Hora contains a sprinkling of smart hideaway bars and houses being restored by foreigners with criss-cross pattern wooden balconies on narrow alleyways around the castle, which have fabulous views of the two bays either side of the headland on which Hora is built.

Ships to Astipalea are scheduled to take about 13 hours from Piraeus, but in practice seem to take forever from the mainland and 2–3 hours from Kalymnos and Amorgos. Because the island is fairly hard to get to it enjoys a feeling of great peace and quiet.

This may change a little following the recent launch of twice-weekly Olympic flights to a new airport on Astipalea from Athens and Kos.

Astipalea must have been more fertile in olden days since the ancient Greeks called the island 'the gods' banquet table' for its abundant crops and the Romans dubbed it 'the fish-bearing isle'. It certainly enjoyed an era of prosperity in the 13th–16th centuries when it was ruled by the Quirini family who built the castle and stamped their arms upon it.

It was the first island taken by the Italians during their occupation of the Dodecanese and they built another fortress near Vathi in the north.

Beaches

The port has a small strip of sandy

beach, but there is a much better curve of sand at Livadi reached by a stiff, but rewarding, half hour walk over the headland, and another prettier cove a further walk beyond that, which is occasionally served by boats from the port. Analipsi also has a peaceful sandy bay where rooms and even small houses can be rented. It is easy to walk from there to the north-west shore where there are two or three remote pebble beaches.

Nightlife and Dining Out

The port is surprisingly well supplied with restaurants and bars and there are more in the town around the castle, including the smart Fisherman's Taverna, and a trio of beach restaurants over at Livadi which makes a pleasant evening's walk to see the sunset or view the stars. Analipsi is much quieter.

Not to be missed on Astipalea

The Venetian castle is a delight to explore, as is the surrounding maze of winding Cycladic streets of the Hora which contain two pretty old churches. It is worth taking a taxi along the island to Analipsi, if only for a day on the beach and a glimpse of a much quieter scene than that in the port.

Worth visiting off Astipalea

The island is a great escape for three or four days. After that, you might start to feel like a sea trip and the obvious alternatives are Amorgos, a dramatic Cycladic island to the west with a spectacular monastery and white villages, Kalymnos, the sponge fishers' island to the east, or Kos, a much bigger island which is soaring in the tourist charts. All have a selection of good sandy beaches.

Kastelorizo

Kastelorizo, or Megisti, is an isolated outpost of Greece and a proud expression of Hellenistic nationalism. The tiny island is over 50 miles and six hours' sailing east of Rhodes and lies in the lee of the Turkish coast with the lights of Turkish villages burning bright only a mile away. There are also Turkish-style houses in the port of Kastelorizo.

It was once the main port between Greece and Beirut with a population of 18,000 and has stayed an undisputed enclave of Greek territory, never making contact with the Turkish coast, thanks to generous subsidies from the Greek Government and maintenance of the population around 200. If it ever falls below that, the story goes, the island will pass to Turkey.

It is all the more remarkable because the island has a turbulent history and has been regularly ravaged by invaders, including the Italians during the Second World War when the island was evacuated in the face of German air raids.

Its Greek name, Megisti (literally 'the greatest') is a complete misnomer, though it is believed to be called after an early settler. The Knights of St John, who built a castle on the hill overlooking the port, gave it its more familiar name of Kastelorizo ('Red castle').

Despite its remoteness, or perhaps because of it, a steady trickle of visitors make the long twice-weekly sea trip from Rhodes and keep the restaurants along the harbour going through the summer. Some of them are returning emigres who were born on Kastelorizo and now live in Australia or the USA. They land in a big natural port of white, red-roofed houses with Italianate archways lying at one end of a rocky bay.

A few, who book well ahead, make the trip from Rhodes in just half an hour by small Olympic planes that land at the equally small Kastelorizo airport.

Beaches

There are no real beaches on the island, although there is some spectacular swimming from rocks and there is a small stretch of shingle at Agios Stefanos. Boats do a 20-minute trip to the tiny islet of Agios Georgios, which has a better beach.

Nightlife and Dining Out

This is quiet and strictly what you make of it.

Not to be missed on Kastelorizo

History has given the island a stately, if crumbling, Castle of the Knights, which towers above the harbour and is well worth a visit. It is reached by a long stairway from the port, which passes by a small museum housed in a Turkish mosque and four white churches. Around the coast by boat from the harbour is a sea cave with stalactites and stalagmites, where seals sometimes swim and the sunlight plays strange tricks in the water.

Worth visiting off Kastelorizo

Unfortunately, it is not possible to visit the Turkish mainland, so the only way out from Kastelorizo is back to Rhodes and the rest of the Dodecanese. Most visitors will welcome a greater sense of civilisation after a few days' splendid isolation on the island.

Nissiros

Volcanic Nissiros is small in area, but big in appearance and offers a contrasting green, fertile aspect to many of the other Dodecanese islands with fruit trees, chestnuts, vines and olive trees cloaking its hillsides. It is all due to the volcano, which supposedly erupted Nissiros away from Kos in ancient times and still smoulders and bubbles away in the huge crater in the middle of the island.

Lava soil is rich and water-retaining. There are many volcanic areas in Greece, but few craters which can be toured and inspected like this one. It makes the island a worthy, yet different, rival to Santorini. The land around the volcano is emerald green and hot sulphur springs and hot water ponds bubble away around the edge.

Nissiros is on the Dodecanese steamer route, but is also on more regular routes from Kos town by ship and from Kardamena harbour by regular caique. Both trips take about 2 hours, passing the islet of Yiali on the way.

You can do it more quickly by the smart Australian catamaran which speeds between Nissiros and Kos and on to Rhodes.

The capital and harbour of Mandraki where the ships dock is a pretty white fishing village with winding streets, whitewashed walkways and a number of comfortable little hotels and restaurants crowned by a Castle of the Knights and the Monastery of the Holy Virgin or Panagyia Spiliani.

It is an emerging Mykonos in the Dodecanese, thanks to its white cubist houses and a series of smart little restaurants along the harbourside. In time it could become as sophisticated as the islands of the central Cyclades.

Nissiros has spectacle and good

eating, but suffers from lack of good beaches and a slight tenseness in the local people that you find on other volcanic islands like Santorini.

Beaches

Nissiros is not a great island for beaches. They are mostly rocky or pebble, but there is a small stretch of sand along the coast from Mandraki and a more businesslike sandy beach along the coast at Pali, which is a half hour's walk and served by occasional buses. There are also some spectacular pebble bays beyond the headland supporting the castle and monastery.

Anyone staying on the island for more than a couple of days should explore the brown sand beaches that run south of Pali along the road to Lies, but you need your own transport or to be prepared for a stiff walk beyond Pali.

It is claimed there is a 'white beach' below the hotel of the same name along the coast between Loutra and Pali, but it is just a small imported sand beach and usually crowded. The only white beaches are on the island of Yiali.

Nightlife and Dining Out

Mandraki has a couple of lively tavernas where meat turns on the spit in summer and music is sometimes laid on, but nightlife is mainly dining out in the town and walks along the coast to watch the sun go down.

Not to be missed on Nissiros

The Castle is certainly worth visiting and you can take in the monastery on the same walk uphill. Its church is cut out of the rock and is plastered with icons, hung with silver and gold. Ten minutes walk to the south of Mandraki is the ancient acropolis dating from 500 BC and called Paleokastro, with remains of its walls and fantastic views over the port. The town has a small museum with pottery, sculptures and icons testifying to the island's past.

On the hillside along from Pali is a crumbling old spa complex called Loutra served by hot water from the volcano, complete with hot baths, café and hens and goats feeding beneath the trees.

There are two other, more formal hot bath establishments going under the same name closer to Mandraki.

But the big sight of the island is the double crater of the volcano, known as Polyvotis. It is a bleak multi-coloured 'Star Wars' setting where sulphuric mud splatters out of the ground with a gurgling sound and pools of water steam and hiss. It is reached by minibus, taxi or bus from the port, which seem to be more in evidence when ships or caiques come across from Kos. They do a lively business – sometimes at extortionate rates when the boats come in – to the crater via the hillside villages of Emborio and Nikia, which are white, surrounded by greenery and give commanding views of the crater and seascape below and across to Kos.

The volcano is 17 kilometres from the port and is the most spectacular extinct crater in Greece – quite different from Santorini's sea-filled caldera. It fills a deep valley 2 miles long by half a mile wide ending in a deep grey pit where you can pick up pieces of pumice stone. Alternatively, you can buy them cheaply from a nearby café.

It is possible to walk to the crater from Mandraki via one of two hill monasteries, but allow 2–3 hours for the trip.

Worth visiting off Nissiros

If you want better beaches or just a glimpse of a different island, Yiali is idyllic and an easy day's boat trip. Kos and Tilos are each about two hours' away to the north and south.

Yiali

Half an hour by boat from Mandraki harbour lies the idyllic little islet of Yiali. All the best beaches on Nissiros are on Yiali, which is mainly a quarry island. It once provided pumice for the Empire State building in New York.

The only buildings are workers' houses, but it boasts three or four lovely desert island beaches on a bay facing Nissiros. You can find good pumice stones there if the supply is running short at the volcano, but need to take food and drink for a day trip as there are no shops or cafés.

Tilos

Tilos is a rare jewel among the Dodecanese islands. It is beautiful, friendly and well-endowed with beaches, scenic walks across herby hillsides and a dozen good restaurants. Yet its local population is declining and it is not crowded with tourists.

Transport problems are part of the explanation. There are 3 or 4 ships a week in summer, only 1 in winter, and it can take 6 hours from Rhodes, 4 from Kos and about 2 from Nissiros. Until recent years the island had no bus or proper taxi.

Visit it soon before it is discovered by more people. A hydrofoil service or small airport, which is planned, could make a big difference.

Most of the island is populated by goats, who seem to graze every

hillside. They also grace the restaurants of Livadia, the port, in summer.

There are only two populated villages, the tiny port of Livadia, which has most of the accommodation and restaurants, and stretches around a large, scenic bay, and the old capital Megalo Horio, which has the local Castle of the Knights and is enjoying a revival, thanks to tourism. They are 7 kilometres apart, which is just walkable when there are no buses about.

There are also rooms and restaurants at Agios Anthonios and Eristos, two of the beaches reached via Megalo Horio.

The third village, Mikro Horio, was abandoned by its inhabitants in the 1960's. They fled a hard life to move down to the coast at Livadia and many didn't stop until they reached America or Australia.

Getting around Tilos has been transformed in recent years by the arrival of a small bus, which runs the length of the island 3 or 4 times a day, and occasional rival services.

Beaches

Livadia has a long, swimmable pebble beach stretching around the bay next to the port. But the big beach of the island, which is pine-fringed and sandy at the southern end, is Eristos. It has two restaurants back in the trees, which grow much of what they serve.

The most exciting beaches are in the north around Megalo Horio. Apart from Eristos, Agios Anthonios has sparkling pebbles and Plaka half an hour around the bay is the desert island beach of the island.

There are two other swimmable coves

at Staffi, reached beyond the castle, and Lethra east of the main road halfway between the two villages.

Nightlife and Dining Out

The main eating out scene is Livadia and it also has a disco/bar, but it is mercifully on the edge of the village and not hugely popular.

Not to missed on Tilos

Tilos is rich in history. It was the island of the poetess Irina, a big rival of Sappho, and once had 7 Castles of the Knights. The best remains are at Megalo Horio.

There is also a spectacular remote monastery at Agios Pandelemonas, high above the coast, which is served by the town bus on Sundays, and the ghost village of Mikro Horio. It has the remains of fine mansions and a small church plastered with beautiful old frescoes. Don't miss it.

There are more frescoes in a tiny church 30 metres above the white Panagia church, which is 30 minutes walk from the port by a dirt road. You have to crawl to get in and disturb families of goats and game birds who live there, but it is worth it for a set of superb paintings of the saints, spoiled only by Turkish invaders, who scratched out their eyes.

There is also a cave above the main road (ask the bus driver), which contains the bones of baby mammoths. It is a bit hard to find and no tribute to Greek archaeology, but worth the trip for a pleasant walk across a hillside full of goat herds.

Worth visiting off Tilos

Tilos is a short sea trip from Nissiros, which is worth visiting for its spectacular volcano. It is also not too far away from Rhodes, Kos, Halki and Simi for a glimpse of totally different islands.

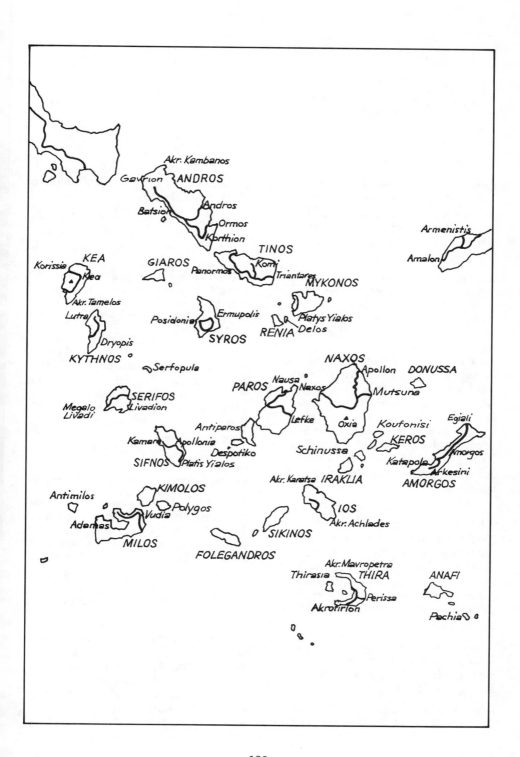

11. The Cyclades

These are the brown isles of Greece. Scorched by the hot sun and the meltemmi wind and unprotected by any mainland nearby, they are strung across the central Aegean like a string of pearls.

They have a common ancient civilisation and common architecture in their white cubist houses and churches. There are forty islands in this group, but only about thirty are inhabited. Six of them have airports, but the most usual means of access is by ferry from Piraeus or from Rafina and Lavrion on the east coast of Attica. The ferries run in three main directions – down the western side of the group; across the northern fringe; or across the middle with two splinter routes, one to Mykonos in the east and the other to Paros–Naxos–Ios–Santorini in the south.

The Chic Isle – Mykonos

Mykonos is lively, fashionable, and photogenic, cosmopolitan and well-developed. It has been called the St Tropez of the Aegean and there are connotations because the island caters for nudists, gays and pleasure-seekers. But in a unique Greek way.

It has almost given up farming and fishing in favour of running restaurants, discos, nudist beaches and gay weddings.

It has also been richly celebrated on film because it is the island featured in 'Shirley Valentine'. And it enjoys direct flights from Britain.

It is not a totally unspoilt Greek island and is not ideal for families. Yet it has great charm and can be great fun. It is stunning to look at and has learned to live with mass tourism better than some Greek islands. It is not covered with high-rise hotels and there is little sense of over-development.

Surprisingly, it was little more than a stopover en route for Tinos and Delos in the 1950s, but it was tailormade for a popular island holiday centre with its dramatic brown landscape, its whitewashed cubist houses, its windmills and its 365 wedding cake churches. There are probably nearer 500 today and many have been endowed by islanders who have become rich through the tourist trade.

In the early days the island had its own rough red wine and a pelican called Peter. You will not find the wine nowadays as agriculture has almost ceased in favour of tourism, but Peter the Second can be seen wandering around the waterfront and sometimes, if you look carefully, you might even catch sight of two pelicans.

The main harbour and the labyrinth of houses behind it make up one of the most spectacular island capitals in the Aegean. It boasts a horseshoe of cafés and restaurants around the harbour and another horseshoe of narrow streets through the town which is lined

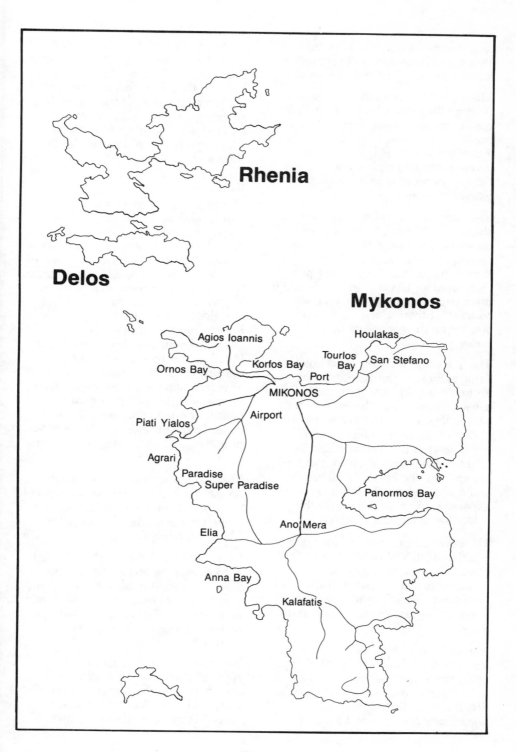

Rhenia

Delos

Mykonos

Houlakas

Agios Ioannis

Tourlos
Bay

San Stefano

Korfos Bay

Ornos Bay

Port

MIKONOS

Airport

Piati Yialos

Agrari

Paradise

Super Paradise

Panormos Bay

Elia

Ano Mera

Anna Bay

Kalafatis

with trendy restaurants, bars, art shops, and boutiques selling jewellery, fashion clothes, furs and handicrafts.

These are the landmarks of any walk through the maze of streets where it is easy to get lost, even after you have been there a week. Local folklore has it that the town was built that way to confuse invading pirates and you can believe the story after a couple of glasses of wine.

You can live well in the town, with hot showers and sunny balconies in a dozen or more small hotels that have sprung up over the past 20 years, though rooms tend to be more pricey than on other Cycladean islands and it often pays to hunt around on your own rather than taking the first offer you get on the gangplank of an arriving ferry.

There are also a dozen small hotels flanking most of the main beaches around the island and it can make sense to live outside the town in high season if you want to have some choice of places on the beach and enjoy quiet sleeps, rather than trip the light fantastic every evening. But bear in mind that the hotels on Kalafatis and Agios Stefanos beaches can be expensive, even for the simple things in life like omelette and coffee.

The best choice for out-of-town stays could be Plati Yialos, which offers a choice of accommodation and restaurants, plus a road to town that is just about walkable, and affordable if you miss the last bus and have to take a taxi.

The sad side of Mykonos is that tourism swells the local population too many times in mid-summer and some of its services groan to breaking point. The buses to the beaches are ridiculously crowded and so are the banks, as though the islanders are trying to squeeze the last penny out of their guests. They don't need to because they thrive on tourism and are visited by some of the richest free-spending tourists to visit Greece as well as back-packers and campers, who can also find places around the shores without too much hassle.

Beaches

The beaches are good, some spectacular, and most of them have restaurants on them. Those away from the town have a liberal sprinkling of topless bathers and two – Paradise and Super Paradise – are frequented by narcissistic nudists, mostly male. The local police usually turn a blind eye, despite notices banning nudism – even where there are loads of lithesome male couples, as on Super Paradise – or they expect bathers to rush into their briefs when they approach and then move away again. People who don't fancy a nudist beach, or one to themselves, can either follow the example of the police or find a good beach elsewhere on the island.

There are welcoming sandy beaches on the north, south and west coasts of the island, beckoning visitors to cool off on the many white hot days for which it is famous.

Venture beyond the beach to the left of town and the one in the harbour, unless you want to be in the company of hundreds of other sun-seekers, and in the case of the one on the left risk a bad scratching on the reef close inshore.

You can find good beaches at Elia, Anna Bay and Kalafatis, all a short walk from the inland village of Ano Mera and in the lee of the offshore islet of Tragonissi. There are two other beaches in the Bay of Panormos and Fteila, which can be reached by hired scooter, car or bus via the village and monastery of Ano Mera.

Within a half hour's walk of town there are other good stretches at Ornos Bay, San Stefano, Korfos and Agios Ioannis. The coast along from Agios Stefanos has two sizeable hotels and there is another at Kalafatis, but they tend to charge highly for indifferent food.

Unless you feel embarrassed or prudish, a day out at the Plati Yialos–Paradise complex is a must. It offers six coves of sand in succession, reached either by small boat from the port or hired scooter or by a doddery little bus from the port, which always seems to have standing room only for its 60 to 70 passengers.

The best sand and eating is on Psarou to the right of the bus stop. Plati Yialos has a choice of restaurants, hotels and the bus stop. Paradise, Super Paradise and Elia can then be reached by boat or walking east over low cliffs. They are good beaches with cheap restaurants, serving a variety of couples decorating the sand. Many on Super Paradise are slender young men with a taste for pastel shades and gold chains. Some of them never swim.

Since two equally sandy coves between Plati Yialos and Paradise are often bare of people it is tempting to conclude that Paradise is closer in spirit to Narcissus rather than Apollo.

Mykonos is often windy, thanks to its position close to the vortex of the Cycladic wind system and its lack of high ground, so it often pays to check which direction the wind is blowing before deciding whether to go to the north or south coast to swim.

Nightlife

Unlike so many Cycladic islands, Mykonos has ample nightlife and dozens of places to eat out. You can eat well on a Greek cuisine spiced with spit-roast pork, chicken and lamb, plus a broad spread of international dishes in almost any price range around the golden horseshoe of streets that threads around the town and find speciality fish restaurants like 'The Waves' beneath the windmills and along Mykonos' own 'Little Venice' harbour. Then you have a wide choice of bars and discotheques.

Like many of the restaurants, they are not cheap, but often worth the money. They serve cocktails and expensive wines. They rarely serve retsina and have long ago given up the custom of serving local wines, which have anyway almost disappeared, but drinks can be imaginative and perfectly chilled. The Nine Muses, the Remetso and Windmill are famous, but try the frenzied silvered dance floor at Piero's for somewhere different to bop or Kastro's Bar for a sophisticated drink.

You can sit high above the sea and study the reflections of the moon or harbour lights across the bay while sipping one of the incomparable Kastro coffees – a variant on Irish coffee – and listening to soft music.

Not to be missed on Mykonos

Mykonos does not have many things to see, apart from its dramatic white port and yellow beaches, but don't miss a visit to the secluded little inland village of Ano Mera and its monastery, which boasts some pretty 500 year-old wood carvings. Nearby around Panormos Bay is an ancient town and Venetian fortress.

The port has a charming little folk museum for wet days and one or two spectacular little wedding cake churches nearby, while the archaeological museum on the road to San Stefano has pottery from Delos.

Worth visiting off Mykonos

The nearby island of Delos is a must for anyone remotely interested in history and archaeology, and can be reached by motor boat from the port, but try to pick a day when the sea is calm.

It is not too difficult to take a bigger ship to Siros, Tinos, Paror or Naxos for a day or two and the island has regular ships and planes to Piraeus and Athens airport as well as Rhodes. But don't bank everything on one ship, especially in July–August when the meltemmi blows hard in the central Aegean.

The Windmill Isle – Paros

A jewel of the Cyclades, Paros has developed rather like Mykonos ten years later, but has not become quite so chic, expensive or gay and is in every way a bigger island. It boasts a wealth of sandy beaches, thrusting coastal villages with white houses and picture postcard harbours as well as a handsome main port at Parikia with windmills, and blue-domed churches framed in green hills, vineyards and pine trees.

Paros lies squarely in the middle of the Cyclades, and its wind system, and enjoys a regular stream of ships from Piraeus which take around 6 hours and go on to Naxos. It also has daily flights from Athens to its new airport; a valley of the butterflies to rival that on Rhodes; bicycles, scooters and cars for hire; and its own wines.

Gentle hills inland surround some of the best vineyards in the Cyclades, producing a variety of flinty red and white wines under names like Lageri, Moulin, Meltemi and Naoussa. They also protect half a dozen coastal villages and as many again inland, which are usually linked by good roads. They include a ring road around the island, which links all the coastal villages, and one main road across the middle of Paros to the east coast via Marathi and Marpissa.

Parikia is a bustling whitewashed town with winding cobbled streets and occasional glimpses of the Parian marble that Pericles and his architects chose for the Acropolis in Athens. It has two campsites and masses of rooms. Life seems to revolve around the quayside where the big ships dock and a windmill serves as the tourist police office and the main bus stop. It has a bus timetable, a list of the main hotels on the island and a sign saying 'Nudity is forbidden', which everyone ignores.

The town straggles along the coast in both directions, to campsites in the north and hotels in the south. It never seems to run far back from the sea, except for the centre, which is a maze of flower-decked white alleyways reminiscent of the grand maze in Mykonos town and is rich in food, leather, souvenir, paper and pastry shops. It can become crowded with tourists in mid-summer, and rooms hard to find, but Paros is an easy island to get around by car, scooter or the frequent buses from the windmill, which go mainly to Naoussa and Dryos via Marpissa and Piso Livadi.

They run along good roads through low hills, with frequent glimpses of vines, corn and cattle, which give a strong impression that Paros can manage well without holiday-makers,

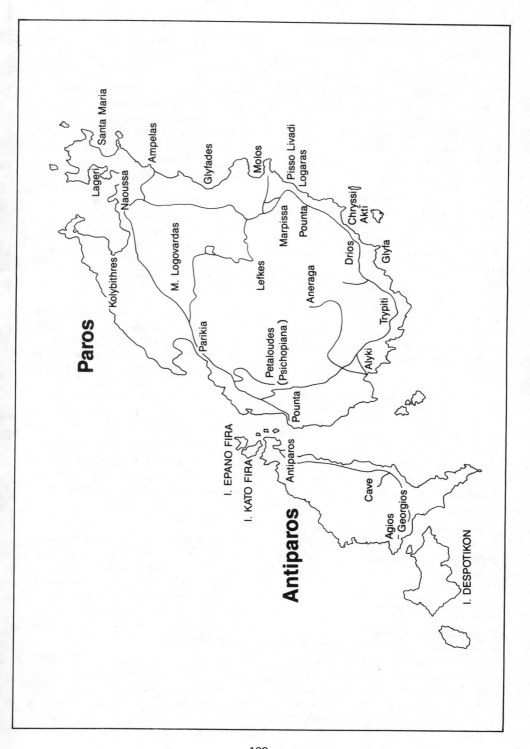

Paros

Santa Maria
Lageri
Naoussa
Ampelas
Glyfades
Molos
Pisso Livadi
Logaras
Kolybithres
M. Logovardas
Marpissa
Pounta
Chryssi Akti
Lefkes
Aneraga
Drios
Glyfa
Parikia
Trypiti
Petaloudes
(Psichopiana)
Alyki
Pounta

I. EPANO FIRA
I. KATO FIRA

Antiparos

Antiparos
Cave
Agios Georgios

I. DESPOTIKON

though the coastal villages suggest otherwise.

Naoussa, around 10 kilometres from Parikia and just about walkable on a cool evening, is a gem of Cycladic architecture with white winding alleyways, hanging with purple bougainvillea, an idyllic miniature fishing harbour and its own rough red wine, best drunk chilled.

Dryos and Piso Livadi are two smaller resorts on the east coast of the island, with a sprinkling of hotels, rooms and restaurants. Piso Livadi also has a small boat running across the straits to Naxos in summer.

The other major coastal village is Aliki in the south-west, which also has hotels, rooms and restaurants. Pounda on the west coast opposite Antiparos is a tiny place with a hotel and landing stage for boats to Antiparos.

Paros has a firm place in history through its export of Parian marble and also skilled sculptors like Ariston and Skopas who learned their trade on the local stone. It was ruled by the Persians, the Athenians, and the Romans, then the Duke of Naxos and the Turks until the War of Independence.

The island was an early participant in the War against the Turks and also contributed one of its heroines, Manto Mavrogenous, who lived the rest of her life on Paros.

Beaches

Paros today is as rich in sandy beaches as it once was in marble. They start right in Parikia, running around the bay on both sides of the port. Livadia beach, which flanks the campsite north of the town, is better than the beach to the south and gets better the further you walk towards the cape. Boats from the harbour serve the coves nearest the cape.

Naoussa also has a healthy quota of beaches with calm seas around the broad sweep of Naoussa Bay and there are others within easy walking or scootering distance on the east coast opposite Naxos. A good sand beach runs to the east of the harbour, there are small coves near the Hippocampos hotel to the west, and there are more exotic coves across the bay at Kolymbithres, set between smooth grey rocks in odd shapes. Kolymbithres is sometimes served by boats from Naoussa harbour and has a restaurant.

Going east from Naoussa the nearest beach is the sheltered cove of Lageri where you can swim out to a small island. Santa Maria, across the narrow neck of the northern peninsular, has a choice of three sandy curves and Ambelas, easily reached by car or scooter, has another sandy stretch flanked by a hotel and restaurant.

Heading south along the Paros ring road you can find more beaches at Glyfada, Tsoukali and Molos, which has two curves of sand enclosed by a big bay and served by three restaurants.

Molos is within easy walking distance of Piso Levadi, which has a campsite and two beaches, one across the headland that supports the monastery of Agios Antonios and the other towards Logaras. There is a third in the bay of Pounda, the second village with that name on the island.

South of Pounda is the most famous, and most photographed beach on the island, Chryssi Akti or 'Golden coast', which is ripe for development and has already seen some in the shape of hotels and restaurants.

Chryssi Akti is within easy walking distance of Dryos, a quiet little village with two hotels and restaurants to match, which also has its own pine-fringed beach. This area is served by the same bus that runs to Marpissa and Piso Levadi.

There are two quiet shingle beaches around the south coast at Glyfa, which are worth remembering when the island is really crowded in mid-season, and Aliki has its own fine curve of sand, though it is hemmed in by the village. Then there is a respectable, but not spectacular, curve of sand at Pounda opposite Antiparos before the ring road turns inland on its way back to Parikia.

Nightlife

You can dine out in style on this island and find plenty of smart bars and discotheques to round off the evening.

Parikia provides good eating at a dozen restaurants, including some along the seafront, in garden settings in the midst of the village and in the two or three little squares that make up its centre.

Naoussa has a similar variety with fish restaurants around the fringe of the harbour and garden restaurants up the winding streets of the village.

The main bar and discotheque scene is in the middle of Parikia a short way back from the waterfront, where half a dozen establishments compete cheek by jowl and boom out rock and Beatles numbers across the bay.

Not to be missed on Paros

Parikia has the Ekatonda Pyliani, the church of 100 gates perched on high in the centre of the town, which was started in the 6th century AD, though

the oldest visible parts date from the Middle Ages. It does not quite live up to its name, but is still a curiosity worth viewing with a huge cypress tree acting as a steeple for the church bells after the last one collapsed in an earthquake. Inside are the bones of the island's patron saint, Theokisti, her hand and footprint as well as some pretty icons.

Near the church is the town's cute little museum, which contains a history of Greece carved out on Parian marble and finds from local temples in the same material.

The buildings themselves are all within walking distance of Parikia with the remains of temples of Apollo and Aphrodite to the north of the port around Livadia Bay and the remains of an Asclepion temple – a temple of healing – and a temple of Apollo south of the port around Souvlia, but they are disappointing.

The wonders of Paros are more modern, and easily reached by the ring road around the island if you have transport. Like the valley of the butterflies (or Petaloudes or Psycopiana), a rival to the one in Rhodes, which is located just off the west coast road between Souvlia and Pounda. It can be reached either by donkey or walking from the coast after taking a bus to Pounda and affords the pleasant sight of thousands of reddish moths swirling around trees and mossy banks in a damp valley, but only for a couple of months each year.

Paros also has a rich quota of monasteries, including Christou Dassos in the wooded area near Petaloudes; Logovardos in a grand position on the Naoussa road, which boasts a wealth of old icons, but bans the fair sex; Agios Theodoros in the south where the nuns do rich

…ios Georgiou a stiff walk …ryos; Agios Antonios, … a hill beside a Venetian …en Molos and Piso Levadi; and …ion in a spectacular isolated position in the hilly centre of the island.

Touring Paros is a delight because there is a surprise view of a monastery or white coastal village around every corner and a round tour of the island can easily be completed in a day.

Worth Visiting off Paros

Paros has 17 small satellite islands which can often be visited by boat after persistent enquiry. Kato Fira and Epano Fira have super beaches, as does Antiparos, which makes an easy day trip from Parikia or Pounda. Naxos is only 1½ hours away by ferry and Mykonos, Siros and Ios are all about 2 hours away by direct ship.

So close to the west coast of Paros that you feel you could swim across, Antiparos is the biggest of the 17 satellite islands of Paros and has blossomed in its own right in recent years.

Its sudden popularity is due to its casual desert island atmosphere coupled with a well-developed main village. There are half a dozen sandy pine-fringed coves within easy reach of the main port, which is an appealing village with half a dozen busy restaurants and a similar number of small hotels, bars and discotheques along the side of a sheltered lagoon-like harbour.

Antiparos is served by 3 or 4 boats a day from Parikia and an occasional one from Pounda directly opposite on the west coast of Paros. They take between 20 and 40 minutes to do the trip and sometimes go on around the island to the cave on the south-east

coast and the bay of Agios Georgios on the west coast.

From most parts of the island you have superb views of Paros across the narrow straits that separate the two islands.

Vulcan's Isle – Santorini

One of the most dramatic events in the ancient world has created one of the natural wonders of the modern world at Santorini – an island which is called after its patron, Saint Irini. It is almost as often called Thira and occasionally Kaliste or 'the most beautiful'.

It could not have looked that way on a fateful day in 1500 BC when volcanic Santorini blew its top. The eruption may have been three to four times the size of Krakatoa in the last century because it left a crater nearly 3 times as big. It landed enough ash and tidal waves on Crete 60 miles away to bury the Minoan cities on the north shore and may have caused the Biblical flood across the Middle East that launched Noah's Ark.

It also launched a legend – of the city of Atlantis sliding into the depths of the sea. And it just could be true because the eruption carpeted the surrounding seabed and beaches with black pebbles and pumice stone, created a sea-filled crater beneath a sheer crescent of cliffs 1,000 feet high and then threw up lava islets in the bay where the volcano still smoulders to this day.

Looking at a map of Santorini and its neighbouring islets, it is easy to imagine that it was once roughly circular in shape with the islands of Therassia and Aspronisi as hills on its western shore and the seawater lagoon around Palia Kaimeni and Nea Kameini in the middle of the high

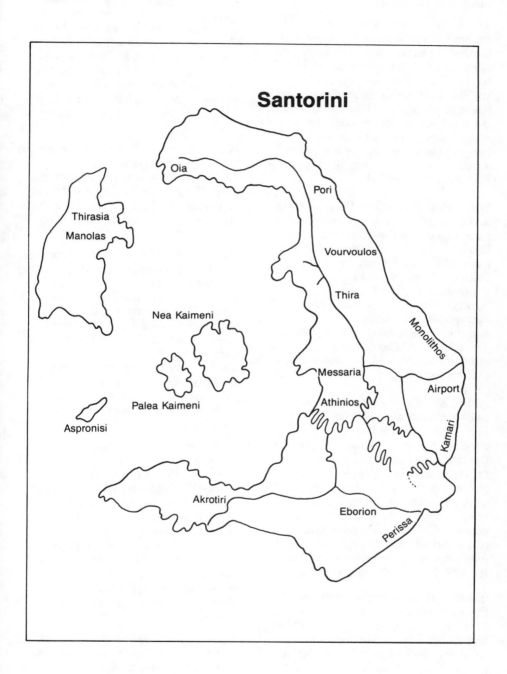

Santorini

Oia

Pori

Thirasia
Manolas

Vourvoulos

Thira

Monolithos

Nea Kaimeni

Messaria

Airport

Palea Kaimeni

Athinios

Kamari

Aspronisi

Akrotiri

Eborion

Perissa

reaches of the island.

Thanks to the eruption, Santorini is the single most spectacular sight in Greece, its main town of Thira or Fira perched 1,000 feet above sea level on the lip of the crater and others sprinkled along the spine of the island like crystals of salt. Thira has some of the most scenic accommodation, restaurants and bars in the world hanging along the edge of the cliff with a bird's eye view of ships like toys in a bathtub 1,000 feet below.

Both sides of the island have big drops and also radiate exotic colours, mainly reds, browns, yellows and blacks in layers across bare hillsides, which make it look as though it has been painted by one of the French impressionists, and they make a strong contrast to the olive green eucalyptus trees flanking the roads and the white villages on the clifftops. The white Cycladic dwellings are interrupted only by an occasional blue church dome.

All the island's roads run past black walls and cultivated fields, where the rich volcanic soil of the island is put to good use, notably in vineyards, where the vines are plaited in circular pig's tails to strengthen them against the high winds that blow across the clifftops. Santorini produces juicy sweet grapes and some of the best wines in Greece – rich reds, sweet roses and smokey whites – which sell under romantic-sounding labels like Atlantis, Lava, Kaldera and Vulcan.

It is easy to explore Santorini since there are regular bus services, tours to its many places of interest, and bikes and mopeds for hire in the town. A hired scooter or moped is an ideal way to see the island, since it is the right size for such machines.

Inevitably the island has roared on to the tourist track in recent years. Cruise ships and ferries from Piraeus, Crete, Ios, and Naxos pull in daily to the three harbours at the base of the cliff, while the island's airport on the east shore enjoys international flights as well as daily Olympic flights from Athens, Mykonos, Crete and Rhodes in summer.

Ascending the 1,000 feet cliff face from the three harbours of Calderas, Athinos and Oia was not easy in the past. The alternative was a stiff walk or a donkey ride at Calderas and Oia and a wait for a bus or taxi at Athinos in the south.

Calderas, the closest port to Thira, is traditionally reached by a steep zig-zag of 587 stone steps two kilometres long. A ride on a donkey or mule, which most tourists and cruise-ship passengers opted for, could be a hairy business, especially after dark. Many people have ended up riding side-saddle and clutching for dear life to the reins of a rampaging mule with their bags tumbling down the steps or trailing along after becoming dislodged.

However, modern technology has provided an alternative in recent years in the shape of a cable-way carrying 6-person bubbles which whisks visitors up the cliff in two minutes. It was built by an Austrian company at the behest of the Nomikos Foundation of Evangelos Nomikos, which then gifted it to Santorini's 14 communities and ensured the future of the donkey drivers by paying them a small commission from each cable-car ticket.

Rooms can be dear and hard to get in Thira in mid-summer, so arrivals by ships at Oia have a case for getting off there and seeking rooms locally, while those arriving at Athinos should think of taking the first hotel bus that touts for trade or the first rooms they come across, which may be in the village of Messaria at a handy road junction in the middle of the island.

Thira town is undoubtedly the most spectacular place to stay but it can be mean and moody, and a good place to be out of when cruise ships call. Then its narrow pebble-dash streets are crammed with camera-hung trippers, who have only an hour or two to bargain for souvenirs and take photos. The sudden influx turns shopkeepers and donkey-drivers into mercenary maniacs for a short time.

Beaches

Most of the beaches on the island are black sand and pebbles, but nonetheless offer good swimming in warm waters with a slight sulphur smell cheek by jowl with chunks of pumice stone.

Almost the whole of the gently sloping east coast is swimmable. The most popular beaches, with regular buses, are at Kamari, three-quarters of the way down the island, which is turning into a sizeable resort in its own right these days, and Perissa near the tip of the south coast. Both are rich in restaurants and have simple accommodation and watersports, while Kamari also has a campsite and discotheque.

To get away from the crowds, aim halfway down the island at Monolithos, where the sand is a lighter hue, but be prepared for a dusty road around the airport and a not-so-pretty coastline. This is not well served by buses, but as a result attracts fewer people, and it has a café.

There are other deserted coves accessible to scooter and moped

riders via the coast road that runs north from Thira to Oia. Akrotiri also has a little beach beneath its archaeological site and it is possible to swim off pebble beaches at all the three ports on the west coast.

If you tire of the popular beaches and find the west coast pebble strips below par, take a boat trip to the nearby islet of Therassia, which has a beach by the harbour and a better one over the hill on the other side of the islet.

Nightlife

Thira has a number of smart bars with smart drinks and smart prices. It also has a variety of scenic restaurants that hang to the cliff. They can be pricey, but worth the money for the unique experience of sipping wine and dining on local fish sitting on a balcony perched 1,000 feet above the sea watching the lights of ships passing below.

The main town also has a clutch of discotheques trading under names like Neptune and Volcan. Kamari also has a disco operating in mid-summer.

Not to be missed on Santorini

Santorini is rich in man-made antiquities as well as the natural phenomena left behind by the volcanic eruptions. A stunning Minoan city is emerging in the south at Akrotiri, which beats any of those on Crete. There are also Graeco-Roman remains at Ancient Thira, a wine factory which processes the fruit of the island's volcanic soil, the rich monastery of Profitis Elias, and the half-deserted village of Oia in the north which bears witness to the force of the last eruption in the 1950s.

Akrotiri, which can be reached by bus from Thira or Perissa, or by a tour which takes in other wonders of the island, is one of the most important archaeological sites of Greece. There, in a dried-up riverbed, a local farmworker noticed the tip of an old building 20 years ago and excavations have uncovered a well-preserved Minoan city which has been buried for 3,500 years under lava.

Thanks to the lava, it is in a better state of repair than any of the Minoan cities on Crete and the excavators are making a better job of reconstruction than Sir Arthur Evans did with his imaginative paint job at Knossos. Akrotiri's houses may be under modern corrugated roofs, but they are proper 2-storey houses with recognisable rooms which could be lived in at a pinch.

The tragedy of the site is that the magnificent frescoes of sea battles, African expeditions, children boxing, fashionable women and exotic flowers have been borne away to the Athens Archaeological Museum for safe keeping and fear of volcanic damage. There is talk of them being returned when a strong museum is built on the island, but action would speak louder than words.

If you study the pictures along with the site, you will soon appreciate that a sophisticated society existed on Santorini from 3000 BC to the big eruption, and may even support my pet theory that the former Atlantis was the centre of Minoan civilisation for a time. The conventional theory is that Santorini was an outpost of Knossos, but it could be turned on its head if a royal palace is unearthed on the island.

Ancient Thira does not set the imagination racing in quite the same way, but is a beautiful little site in a dramatic setting. Mainly Roman, with a market, gymnasium, theatre, baths

and Temple of Apollo, it is perched on a shelf above the sea in the south-east of the island with a stunning view towards Anafi.

Profitis Elias is a declining monastery set on the highest peak of Santorini in the lee of a radar station, but its two resident monks are seeing a lively tourist trade these days, thanks to coach tours. And its museum of household items and religious treasures gives an unusual glimpse of religious and island life over the centuries, including a school which flourished underground during the Turkish occupation.

A visit to the half-deserted village of Oia at the northern tip of the island is a must for anyone spending more than a few hours on Santorini because it gives a glimpse of what the villages looked like up to the 1956 earthquake. Some of the old houses are being tastefully restored as guest houses to give an even better impression.

Another pilgrimage worth making is by boat to the two smoking islets in the bay below Thira town, where the volcano still smoulders amidst black cinders. Vegetation is gradually returning, but the scene still resembles something from 'Star Wars'. The only sign of human activity is white paint graffiti plastered over the rocks by the harbour by visiting vandals.

Worth visiting off Santorini

People who have stayed on Santorini for a few days can find the atmosphere a trifle oppressive. It is the feel of an island living next door to a volcano, which sees too many day visitors. However, there are plenty of easy escapes.

The easiest is access to the satellite isle of Therassia, which is delightfully unspoilt beside its parent island. It has rooms and beaches on both sides, so it is a good place for a short stay. Another is by regular ferry to the smaller islands of Anafi, Sikinos and Folegandros.

It is also easy to find a sea connection to Ios, if you want good yellow beaches and don't mind crowds of young people and a booming discotheque scene. Naxos and Amorgos are other good bets by sea, while Olympic Airways offers the chance of flights to Mykonos, Crete and Rhodes.

Andros

One of the two biggest islands in the Cyclades along with Naxos, Andros is also one of the most fertile and well-populated – entirely by sea captains, you might think, if you view their mansions in Andros town, or by Athenians if you see a settlement of their holiday villas.

Andros is relatively close to Athens and the Attic mainland, being 2 to 3 hours by ship from Rafina, so it is an appealing island to those who don't relish a long sea voyage. It also boasts a quartet of pretty coastal villages, sandy beaches and interesting sites, so that it has plenty to offer visitors of all tastes, and its countryside is varied in appearance.

There are green meadows and gentle hills around the shore with cypress trees, olive groves, fruit groves and even grazing cattle. The interior offers contrast with bare hills and high mountains stretching up to 3,000 feet in the case of Mount Kouvara and a selection of exciting walks to colourful hill villages.

Regular ferries – two or three a day in summer – run to the port of Gavrion, which is set on a big natural curve of a harbour in the north-west of the island. It is not the comeliest village on the island, but is a lively place to stay and has bikes and scooters for hire as well as regular buses to the other three main villages, Batsi, Andros and Korthion.

Batsi, 8 kilometres down the west coast, is the main holiday resort and it is easy to see why the moment you arrive. The centre is a busy fishing harbour with successive tiers of red-roofed houses and the village spreads out along the coast running around three bays which contain small hotels, rooms and a string of restaurants.

Where Batsi is pretty, Andros is grand. The island capital or Hora, which is almost a town rather than a village, stands proud on a headland on the east coast with tall mansions and a paved pedestrian walkway. That leads to a small tree-lined square where you can take coffee and cakes with a view of the sea and a small tower on a rock off the headland.

Korthion, reached by buses that run along the high cliffs of the west coast and then inland through a spectacular valley of villages and fertile fields to a bay south of Andros town on the east coast, is a slightly depressed, but honest, village straggling along the coast. It has rooms and restaurants along alleyways leading off the main street.

Beaches

Andros is blessed with long, sandy beaches and most of them are strung between Gavrion and Batsi. There are two or three in the bay of Gavrion, four or five along the road to Batsi and more in that village and beyond, including a nudist beach with taverna about half an hour south via a walk along the cliffs.

The best sandy beach along this coast,

and the longest, is Chryssi Ammos between the two west coast ports. It is about half an hour's walk south of Gavrion and seems destined for development, but mercifully had only one good beach taverna run by a character called Little John on my last visit. If you do find this beach too crowded, it is easy to walk over the headland towards Batsi where there is another sandy cove, which is usually less populated.

Andros town puts up keen competition to this coast with its own sandy beaches. It has one on each side of its harbour below a steep cliff and two more a short way along the coast at the village of Stenies in the bay of Yialia. One has a friendly taverna and the other a desert island atmosphere when there are not too many people around.

Korthion has its own curve of sandy beach and there are other pebble and shingle stretches around the island, including one at Paleopolis a thousand steps down from the coast road, near Vasami north of Gavrion, and in a series of coves on the east coast above Andros reached by road across the island from Batsi.

Nightlife and Dining Out

Gavrion and Batsi are well-endowed with restaurants and have three discotheques between them, just along the coast. Batsi also has a thriving cinema.

Andros also has a number of good restaurants and a discotheque though it is the kind that only seems to be active for a few days each summer. Try the local wine, which is usually resinated, and the pastry shops, which serve a rich line in custard pastries.

Not to be missed on Andros

Try to see all four main villages and explore their hinterlands. Walk or drive inland from Batsi and you reach the delightful convent of Zoodos Pigi (the 'spring of life'), which specialises in weaving and has icons dating back to the 1300's. The nearby village of Kato Katakoilos is worth a visit, and Arni, much further inland along the winding mountain road is a must for people who treasure pretty hill villages.

A short walk inland from Gavrion is Agios Petros where an old stone tower rises from the hills. Amolochos is a much longer walk, but a pleasant ride, by mountain road from Gavrion into the northern hinterland of the island.

Andros is a first-class centre for walks into the surrounding countryside. There is a way from there to Arnia via another pretty hill village called Apikia, which has the monastery of Agios Marinas and produces mineral water.

Another walk leads to a medieval village at Messaria, with the ruins of the Byzantine church of Agios Tachiarchos below, and a good way beyond that the island's most splendid monastery, Panachrantou, which is suspended from the side of Mount Gerakonas and is rich in icons. Aladino in the valley below has a cave festooned with stalactites and stalagmites.

Both Andros and Korthion have castles, including the ruined Paliocastro a short walk north of Korthion, all built by the Venetians. Paliopolis is a charming old village on the west coast, which was the site of the old capital of Andros. It is now reputed to be under the sea below the high cliff.

Worth visiting off Andros

Andros enjoys regular ferry connections to Rafina, a bustling ferry port on the Attic coast, and to the island of Tinos, which it almost touches at the nearest point. Ships run on to Mykonos and Siros which are totally different islands in character and appearance.

The Virgin's Island – Tinos

Tinos is the Lourdes of Greece where the Orthodox church bows to Catholicism and an island saint is replaced by the Virgin Mary. It was born as a shrine of the Catholic church in 1822 during the War of Independence against the Turks when, the story goes, the Virgin appeared before an 80-year old nun and told her that a precious icon was buried in a field near the main port. The islanders searched and found a jewelled icon, so they built the shrine of the Annunciation on the spot.

Today the shrine and the icon are housed in a white marble church or cathedral, Panagia Evangelistria, which is hung with gold and silver votive offerings. It dominates the town and the harbour of Tinos and lies at the top of a broad avenue which runs up from the sea and is lined with tourist and religious shops selling icons, candles, silver offerings and ornaments in the shape of crucifixes.

Near the cathedral are seats and arcades where pilgrims and sick people gather for a blessing from the miraculous icon, which is believed to have curative powers. Even on the outside the walls are hung with silver offerings shaped like legs, arms or other parts of the body the sick want cured.

Tinos is reached in about 4 hours by ferry via Andros, skirting some weird cliffs where the islands almost touch, which could pass for the Scylla and Charybdis of the ancient world, or in

5½ hours by ferry from Piraeus which usually goes on to Mykonos. These ships can carry hundreds of the faithful, especially in the festive periods of March and August, who shoot out of their holds en masse and rush up the main street for the church, making the tourist passengers bound for Mykonos wonder whether they are on the right route.

A few years back the islanders indulged in a most irreligious act when Peter, the Mykonos pelican, flew over for a visit. They clipped his wings, so that he would stay on Tinos and bring them luck – and perhaps tourists. A fleet of caiques set sail from Mykonos to battle for its pelican, but he was returned after a telegram from the Government in Athens ordering the release of the Mykonos mascot.

Despite this incident and the heavy concentration of the port upon the holy place, Tinos is a pretty and welcoming island for visitors seeking more worldly pursuits. It boasts a picturesque port with blue and white buildings, over 1,000 churches in matching colours scattered over the island and white dovecotes built by the Venetians on every hillside. It also has occasional outcrops of greenery and sandy coves to relieve the brown landscape.

Beaches

There is a long sandy stretch of beach to the west of the port by the Tinos Beach Hotel as far as Kioni, but it can get crowded. There are more remote coves to the east of the port at Agios Fokas, Xera and Porto. Further along the coast is the enclosed bay of Agios Nikitas with a good beach, rooms and restaurants.

Take a bus along the island's main road to Panormos in the north-west and there is another passable beach, but better is the enclosed sandy bay of Kolimpidria halfway along the north coast.

Nightlife and dining out

Tinos has a good selection of restaurants in and around the main port. It also has busy open-air cinemas and the big hotels occasionally put on entertainment in the evenings, but it is not a swinging island like nearby Mykonos.

Not to be missed on Tinos

The cathedral is one of the great religious shrines in Greece and should be seen for the jewelled icon, and displays around its courtyard and the monument in the crypt to Greeks torpedoed on the original ferryboat 'Elli' in the harbour by an Italian submarine in August 1940. Near the church is a sanctuary of the arts – an archaeological museum with Roman remains and finds from the Temple of Poseidon and his wife Amphitriti near Kioni, plus a Byzantine museum with religious objects, a sculpture museum and an art gallery.

The sanctuary of Poseidon at Kioni extends the cultural round along with Pirgos in the north, which is the home of Tiniote artists and sells their works.

Exombourgo, the hill behind the port, has a Venetian castle with three churches in its walls and Vriokastro beyond Agios Fokas has the remains of an old town.

Worth visiting off Tinos

Andros, the island 1½ hours west of Tinos, has a completely different look about it with high, green hills and long yellow beaches, while Mykonos 1½ hours east has more razzamatazz, nightlife and nudist beaches. Siros, 1 hour away and directly opposite Tinos port, is the great boat junction of the Aegean and has its own charm as a holiday isle.

Siros

It is easy to under-estimate Siros as a tourist island since foreign visitors are vastly outnumbered by Greek residents in the throng that alights from the many ferry boats calling there.

Visitors who disembark tend to view it simply as a stopping-off point on longer journeys because the island is virtually the Crewe Junction of the Aegean, offering the best opportunity to travel between islands on different shipping routes without the chore of returning to Piraeus. But Ermoupolis, the big and bustling capital, the coastline with its many sandy beaches and the typically Cycladean inland scenery all repay closer exploration. And while few casual visitors linger long on Siros there is a hard core of regulars, mainly British and German, who return year after year.

Much of its charm lies in its independence of the tourist industry, its strong sense of being a reasonably prosperous Greek community getting on with its everyday business with neither the need nor the desire to prey upon the visitor.

This independence owes much to Siros's proud history. Originally settled by the Phoenicians, after whom the resort Finikas is named, its heyday was in the 19th century when the capital Ermoupolis, founded during the War of Independence by refugees from Psara and Chios, became the chief port of Greece.

Piraeus has long since overhauled it but evidence of its former glory and prosperity remain in the Apollon Theatre, which was copied from La Scala, Milan and once staged Italian opera, the fine Palladian-style buildings around the Plateia Miaulis and the magnificent, if now somewhat neglected, villas of former Greek shipping tycoons in the resorts of Dellegrazia and Finikas.

As is still the case in Greece today, prosperity was repaid by piety and Ermoupolis is dominated by two hilltop cathedrals, one Orthodox and one Catholic.

Siros is easily accessible from the mainland with at least two ferries a day making the four and a half hour journey from Piraeus plus a daily boat to the Attic port of Rafina. Once on the island, communications are also good with regular buses from the quayside terminus plying through the brown, hilly landscape to the major villages and beaches.

The island also has a small airport, which whisks Olympic Airways passengers from Athens in just half an hour.

Beaches

You can swim while awaiting your ferry at the recently constructed bathing area on the north side of the port while there's a larger pebble beach about half an hour's walk north of the town. To enjoy Siros's abundant sand take the bus to Vari, Megas Gialos, Finikas, Galissas or Kini. The first three tend to be crowded at weekends or during the Greek school holidays, but Galissas and Kini are both pleasant small resorts with rooms to rent and restaurants. Heading north from Kini, a lane meandering through a fertile lovingly-cultivated valley leads to an impressive expanse of sparsely-populated golden sand.

Nightlife and Dining Out

Meals, like accommodation, tend to be inexpensive on Siros as they are geared to local residents rather than rich tourists. The former bevy of restaurants around the main square of Ermoupolis are now fast food joints or pizza parlours but you can still eat well along the harbourside, the final restaurant with the corner site being the best for traditional Greek vegetable and bean dishes.

Galissas has a cheap and cheerful self-service restaurant, good on vegetarian dishes, on the beach while the terrace restaurant at one end of the beach in Kini serves fish in a romantic setting. The island's nightlife centres on the Aphrodite Disco in Galissas, much liked by local gilded youth. Avoid rooms near it if you don't want to be woken up by the roar of motor cycles at its 3am closing time.

Not to be missed on Siros

The maze of steep streets leading up the twin hills behind the harbour are a must for photographers. Bright geraniums and carnations cascade from the window ledges of typical white Cycladean houses while dilapidated balconied mansions, now often deserted, provide a reminder of past glories. Vrontathis Hill, crowned by the Orthodox cathedral, offers views of neighbouring Tinos and Mykonos but the other hill, Ano Siros, is more interesting with its medieval Venetian town dominated by the Catholic cathedral of St George and the Capuchin convent of St Jean.

In the country, traditional Cycladean farms, complete with the inevitable dovecotes, grow superb produce in bamboo-fenced fields nestling in carefully-irrigated green valleys.

Worth visiting off Siros

As Siros is the main junction of the Aegean ferry system, it is easy to get to a number of other islands, and relatively quick too. It has regular ships to Tinos, which makes an easy day out to see that island's cathedral and port, and to Paros, so it is often easy to take in that island's port and beaches in a day trip.

It is possible to go on from Tinos to Andros and from Paros to Naxos, but you will need an overnight stay to complete the round trip. The same goes for Mykonos, which also has regular ships from Siros, but rarely with an easy return boat the same day.

Mykonos makes a great contrast with Siros as an island that is almost solely dedicated to tourism these days, and also offers a more sophisticated line in nightlife.

Treasury Island – Delos

A terrace of lions has become the modern symbol of Delos, the sacred island of Apollo, which was one of the big centres of culture, oracles, religion and political power in the ancient world.

At that epoch it could be believed that this small island was the centre of Aegean civilisation with the other Cyclades revolving around it like a clock.

Today however it is one of the two big satellite islands of Mykonos, to the west of its parent island, and is smaller than neighbouring Rinia or Great Delos. But even now, once you are on Delos, you are surrounded by the past and overwhelmed by its beauty and importance as an archaeological site.

The island became a sacred sanctuary of Apollo as a result of an ancient legend that told that it wandered around under the waves until Poseidon raised it out of the sea on diamond pillars to be the birthplace of Apollo and his sister Artemis. For many years it was forbidden for anyone to be born or die on the island, so a sudden heart attack or birth pang would win a swift passage to Rinia.

It is not only one of the most impressive sites in Greece, but in the whole world because it is so comprehensive and so well-preserved. It was a rich sanctuary from around 1,000 BC to around 150 AD, ruled over in turn by the Ionians, the Athenians and the Romans, who built treasuries, temples, harbours and a thriving commercial city for the many inhabitants. Then it was almost uninhabited for the next 18 centuries, so that it was frozen in time and the remains of its golden age were not disturbed too much.

The ancient city covers a large part of the west side of the island and offers a galaxy of delights to modern visitors. There are four major temples including three sacred to Apollo, the Sacred Way, the Lions' Way, a theatre stadium, gymnasium, shops and the Treasury – which gets less attention than it deserves in view of the way it concentrated the minds of the Athenians, their allies and their successors on Delos for centuries.

Many visitors are diverted by a curious collection of brothels in the midst of the town, they are reminiscent of those at Pompei, and a row of giant phalluses that testify to the rich lifestyle of the ancient inhabitants as well as to the free-thinking cults of Apollo and Dionysus. Let your imagination run in the House of the Trident, the House of the

Dolphins, the House of the Masks and the House of Cleopatra. The superb mosaics help, especially the one of Dionysus riding a panther.

But the whole city is fascinating from the harbours to the market place, the streets, fountains and the theatre, and the whole scene is complemented by the museum, which contains all the finds not removed to Athens.

Too many tourists arrive by cruise ship for a 2-hour visit or come over on the morning caique from Mykonos, which takes nearly an hour and returns around lunch-time – and can provide a bumpy crossing when the sea is rough, as it often is in this part of the Cyclades. Delos merits a longer visit from anyone interested in archaeology or just savouring the atmosphere of the Greek islands.

Although most of the inhabitants of the island are lizards or archaeologists, it is possible to stay overnight by camping or booking a room at the island's only hotel. The reward is being able to view the site around sunset or sunrise without the crowds and to have time to explore the rest of the island.

It is well worth climbing Mount Cynthos in the middle, which is only 350 feet high, but gives a superb panorama of the Cyclades on a clear day and also plays host to the Sacred Cave where the oracle of Apollo was sited.

Antiparos

Clinging close to its west coast Antiparos is the biggest of the 17 satellite islands of Paros. It has an appealing little village with six busy restaurants and the same number of small hotels along the side of a lagoon-like harbour.

Beaches

Antiparos rivals Paros for sandy beaches and they are closer together, half a dozen within easy walking distance of the port. The curved beaches backed by pines and scrub, give Antiparos, as much as any island in Greece, a desert island atmosphere. That is true even though there are three or four boats a day from Parikia and Pounda, and the port now has rooms for 2,000 visitors, and half a dozen bars and discotheques.

Boats also run along the coast facing Paros to a small beach from which a rough track runs uphill about two kilometres to a long sloping cave.

Whether on foot or boat, the journey does open up some of the wonders of Antiparos. It has three good curves of sand just south of the port, within easy walking distance, plus one across the headland from the port and a long stretch of dune beach to the north between Antiparos and Kato Fira where there is a camp site. There are plenty of other remote swimmable coves just off the single road that runs south along the coast and others across the southern headland at Agios Georgios, which are sometimes visited by boat in summer. Kato Fira has yet more remote beaches reached by boat from the port.

Nightlife

The port has a string of good restaurants on the shore, along the main street and in garden settings in the backstreets. It is surprisingly lively at night.

Not to be missed on Antiparos

Antiparos is a beach island, but it has a cave in the south of the island, which has been visited from ancient times. Access is now made easier by electric light, cement steps, a boat down the coast, a café by its mooring posts, and donkeys which stand on the beach and spare the effort of a half hour walk uphill in the summer heat.

It is a sloping underground chamber filled with stalactites and stalagmites and makes a pleasant excursion from the main village by road or boat. Further on by road and sometimes by boat is the church and beach of Agios Georgios on the other side of the island.

The island has no monasteries, but there are two old churches in the village, two more inland on high ground, which make good walks on a cool day, plus a little chapel by the cave.

Worth visiting off Antiparos

Boats go occasionally to offshore islands like Despotikon and Strogilo in the west and Epano Fira and Kato Fira to the north, which have superb, and usually deserted, sandy beaches.

It is also worth taking a boat across to Pounda on the nearby coast of Paros for a swim on a different kind of beach and to Parikia for a day out shopping and sight-seeing.

The Duke's Isle – Naxos

With expanses of golden beaches, a quaint old port crowned by a Venetian castle, superb mountain scenery, discos galore and a little easily assimilated culture, it is hardly surprising that Naxos has become a top destination for tour operators.

However, it is the biggest island in the Cyclades and large enough to absorb the invasion. Only during the evening promenading along the harbourside and on Agios Georgiou, the nearest beach to town, do the crowds seem

excessive. Inland Naxos is a different scene – a lonely, romantic landscape with tall mansions and dovecotes dotting the hillsides.

Naxos was inhabited from 3,000 BC and has remains of a Cycladic town at Grotta. In mythology, later to provide inspiration for an opera, Theseus took the Cretan princess Ariadne there after slaying the Minotaur, subsequently deserting her to return to Athens. Ariadne found solace in marrying the god of wine, Dionysus.

Later generations of Naxians were pioneers of carving in marble, making the famous lions of Delos and giant kouros statues of young men, two of which can still be seen on the island. Small wonder, then, that the Venetian adventurer, Marco Sanundo, chose it as his Aegean capital and ruled the Cyclades as Duke of Naxos from 1207.

Naxos has recently acquired an airport close to the main beach area south of the port, which has made it more accessible than the 6-hour sea journey from Piraeus. Visitors who brave the longish sea journey sail into a harbour dominated by the massive Portada of the unfinished temple of Apollo. The noisy, brilliantly lit disco in the Portada's shadow is a more recent addition to the island's amenities.

Behind a busy, slightly tatty frontage the town is magical with tiny alleyways and carved stone steps rising through archways and tunnels to Venetian mansions, the 13th century cathedral of Ypardiard and the white walled Venetian castle on its summit, from which the Dukes of Naxos ruled for centuries.

Rooms to rent will be offered in grille-fronted homes that are little more than medieval cells – quaint, but not for

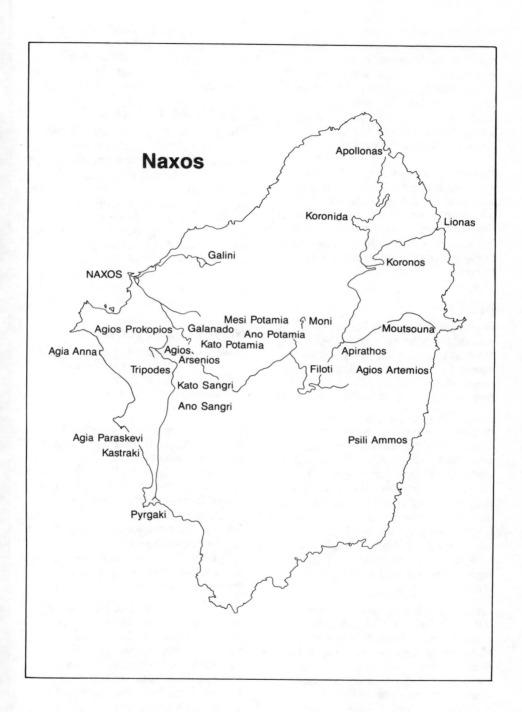

Naxos

Apollonas

Koronida

Lionas

Galini

NAXOS

Koronos

Mesi Potamia   Moni

Galanado   Ano Potamia

Agios Prokopios

Moutsouna

Agios

Kato Potamia

Agia Anna

Arsenios

Apirathos

Tripodes

Filoti   Agios Artemios

Kato Sangri

Ano Sangri

Agia Paraskevi

Psili Ammos

Kastraki

Pyrgaki

lovers of modern comfort or privacy. For more modern rooms it is best to move to the fringe of town. But whether you want to escape the heat of the midday sun or enjoy a romantic evening stroll the old town with its fascinating traditional Greek shops, tourist boutiques and garden restaurants repays exploration.

Bus services, leaving from the port, are adequate for exploring the south west and north east of the island. If you want to investigate the beaches of the north west there's no alternative but to take a motorbike or moped and brave the less-travelled road past the town tip.

Beaches

Byron fell in love with Naxos when he walked the island's beaches below the main town and it became his dream island. Even today it is possible to find deserted beaches on Naxos. You just have to travel a little further each year.

Agios Georgiou, the first beach heading south down the coast out of town is now generally packed while over the headland Agios Prokopios and Agia Anna are no longer the tranquil, uncommercialised retreats they were. But they have windsurfing and other watersports. If you want a less crowded beach, head further south or take a bus to Pyrgaki and walk north up the coast to beaches at Alyko, Kastraki and Agia Paraskevi for greater seclusion.

Apollonia in the north has a popular but not particularly attractive beach while the track from Apirathos to Mutsuna on the east coast yields two beaches, one boasting a café, and there are two good sandy beaches a few kilometres south at Psili Ammos and Agios Artemios. More deserted stretches of sand – debris strewn in rough weather – can be reached down river valleys leading off the main track on the north west coast, but you need a scooter or taxi to reach them.

Nightlife and Eating Out

The disco on the harbourside provides just a hint of Naxos' appeal for those who like to dance the night away. At a recent count Agios Georgios had 8 discos and there are others among the new building developments heading south out of town. For a quieter evening try the garden restaurants in town – a good one is Manolis – or eat the local speciality of grilled octopus and drink Naxos lemon liqueur while watching the world go by at one of the harbourside bars.

Not to be missed on Naxos

A walk through the backstreets of the town is a must for the castle and cathedral. After that, the best sightseeing route is to take the Apollonia bus.

It runs through the vineyards which yield the rough, fruity Naxos wine and across wooded hills offering spectacular views, taking in Sagri with its fortified monastery, Halki with its ruined Byzantine churches, Filoti which is a short walk from the cave of Zeus on the slopes of towering Mount Zas and Apirathos where life is one long leisurely cup of coffee for the men of the village and the tourists who join them at their cafés.

One of the kouroi is on the outskirts of Apollonia while the other lies in a beautiful garden at Kouronochori to the east of Naxos town. Another Venetian castle stands at Epano Kastro a short walk from the Apollonia road and there are half a dozen more stretching across the south of the island from Plaka beach almost to Psili Ammos.

Worth visiting off Naxos

With a small airport and Piraeus seven hours away by sea, Naxos is not ideal for those wanting to see much of Greece beyond the Cyclades. However it has frequent connections with the neighbouring islands of Paros and Amorgos while summer tourist boats link it with Mykonos, Ios and Santorini.

Visits are also possible to the islands of the 'Little Cyclades' – Donoussa, Schinoussa, Iraklia and Koufonissi – but infrequent boat schedules may require you to stay for as long as a week before there's a return trip to the civilisation of Naxos.

Amorgos

Rising like a steep, narrow wedge from the sea, Amorgos is the perfect island for anyone wanting to combine life in a traditional Cycladean community with basic creature comforts.

All will change when the road crossing the spine of the island from the capital Hora to the northern port of Aegiali is finally completed, but until then the donkey and the caique reign supreme.

After the twelve-hour trip from Piraeus most boats call at the main port, Katapola. Set on a deep bay with indifferent pebbly shores, it's a relaxed, easy going place with some good quayside restaurants. But the real jewel is Hora – sometimes called Amorgos – six creaking kilometres uphill on the local bus. Here is a paradise of vine-shaded white streets clustering around the base of a 13th century castle, plus smarter restaurants and bars and essentials like the island's only bank and post office.

Hora has two adjacent pebble beaches of Agia Anna, forty minutes walk away down a steep hill, but lovers of golden sand may prefer Aegiali. Some of the Piraeus boats call here en route from Katapola and there is an erratic caique service but the only overland link has been on foot (approx four hours walk) or by four wheel drive jeep on the unfinished mountain road.

Aegiali, set on a pleasant sandy bay with further and more private sandy coves to the north, offers a small hotel open only in summer, two campsites and a plentiful supply of rooms many at the fast-growing Lakki complex, half way along the beach.

Beach apart, the main charm of Aegiali lies in its three satellite hill villages, Potamos, Langada and Tholarion. Though a bus now runs to the last two, the old donkey routes from the coast up well-worn cobbled tracks offer walkers spectacular views of the island's hills and coastline. In the villages, particularly Tholarion, life in the tiny huddled houses with their outdoor bread ovens has changed little since the Middle Ages.

Amorgos is a dramatic island with great scenery. It made a perfect setting for Luc Besson's haunting fantasy film, 'Big Blue', about a mythical contest between two deep sea divers.

Beaches

Aegiali has the best sand. There is also a long sandy beach on the island of Nikuria opposite Agios Pavlos on the north west coast but it can be reached only by hiring a boat. The beach at Agios Pavlos itself is weedy and debris-strewn and there is little but rock bathing to reward those who trek along the spine of the island from Aegiali to east coast spots like Ormos Charalas.

Nightlife and Dining Out

The most sophisticated restaurants, bars and cafés are in Hora and Katapola. In Aegiali the self-service restaurant at the Lakki complex is good at lunchtime but often limited in the evening. The restaurant in the main street is the best bet for dinner, though the two lining the steps leading up from the quay offer superb sunset views and one, the Kretikos, has potent and inexpensive red wine from its proprietor's native Crete. As you enter Langada on the donkey path from Aegiali, take a rest at the terrace restaurant. Service is leisurely but the view of the bay from the bougainvillea-hung balcony is unforgettable. Discos tend to be of the here-tonight-and-gone-tomorrow variety.

Not to be missed on Amorgos

Clinging like a large white bird to a sheer cliff overlooking the sea, the 11th century monastery of Khozoviotissa is one of the most spectacular sights in the Cyclades. Twenty minutes walk from Hora, it is open to visitors daily from sunrise to 3pm, though modest dress with fully-covered arms and legs is a must.

Its remaining two or three monks guard treasures including the miracle-working Icon of the Virgin, graciously serve coffee to visitors and contemplate a view of nothing but sea.

Remains of ancient cities near Katapola and Arkesini in the south of the island and of Roman era vaulted tombs near Aegiali are hard to find and of interest only to keen students of ancient history.

Worth visiting off Amorgos

There are ferry connections with Naxos and the Little Cyclades to the west and Astipalea in the east, but allow plenty of time for both journeys, especially if the ship is calling at both Katapola and Aegiali.

Naxos is a lot more developed for tourism around its port, but is also a high and handsome island with tall mansions dotting the landscape and good beaches stretching miles down the coast from the main port. The Little Cyclades are less developed and only served by occasional ships, but have small island charm.

Astipalea is the Dodecanese equivalent of Amorgos, a dramatic island with a castle and Hora high above its port. It provides a relatively easy ferry connection to Kos and the rest of the Dodecanese islands.

Anafi

The southernmost inhabited island in the Cyclades and nearly the most easterly too, Anafi is about 2 hours by sea from Santorini and is the furthest many of the Cyclades ferries go. It also has occasional connections with Crete and Rhodes, but always seems remote from other islands and a trifle forbidding.

It is said to have risen from the sea as a submerged mountain peak at the behest of the Argonauts and looks that way to this day as you approach the port on the south coast. It is rocky and sparsely inhabited with only one real village, one half-decent beach, one harbour and one monastery.

Thanks to those credentials, it is a haven of peace and quiet for anyone seeking refuge from the main tourist routes. There are a few rooms to let in the harbour and in Hora, the main village uphill from the landing stage, and two restaurants in each place. The steep path between the two makes a nice evening walk, though it is better to do the uphill bit later when it is cool.

The shingley beach is at Klisidi a short walk over the cliffs east of the harbour and further along near the south-east promontory of the island is the white monastery of Kalamiotissa, a walk that passes the remains of a temple of Apollo. There are also the remains of an old castle in the north of the island for hill-walking enthusiasts.

Anafi is a long boat journey from Piraeus and a much easier way to get there is to fly from Britain or Athens to Santorini and continue by boat from there.

Island in the Sound – Ios

A dramatic-looking island mid-way between Naxos and Santorini, Ios has the look of a classic Cycladean island with a stark brown landscape crowned by windmills, 300 domed churches and two chalk-white villages in Ios bay where the ships dock. It also boasts half a dozen sandy coves, though only two in the port of Ormos or Gialos and across the hills via Hora at Mylopotamos are easily accessible.

Ios is not a typical 'unspoilt Greek island'. It has rocketed on to the tourist track like no other Aegean island over the past twenty years and has almost been taken over by a young crowd of visitors, who like to party, disco and sleep on the beach, and don't mind crowds of fellow-teenagers and students so numerous they almost hide the native Greeks in mid-summer.

It is a little mysterious what attracts so many, except a feeling of safety in numbers and a promise of fun in the dozens of discotheques, tourist shops and bars that now line the streets of Hora or Ios and boom through the night.

A new road around the 'golden triangle' of Gialos, Hora and Mylopotamos ensures a regular bus service and keeps the two easily accessible beaches teeming with people. Ios is the nearest thing to a Greek island holiday camp with far more locals employed in tourism than fishing and farming.

However, the island is undeniably pretty, especially the port with two headlands running out to sea, and the rest of the island is well worth exploring for those prepared to walk or take boats around the coast. Ios can be recommended to young ravers who don't mind a long boat journey, crowded beaches and everyone speaking English or German, and can sleep to the beat of discotheques in the main town.

Beaches

Apart from the two long sandy stretches by the harbour and in Mylopotamos bay, which can be reached by bus or a short walk from the harbour or Hora, Manganari Bay in the south and Psathis Bay in the east are good beaches and are served by daily caiques from Gialos. You can start to escape the crowds there.

It is also possible to walk the 5 kilometres across the narrowest part of the island to Psathis and Agios Theodotis Bay, which has a fine sand beach, and to walk to Theodotis from Psathis, but allow plenty of time for such ventures and use the cooler parts of the day since walks across the hills of Ios always seem to take hours.

Nightlife and dining out

There is no lack of nightlife on this island, provided you don't mind crowds and aren't looking for anything too sophisticated. Both Gialos and Hora are rich with restaurants and discotheques and even Manganari has a hotel and restaurant.

The big centre for bars and discos is Hora, which had over a dozen of each at the last count going under names like The Foxy Fox, Spiro's Bar, Romeo, Windmill, the Petris Club and the Ios Club.

Not to be missed on Ios

Ios is not a great island for sight-seeing, but don't miss a boat trip around it, which can take in the beaches, plus the monastery and Paliokastro on Agios Theotis Bay and the pretty church on Kalamos Bay.

Homer's tomb is at Plakatos in the north, where there is an old town and tower, a good day's return walk from Hora.

Worth visiting off Ios

It is easy to take a day trip to Santorini to see one of the wonders of the world and the possible site of Atlantis. There are also quick connections to the nearby islands of Sikonos and Folegandros for anyone seeking peace and quiet.

Ios also has regular ferry links with Paros, Naxos and Amorgos.

The island is a long, long way from Piraeus and the quickest way to get there is to fly via Santorini.

Sikinos

Sikinos and Folegandros lie a short distance west of Ios and rather further east of Milos and offer a refuge from the crowds the bigger islands sometimes attract. They are often treated as twin islands, but have totally separate identities and differ sharply from each other, except that both have beautiful Cycladic Horas or main villages.

Sikonos is closer to Ios and a regular caique service runs from Ios and on to Folegandros to supplement the island ferries. It docks at the port of Allopronia, which has a sand beach, two restaurants and a few rooms. From there a cement block road runs uphill to Hora and it was a walk of 1 hour on the last visit with no sign of the daily bus that links the ports and main villages of other islands in the Aegean.

It is worth the hike in the cool of the evening because Hora is an untouched pretty village with more rooms, restaurants and a ruined monastery, Zoodochos Pigi, on the hill above.

Sikinos produces one of the best wines in the Cyclades, a lightly resinated variety which only seems to exist on the island. It is about 12 hours from Piraeus by ship, but more easily accessible by plane to Milos or Santorini and onwards by ship.

Beaches

The beach at Allopronia is sandy and swimmable, but not so pretty. There is a much prettier beach on the other side of the island, but it is a long haul on foot.

Nightlife and dining out

There is a lively evening eating scene in the tavernas in Hora and the port's restaurant can be lively on occasions. The hotel/restaurant on the road just above the port has a discotheque, but the premises are rarely in use.

Not to be missed on Sikinos

Visitors staying in the port should take the walk to Hora, and if they are energetic and the weather is cool, should walk on 1 hour from the main village to Episkopi, the site of ancient Sikinos, which has an Orthodox church built on a temple of Apollo complete with two Doric columns.

Worth visiting off Sikinos

This island can be a trifle claustrophobic after a few days. Fortunately, it is an easy caique ride from Ios in one direction and Folegandros in the other. Each in its way has more life than Sikonos.

Folegandros

Folegandros proves the rule that two Greek islands which are close together geographically are miles apart in nature and atmosphere. It offers a sharp contrast to neighbouring Sikinos, with which it is so often grouped and with which it shares island steamers and smaller boats running between Milos and Ios.

It is a long island, squeezed in the middle like a soft balloon, and lives up to its name – 'rocky and arid' – with a rocky and barren coastline which sometimes rises grandly and mysteriously 1,000 feet above the sea. But the island is also warm and friendly, with a welcoming white harbour at Karavostassis, two pretty white villages on the high spine of the island in Hora, its main village uphill from the port, and Ano Meria, a long village in the west.

Folegandros also has a surprising number of good sandy beaches tucked away in coves around the coast. The easiest way to get there is by plane to Santorini or Milos and on by boat as a ship all the way from Piraeus takes about 11 hours.

Beaches

Karavostassis has a reasonable beach around the bay beside the port, where sand peeps out occasionally between the pebbles, and other swimmable coves to the south of the port. Livadi is the best of the series, a sand beach backed by pine trees and a flat strip of marshland.

But, as is customary in Greece, the best beaches of the island are further afield and require a little effort and travelling.

One such is Angale, a small village reached by walking along the ridge of the island and turning left by the windmills towards the south coast where it is squeezed to its narrowest point. It boasts two restaurants and is sometimes served by a donkey man for the return trip uphill. Further west is Agios Nicholaos, a sheltered beach a short walk of 15 minutes along the coast from Angale, and Livadaki, even further west by the Asprorountas lighthouse can be reached by walking south from the western end of the village of Ano Meria from the last bus stop travelling in the direction.

Yet another small beach lies at Agios Georgios, by a small chapel, reached by walking north from the same bus terminus.

The most stunning beach on Folegandros is Katergi, 1½ hours walk south from Karavostassis via the village of Livadi and across the foothills to the coast, or half an hour's boat trip from the port. It has a beautiful desert island atmosphere, thanks to a long curve of pale sand and a small island in the bay, and is often deserted. Caiques from the harbour will drop you there for a fixed fee and return a few hours later to complete the round trip.

Nightlife and dining out

Karavostassis has two good restaurants, including the Remezzo where the strains of classical music can add a touch of sophistication to an atmosphere and cuisine that are more reminiscent of Mykonos than a remote island like Folegandros. They are matched by two others up in Hora, including one in the main square specialising in roast meat.

There is a discotheque on the outskirts of Hora by the road to the port, which makes brave efforts to attract visitors, but only gets a good crowd in high season.

Not to be missed on Folegandros

Hora is a jewel among Cycladic villages with pretty flowered squares, narrow streets and terraced vineyards tumbling down to the sea from what used to be a castle. It is served by an occasional bus from Karavostassis, which also runs along the spine of the island to Ano Meria once or twice a day.

It is well worth taking the bus uphill, but the walk back down is a delight on a starlit night. There are many other good walks from the middle of the island, north of Hora to the 'golden cave' or Chrysispilia, which is hung with stalactites and stalagmites, and from Ano Meria to the coast at Angali, Agios Nicholaos, Livadaki and Agios Georgios. Livadaki is the site of the Asprorountas lighthouse.

Worth visiting off Folegandros

The regular ships running to Sikinos and Ios makes it easy to visit contrasting islands, but check return times carefully. Ios offers a glimpse of bright lights and razzamatazz.

Kimolos

Kimolos is the only one of the three satellite islands of Milos that is inhabited and easily accessible. It has regular boats from Milos and is also a regular call for Piraeus steamers plying between Milos, Sifnos and Folegandros.

Called after the chalk ('kimolia') which it once produced, Kimolos used to be joined to Milos, but is now separated by a deep gulf. It is a haven of peace and quiet with a succession of good sandy beaches, which can be viewed at leisure from the deck of the boat from Milos.

The south side of the island is green and inhabited at the little port of Psathi and the village of Kimolos or Hora, which is about 20 minutes walk uphill from the harbour. It is a pretty white Cycladic village with winding streets, rooms to let and some good honest tavernas. The stiff walk uphill explains why donkeys are still widely used on this island.

The main businesses of the island are fishing, farming and fuller's earth. It has not yet made many concessions to tourism.

Beaches

There is good swimming close to the harbour from smooth rocks that run north of there along two sheltered bays. There is also a succession of six sandy bays running south from the harbour, which are reached by a stiff walk from Hora and go under names like Aliki and Mavro Spilia. Aliki has a restaurant and a few rooms, but the best beach is a wide strand of coarse sand half a mile long which is about half an hour's walk south of the port or the village.

There is another beach at the tiny

village of Klima to the north.

Nightlife and dining out

Is confined to restaurants in the village and one or two on the coast.

Not to be missed on Kimolos

Hora has a 17th century church and there are some remains of a Venetian castle nearby at Paliokastro, which contains another old church. An ancient cemetery is being excavated in the south of the island where Kimolos was once connected to Milos.

Worth visiting off Kimolos

Visitors staying on Kimolos for a week should certainly make the short sea trip to Apollonia on Milos and see something of the parent island. It is also easy to take ships to Sifnos and Folegandros for glimpses of other islands. It is possible too to take a caique from Psathi to the islet of Poliegos uninhabited except for goats and the odd goatherd. There is good swimming from three or four sandy coves facing Kimolos and a splendid feeling of isolation.

Milos

Milos is shaped like a horseshoe around a big enclosed bay, which makes a wonderful natural harbour for the main port of Adamas and also contains a wealth of calm sandy bays for swimming. It is easy to see that there has been a volcanic eruption similar to that on Santorini in ancient times and the sea has flooded the crater, both from the shape of the great harbour – which is 3 miles across at one point – and from the coloured rocks along its shores.

There are outcrops of sulphur, gypsum and obsidian, a glassy stone prized by the ancients for arrow heads, all over the island. There are also exotic rocks sprouting out of the sea like the Arkoudes in the harbour and the stubby white Glaronissi near Apollonia. And there is a small geothermal power plant at Zefyria pumping hot water from underground springs.

The great harbour was used by the French during the Crimean War and the First World War, and they made Milos famous by carrying off an armless statue of Venus to the Louvre, where it became known as the Venus de Milo. The island's other big claim to fame is its quarries, where some of its exotic stones are mined. There are plenty visible around the harbour near Zephyria.

But Milos deserves a better reputation because it is a first-class holiday island. Although it is around 8 hours by sea from Piraeus and bus services leave something to be desired, it also has regular local air flights from Athens and scooters and bikes for hire in Adamas. It also has more sandy coves than all its immediate neighbours put together.

Yet, apart from Adamas and Apollonia in high season, it is not touristy compared with the popular northern Cyclades and it offers a good refuge for anyone seeking peace and quiet with reasonable access to civilisation, adequate places to stay, good swimming from both inner and outer shores, and good walking over the rippling hills around the harbour.

Beaches

Adamas has sandy beaches on both sides of the port with tamarisk trees and pines hanging over the sand and dipping into the sea in places. There are six more sandy coves across the bay at Emborion, a tiny holiday village boasting good home cooking and a few rooms which can be reached by small boat from the quayside at Adamas. It may soon be accessible by road right around the bay from Adamas, which will make a spectacular drive.

The sandy coves continue around the bay at Patrikia and Hivadolimni, where a small curved beach is fringed with pine trees and backed by a small lake.

Apollonia, which is a fishing village with boats to Kimolos, has an enclosed sandy beach of its own surrounded by pine trees and there are others at Mandrakia, Pyropatamos and Platina beneath the three white hill villages of Plaka, Tripiti and Triovossalos, though Klima has only a pebble beach.

The west and east shores of the island also have beaches, but they are a trifle inaccessible since the buses usually go only as far as Zefyria. It is worth taking a taxi or scooter ride to Agathis or Agios Ioannis in the west or to Paliochora and Agios Kiriaki in the east. Both have simple restaurants with rooms and Paliochora has a spectacular cliff-backed sandy beach with a hot spring a short walk along the coast surrounded by purple and yellow stones.

Nightlife and dining out

Adamas has a good variety of hotels and restaurants along the quayside, which are lively at lunchtime and in the evenings, and two discos come to life around the port in summer time. Apollonia also has a lively dining out scene in the evenings, especially around the square.

Not to be missed on Milos

It is a good idea to rent a scooter, bike or car to see the island from Adamas,

since buses are limited to two or three main routes, and the first trip should be 5 kilometres up the hill to the island capital of Plaka and its two satellite villages, Tripiti and Triovossalos, which almost run into one another.

It is worth doing this just for the view, but Plaka is also a picturesque village with two big churches, a Venetian castle and folk and archaeological museums. Steps above the village lead to the castle or Kastro, which was also occupied by the Turks and by Greek pirates for a time over the centuries. The museums are in the village near the bus stop and contain a variety of ancient statues, pottery and items from Cycladic life.

From Plaka you can easily walk downhill to Klima, a picturesque, but rather windswept old fishing village where the Romans once landed on Milos. There are few traces of them by the sea, but on the way is a splendid old city where the Venus statue was found, which has a nice little theatre overlooking the bay and one of the best-preserved warrens of catacombs in the Mediterranean.

The catacombs are lit by candles when they are open to the public, but have been closed for repairs over recent years. Fortunately, the same fate has not befallen the theatre and a touring company gives shows there in August.

The other main road out of Adamas goes to Apollonia, which gives a completely different view of the island and has boats both to the nearby island of Kimolos and to the offshore Glaronissia (or 'gull islands') which are spiky outcrops covered with rock crystal. A short walk away is Philakope, which has fascinating remains of houses, roads and a palace from the Cycladic period.

A third trip worth doing is to Zefyria, which was the capital of Milos for centuries. It is reached via a salt lake at the head of the big bay. It is a pleasant old village, is partly-deserted and offers good walks through gentle hills and cane groves in the surrounding countryside and to the east and south coast beaches about 3–4 kilometres away.

You can also walk from Zephyria or Hivadolimni inland to Loutra Provata, which has the remains of a Roman village and a spring with curative waters.

In summer boats go around the island from Adamas to view the rock wonders of Glaronissa, Arkoudes, Kleftiko and Triades and the cave of Sykia.

Worth visiting off Milos

Boats usually run from Apollonia to Kimolos, Sikinos and Folegandros, which are all smaller islands than Milos with different character, but the similarity of good beaches and Cycladic buildings. They sometimes run as far as Santorini or Ios.

Kimolos is only an hour or so from Apollonia, so it can make an easy day trip, but allow a lot more time for Folegandros and Sikinos. The volcanic island of Santorini or Thira is one of the wonders of the world, with a lot to see, so give it the time it deserves – at least two or three days.

Ships on the Western Cyclades route run in the other direction to Sifnos and Serifos, which are again different in appearance from Milos, reaching higher and looking more barren. The sea journey takes about 1½ hours to Sifnos and the same again to Serifos.

Athens is easily accessible by plane in about ¾ of an hour, but book well in advance for a day trip or a return over two days, as the planes are small and not too frequent.

Finally one should mention Antimilos, the most remote of the satellite islands of Milos, with only occasional caique trips from Adamas. It is questionable whether the trip is worthwhile unless the sea is like a millpond. It takes two hours each way and when you get there you find a barren, rocky little isle with a great feeling of isolation which is inhabited only by chamois or wild goats.

Sifnos

Sifnos is a dramatic island with a barren brown landscape, chalk white villages and three long sandy beaches. This combination explains why it has become the most developed tourist island in the Western Cyclades, even though it is about 6 hours sailing time from Piraeus.

Ships dock in a narrow gulf at the port of Kamares, which cannot be seen from the sea until the ship is in the gulf. The port has a sandy beach of its own, a smattering of hotels and restaurants along the quayside and both buses and boats to other parts of the island.

The buses go up to Apollonia, the capital, to nearby Artemon, and to the most famous beach, Plati Yialos, which is fast developing into a seaside resort. The boats do a circular tour of the island daily in summer to Plati Yialos and Vathy, another beach resort via the church of Chrysopigi. On both routes you may be stunned by the sight of over 300 churches, the biggest having unusual crimson domes topped by white or gold crucifixes.

Sifnos was wealthy in ancient times thanks to its gold mines, which were worked by the Phoenicians, but fell foul of the Delphic oracle, which demanded a golden egg as an annual tribute. The island sent a gilded rock instead and its mines were flooded by the sea. They remain that way to this day, but the island has its golden beaches to console it.

Beaches

The most famous beach on the island is the long stretch of Plati Yialos on the east coast, which is deserted in winter, but turning into a sizeable resort in summer. It has a bus from Apollonia and a boat from Kamares. Its big rival on the opposite coast is Vathy, which has a village on a curving bay. But there are also beaches of quality at Faros and Apokoftos beside the monastery of Chrysopigi, which is set on a rocky promontory.

Nightlife and dining out

Sifnos is famous for its cooking and its olive oil, as well as its wine and pottery, so you ought to dine well on the island. Kamares has a good selection of quayside restaurants and the linked white villages of Apollonia and Artemon on the high plateau also have plenty of tavernas. Incredibly, both villages have discotheques too, though they are only active in high summer.

Not to be missed on Sifnos

It is a good island to walk around, using simple stone paths across a barren brown landscape. Apollonia and Artemon have the bank, the post office and the folk museum, where local pottery and textiles are on show, but the most dramatic village is a good half hour's walk away at Kastro.

This is the old capital, set high on a cliff with a sheer drop to the sea

below, and it has a Venetian castle and houses to match with medieval coats of arms above their doorways, separated by narrow alleyways. It also has some fine old churches and a beach of sorts below the cliff for those who can find the way down.

Sifnos has three spectacular white monasteries dating from the 17th century; Chrysopigi on its holy rock; Vrissi in the village of Exambello; and Taxiarchos, which is set on high between Vathy and Plati Yialos.

Worth visiting off Sifnos

Ferries on the Western Cyclades route run to Milos and Kimolos to the south as well as to Serifos to the north, which are all slightly quieter, less developed islands. Occasional caiques also run to Paros, which is no great distance away to the east and ought to be a regular ferry run. They go from Plati Yialos in high season.

Serifos

Serifos lies between Kithnos and the more popular tourist island of Sifnos to the south, about 5 hours from Piraeus by the daily ferries that ply the Western Cyclades. Its name means 'barren rock' or 'bare place' and it is often described that way, but that belies the beauty of the island.

It is warm and welcoming in the port of Livadi and spectacular in the whitewashed main village of Hora, which is sprinkled across a rocky hill high above the port. It has plenty of good simple accommodation and restaurants around the long pine-fringed bay that flanks the harbour, two fertile valleys inland, and an abundance of pretty sandy coves hidden away around the shore of the island.

Most visitors stay in Livadi where they land, and it has easy access by walking to the beaches around the south coast, by bus to the west coast villages of Megalo Livadi and Koutalas, to Galani with its monastery in the north, and to Hora, which is also walkable in under an hour.

Hora is a spectacular village with great views of the surrounding Cyclades, the remains of an old castle and the island's post office near the square where the bus stops. One or two restaurants are also developing.

Beaches

There is a series of good sandy coves within walking distance of Livadi around the south coast, including Psili Ammos, Ambeli, Livasaki and Karari.

Go west and you will find others at Megalo Livadi and more still at Sikania in the north. There are also beaches near Galani and Kallitsos.

Nightlife and dining out

Livadi bay has a good selection of restaurants and the occasional music/disco bar sited along the seashore. Hora is also developing one or two restaurants. Try the local sweet brown wine chilled.

Not to be missed on Serifos

Hora is a spectacular village. It was fortified in bygone days with a Venetian castle and walls, and they still peep out through the walls of houses in the village. Well worth an evening stroll from the port to see the town and the view.

Megalo Livadi has a 'white castle' dating back to medieval times and at Mesa Akrotiri in the middle of the island there are two caves festooned with stalactites and stalagmites.

The most spectacular monastery on the island is the fortress-like Taxiarchon monastery in the north beyond Galani, which dates from the 15th century and has some beautiful frescoes in a slightly tattered state. Panagia village on the way has a 10th century church of the virgin which gives its name to the place.

Worth visiting off Serifos

Kithnos to the north and Sifnos to the south are as different from Serifos as they are from each other, though the three islands all have good sandy beaches and Serifos and Sifnos have a similar brown landscape. It takes about an hour each way.

Kea

Kea or Tzia, to give it its Venetian name – lies only 24 miles off the coast of Attica and can be reached by daily ferry from the industrial east coast port of Lavrion in under two hours. So the total journey from Athens can be around 3 hours, putting the island closer to the capital than most Aegean isles. The sea voyage is around the electricity and coal island of Makronissi. Kea is the first big island you see from island ferries heading for the touristy Cycladean islands like Mykonos, Paros and Naxos once past Cape Sounion.

Yet Kea seems more remote than those islands, like the rest of the chain known as the Western Cyclades, with which it shares a ferry once or twice a week. It is easy to get away from people in its rugged interior and the island seems to get more Greek visitors than foreign tourists.

It is a commercial island. You can see the remains of an old coal mine across the bay from the port of Korissia

where the ferries put in and it does a
lively trade in almonds, acorns, figs,
grapes, citrus fruits, cheese, honey
and red Mavriti wine.

But it also has pretty whitewashed
villages, fascinating archaeological
remains and a number of sandy coves
tucked away between rocky headlands
around its coast.

Beaches

Korissia is a bustling little port in a
well-sheltered bay approached
through two headlands and boasts a
hotel, rooms and harbourside
restaurants, so it is a sensible place to
stay. It is within walking distance of
the north coast resorts and beaches of
Vourkari and Otzia, and also the
island capital of Hora (or Kea or Ioulis)
which is linked to the port by a good
tarmac road and an occasional bus
service. A rougher road leads from
there to the beach resorts of Pisses
and Koundoros.

Hora stands high on a hill and has
cobbled streets, a square and remains
of both ancient and medieval
buildings. It also has the island's main
bank and post office.

Not to be missed on Kea

Kea was a more important island in
ancient and medieval times. The
Minoans colonised Agia Irene close to
Vourkari and used the big bay that
connects it to Korissia as a safe
anchorage for their fleet in this part of
the Aegean. Their palace was on the
site of the present day church and
ruins are visible under the sea close
by.

Later the island boasted four
important towns, Ioulis, Poiessa,
Karthea and Koressia – and it was the
administrative capital of the Cyclades

in the Middle Ages before Syros and
Piraeus were big ports. The Venetians
built a fortress in Hora and the Turks
stationed their consuls there.

Kea has three monasteries, the most
impressive being Panagia Kastriani. It
is also worth walking up to the summit
of Profitis Ilias, the highest point on
the island, from which you can see half
a dozen other islands and Cape
Sounion on a clear day.

Koundoros Bay in the south-west of
the island is the site of the island's
biggest hotel, the Kea Beach Club,
built on a promontory overlooking a
sandy bay.

Kithnos

Served by regular ships from Piraeus
that run down the Western Cyclades,
and occasional ships from Kea,
Kithnos is a charming little island
which supports fishing and farming,
and has a number of brown sandy
beaches fringed with pine trees. It is
even quieter than Kea and is about 4
hours from Piraeus.

Kithnos is called after an ancient king
of the Driopes, Kithnos, who ruled the
island in the 6th century B.C. from the
seaside village of Driopi.

The main port, where the island
steamers call from Piraeus and
Serifos, is Merichas. It has rooms,
restaurants and a sandy beach plus
occasional buses to the island's capital
of Hora or Kithnos 9 kilometres away,
which has the main bank and post
office. There are also buses to Driopi,
which stands on a headland over the
sea, and to Loutra, which is a spa
village with thermal baths and a hot
stream running into the sea. Both are
reputed to cure arthritis.

Beaches

Kithnos is blessed with a series of good sandy beaches along the coast within easy walking distance of Merichas. Loutra also has a sheltered sandy beach and there is another around the bay below Driopi. There is a fine beach by the monastery of Panagia.

Nightlife and dining out

Loutra has a discotheque of sorts, but nightlife on this island is mainly dining out. There are busy restaurants at Merichas and Loutra and another in the island's simple whitewashed capital. Be sure to try the sweet brown wine which is native to most of the Western Cyclades. It is best drunk chilled.

Not to be missed on Kithnos

The roads to Loutra and Driopi run along fertile valleys and both are worth a visit to see seaside resorts which are both different from, and prettier than, Merichas. Loutra has a fort and there is a ruined castle and medieval houses at Katakefala along the coast.

Worth visiting off Kithnos

Kea is a completely different island in one direction and Serifos in the other. Both have good beaches and Kea some interesting remains.

The Little Cyclades

This chain of small islands, which can be glimpsed from the eastern shores of Naxos, is strictly for lovers of the simple life. Rooms are few and nightlife non-existent.

The Little Cyclades are on the shipping route from Naxos to Amorgos and also see an occasional catamaran from Amorgos.

Schinoussa

Schinoussa is possibly the quietest of the Little Cyclades. It has a simple restaurant at the harbour of Myrsini but most of the 100 or so population live in Chora, less than a mile away up the hill. While the other islands in the group have golden sand, the Schinoussa beach, ten minutes below Chora on the south-west coast, is grey and coarse.

Iraklia

Iraklia also has a hill village but the port of Agios Georgios, set in a fertile valley is now becoming more important. It has a large cave and a Greek fort with a tower.

It is the prettiest of the Little Cyclades and has a port beach fringed by tamarisk trees, but it does not have the variety of beaches that Donoussa and Koufonissi can boast.

Donoussa

Donoussa's main village is at the harbour, which is set on a sandy bay. Donoussa is strong on sandy beaches. There is one each side of the port and another good stretch can be found in the north-east of the island.

Koufonissi

Koufonissi is beginning to be discovered by both Greek and British holidaymakers.

The harbour is long and rambling, but offers good eating. There are prettier stretches of coast around Porion and Forikas, which has three adjacent sandy bays.

Keros

Keros is an important archaeological site with remains of very early inhabitation as well as medieval ruins in the north but attracts few visitors.

12. Athens and the Mainland

City of the rock – Athens

Athens, the unchallenged capital of Greece for 150 years, is a tawdry city but it has many beautiful things in it.

It is dirty, noisy and hot. It lacks the architectural unity and wide avenues of Paris, London, Rome, Madrid, Amsterdam and Istanbul. It sprawls into the port of Piraeus and together they house over three million people – a third of the Greek population. They also share an unhealthy cloud of pollution called the Nefos.

Yet no other city in the world can touch Athens for its history, symbolised by the Rock of the Acropolis, where four proud white temples preside over the chaos below. Few cities can match it for the charm and friendliness of its people, who are linked in spirit, if not in appearance, to their ancient forebears who built the Acropolis and its most famous temple, the ladylike Parthenon.

Melina Mercouri, one of the most spirited of modern Greek women, who did a lot to popularise Greece with her performance in 'Never on Sunday' and has in recent years been the Minister of Culture in the Papandreou Government, put it this way: 'Paris is like a beautiful woman with great charm, whereas Athens is like an ugly woman with great charm.'

Seen at its best, sparkling in the Mediterranean sun, and surrounded by green hills, from a high vantage point like the Lycabettus or the Acropolis, the city has an appearance of order and charm. But at street level it is ugly and heaving. It is a jumble of unplanned cement and steel buildings bristling with Coca Cola signs and lampshade shops orchestrated by the squealing tyres and horns of its huge car population.

In summer the city heaves even more because a tourist population that is almost equal to the resident population descends on Athens and the city bakes in a valley between the hills. When there is no breeze it is like standing in front of an open oven.

These are all problems of an unplanned city that grew up around a little 19th century village nestling in the Plaka district under the Acropolis. It was picked as the capital by King Otto, the German prince who became the first modern king of Greece and wanted to restore the city's splendour from its Golden Age in the 5th century BC.

Otto added a few neo-classical touches to the village, but it stayed a small planned town until the 1920's. Then it suddenly mushroomed into the jerry-built suburbs that run down to Piraeus when over a million Greeks were expelled from Turkey and most of them decided to seek their fortune in the capital.

That damage has been done over again in the years since the Second

World War as another million Greeks have given up trying to scratch a living from poor smallholdings in the countryside. They have turned the Athens–Piraeus sprawl into a concrete jungle of small factories, workshops and makeshift multi-storey flats.

Yet the heart of the city around the Acropolis, the Pnyx and the Lycabettus, which is the mecca of the tourists, although surrounded by this urban nightmare, remains pure and proud. It is unchanged in character, though gradually eroding under clouds of acid rain that rise over the steel factories, refineries and shipyards of Piraeus and Elefsis and find their way right up to the high columns of the Parthenon.

The erosion is not visible to visitors, who may pass through Athens without even noticing the Nefos. But they should see and wonder at the treasures that lie in the city centre, in a rectangular area about 1 mile by 1½ miles with its corners in the Acropolis, the National Gardens, the Lycabettus and the city's superb Archaeological Museum.

Within that area lie a dozen Wonders of the Ancient World, led by the four temples of the Acropolis, the twin theatres of Dionysus and Herodus Atticus lying beneath the rock, the Theseion and Agora only a stone's throw away, and another stone's throw away Hadrian's triumphal arch and the huge pillars of the Temple of Zeus. There are also four splendid museums – the Archaeological, the Acropolis, the Byzantine and Benaki – two memorable squares in Syntagma and Omonia, the stately steps of the Plaka district under the Acropolis, and the cool green areas of the National Gardens, the Lycabettus, the Pnyx and the Areopagus.

If Athens isn't a city to wonder at, it is a city to wander in, seeking out its individual marvels. And not all of them are ageless and carved in stone.

Athens is a lively commercial city close in character and geography to the orient. Its streets and squares are busy with markets, shops and cafes where people seem to sit all day talking love and politics. The traffic noise competes with the cries of hawkers and touts selling anything from sponges and postcards to sandals, shoe shines and State lottery tickets. By night the tinkle and beat of bouzouki music pours forth from the garden restaurants of the Plaka beneath the Acropolis and Kolonaki beyond Syntagma Square.

The spirit of ancient Greece and modern Greece somehow blend together to raise the city above the chaos and confusion of its ill-planned streets and suburbs, and make it a place of pilgrimage. Everyone who loves Greece should visit it once, if only for a few days.

Location and travel

Athens lies close to the west coast of the Attic Peninsular and almost exactly at the centre of Greece. Its airport is easily the busiest in the country handling most international flights and the adjoining port of Piraeus harbours nearly as many big ships as all the other ports in the country put together because they radiate from there to neighbouring countries and to nearly a hundred islands.

It takes 3½ hours to fly the 1500 miles from London to Athens and it takes three days or more by coach, rail or car via the heel of Italy.

The biggest snag to flying in and out of

Athens is that you have to pass through Athens Airport, one of the horrors of the modern world. Like the city, it heaves in the summer and expansion never seems to keep up with the crowds. It can be chaotic, frustrating and uncomfortable.

It has three terminals on two sides of the landing strip. The terminal on the inland side is called the East Airport and is used by foreign airlines. The West Airport is on the seaside and is used only by Olympic Airways, but to add to the confusion it has two terminals, domestic on the left and international on the right when viewed from the coast road.

They were built in that peculiar way to satisfy Greek logic and a fast-expanding tourist population, but have never been logical nor have they kept pace with the relentless march of tourism.

There is no underpass beneath the airstrip, so you have to take a bus or a taxi between the two. The airport buses are only half-hourly and don't run all night, so if you end up at the wrong terminal or are in transit from a British Airways flight to an Olympic domestic flight, you may have to take a taxi. The good news is that taxis are cheap in Greece – it should not cost much more than £2 to £3.

It is easier to travel between the airport and the city, but not that easy. There is a bus every 20 minutes connecting the East Airport and the corner of Syntagma Square, but the bus from the Olympic Airport sometimes stops short of the centre of town. It is better to walk 100 yards out on to the coast road and take a service bus into the centre of Athens, asking which goes to Syntagma Square, or to ask the price of a taxi and pay a small premium to avoid a lot of hassle.

Pray that you never have to spend more than the normal queueing time in the East Airport in high summer. There are never enough staff for either the check-in desks or the passport counters, nor enough chairs to sit down when more than two big jets depart around the same time. The front hall of the airport often looks like the aftermath of a revolution with tired tourists sitting and sprawling on their luggage and any space they can find on the floor.

If you do have hours to kill at the airport during the day, think of going down to the coast for a swim or a meal. There are places near to the Olympic terminals. If you are stranded at night, the best places to sit and catch forty winks are the arrivals section and bar of the foreign airlines terminal and the departure section and bar of the Olympic international terminal.

Beaches

There are no beaches in Athens and none fit to swim from within miles of the port of Piraeus because of pollution. You may remember Melina Mercouri jumping off a boat for a romp in Piraeus harbour in 'Never on Sunday', but that was a stunt that shouldn't be repeated today in those oily waters.

In both cities stick to swimming pools. A handful of the big hotels in Athens have pools, including the St George Lycabettus and the Divani-Zafolia Palace and the city has an Olympic swimming pool beside the National Gardens. Piraeus also has one at Zea Yacht Marina.

But the obvious solution if you are in Athens and want to spend time on the beach is to travel out by bus or taxi to one of the resorts on the coast of the Attic Peninsular. There are more than a dozen resorts on both the east and west coasts of Attica and the general rule is that the further you go from the city the cleaner the water becomes and the further you are from the slipstream of jets going in and out of Athens Airport.

Take the coast road towards Sounion, which Anthony Perkins took as a suicide trip in the film 'Phaedra', but can safely be approached by bus from Leoforos Olgas or Mavromateon Street near the Archaeological Museum. You will start to see beaches before the bus passes Athens Airport at Faliron, Alimos and Ag. Kosmas. There are also tennis courts in the sports complexes beside the coast road. This is the start of the 'Athenian Riviera', or Apollo Coast, but this strip is best left for a quick dip during a wait at the airport.

Go as far as Glyfada, Voula and Kavouri and you will find three organised swimming and sports complexes with a small entry fee, clean changing cabins and passable stretches of sandy beach with windsurfing and water-skiing just 20 kilometres from the centre of Athens. Glyfada also has an 18-hole golf course and tennis courts.

There are a few stretches of beach between the complexes, just off the coast road, which have no entry fees and a string of pretty restaurants serving good seafood for those who prefer swimming outside a compound. The big snag with this stretch is that the coast road is busy and it is beneath the approach run to the airport, so you do hear the roar of a big jet every few minutes.

To escape the jets, you have to travel further along the road to Vouliagmeni,

Varkiza, Lagonissi, Saronis or Sounion, a pretty cape 70 kilometres from Athens.

Vouliagmeni is a spectacular yacht harbour with water-skiing, and another beach and sports complex on a pine-fringed peninsular, but it is again swimming from a compound with entrance fee. Varkiza is less formal and is surrounded by natural rocky coves where you do feel you are at last getting away from the urban environs of Athens, but swimming is off shingle. Lagonissi is a bungalow complex with restaurants, tennis courts and a passable beach. One of the best sand beaches along the whole coast is right at the end just below the spectacular Cape Sounion with its temple of Poseidon.

The beaches are less organised on the east coast of Attica, but the resorts are honest and the bus journey from Athens by the country route affords a glimpse of Greek mainland life with both wine and cement factories dotted along the road.

You can take buses to the fishing and ferry ports of Rafina, Porto Rafti and Lavrion or to the historic sites of Vraona and Marathon, which is only 40 kilometres from Athens. Hotels have sprung up along both these stretches of coast opposite the island of Evia and separate resorts have developed along the Bay of Marathon at Mati, Nea Makri and Agios Andreas where there are some pretty pine-fringed shingley coves to swim in.

If you are more adventurous, you can take a ferry from Rafina or Lavrion to the islands of Evia, Andros or Kea for the day, to find a sandier beach, but make sure before you visit Andros or Kea that there is a convenient ship back unless you want to stay overnight because the journey takes

1½–2 hours each way by ship and the bus from Athens 1 hour. Unfortunately, the two do not always connect.

West of Athens lie other beach resorts at Kineta, Agii Theodori, Loutraki and Porto Germeno. They are mostly pebble beaches and the approach road is a busy motorway along an industrial coast. But Porto Germeno is a lovely spot to spend a long weekend. A picture postcard port with sandy beaches, fish restaurants, hotels and old castle, it is isolated at the end of a long wooded valley on a picturesque coastline of bays and beaches curving around from Loutraki.

Give the isle of Salamis a miss unless you desperately want to see where Xerxes sat to watch his fleet destroyed, but Aegina makes a good day out to glimpse island life and try out a good sandy beach. It can be reached in 1½ hours from Piraeus by regular ship and half an hour by occasional hydrofoil from Zea Marina, while Piraeus is less than half an hour from Athens by underground railway.

Football (podosfero) is a big sport in Greece. You could say a national obsession. Everyone from the cradle to the grave knows names like Manchester United and Tottenham. The place to watch it is in the new olympic stadium in Halandri or in the Karaiskaki stadium at Piraeus. The city horse-racing stadium is also down towards Piraeus where Singrou Avenue reaches the sea.

Nightlife and dining out

Nightlife in Greece usually means eating out in the open air, preferably with music and dancing, and in Athens that means that Plaka. The old village nestling beneath the rock of the Acropolis is the Montmartre of Athens with steps, narrow streets and stately houses with gardens dating back to the early 19th century.

Many of the old houses now serve as tavernas with tables inside candle-lit cellars and outside in the gardens or on the pavement or levels between the steps. In summer they swing to bouzouki music, live and canned, and to the sound of cash registers because the Plaka sells its atmosphere at a premium in the tourist season, and charges especially high rates to tourists who accept an invitation to smash plates.

But it is always possible to find somewhere on the fringe that is cheaper than average and it is often worth paying a little extra for live music and dancing, plus night-time views of the city and illuminated Acropolis. Guided tours which offer 'Athens by night' invariably include a visit to a Plaka taverna.

You may find that the most exotic places and nightclubs don't really get going before midnight, but it is easy to fill in time wandering from one place to another, pausing only for a bottle of wine and snacks to soak it up. This kind of taverna crawl should appeal to people staying in a big hotel with full board who don't want to miss their dinner there, but still want to sample the Plaka.

Another spectacular place to see Athens by night is from the Lycabettus hill, reached by funicular or a long walk through the fashionable Kolonaki district. You may dine or drink at a restaurant or cafe on the summit or in one of the streets below where you can also find fashionable clubs, including some with live music.

You may need a long purse for Kolonaki, and the same is true of

Tourkolimano or Mikrolimano, the U-shaped yacht harbour in Piraeus where many people go to eat fish and see the moonlight reflecting in the harbour. A good value, but not cheap, restaurant in Athens is the Corfu, off Syntagma Square. For a cheaper meal in Athens, try one of the grill houses around Omonia Square, where lamb, chicken, suckling pigs and guts are roasted on rotating spits.

You can either down three courses with wine at a pavement table or wander through the arcades sampling snacks on sticks and wrapped in pitta bread.

Another reasonably-priced evening out is at the Daphne wine festival held in an 11th century monastery through the summer and reached by a 20-minute bus ride from Athens. Once you have paid your entrance fee, the wines are on the house and there are many barrels to tap.

There are cafes in Omonia and Syntagma Squares where you can sip a drink and watch the world going by, and there are others like Floca's and Sonar's just off Syntagma where well-to-do Athenians gather to eat cakes and ice-cream.

Cinemas, showing Greek and foreign language films, are cheap and plentiful along the main streets in the centre of town such as Stadiou, Venizelou and Patission. Many are open-air in summer. For programmes, ask at your hotel or buy a local English-language paper like the 'Athens News'.

From the same sources you can learn about live theatre or puppet theatre performances. A festival of old and modern Greek theatre runs through the summer at the Herodus Atticus theatre under the Acropolis and the theatre on Lycabettus hill, but you need a translation to follow the drama because the language is Greek.

There is not the same problem with sound and light shows of the Acropolis and music at the Herodus Atticus, which ranges from classical to Nana Mouskouri. Nor at discos and jazz clubs, which are mainly in the Plaka or Kolonaki. Again the 'Athens News' is useful, but if in doubt try the Half-Note for jazz, the Kyttaro for live rock music, or Quasimodo's for traditional Greek music.

A rich history

Athens has a rich history, spiced with a little mythology, and it is well-documented because the city was the home of historians like Herodotus and Thucydides around the time it enjoyed its Golden Age in the fifth century BC.

It is often the history of Greece because Athens headed the city states of that age, remained the big centre of culture during the Roman Empire, and has been the capital of Greece all but a few years since it won its independence from the Turks in 1833.

Other cities have been made the capital of Greece – Corinth, Salonika and Naufplion among them – but have never lasted long. Other cities have been superior in force, notably Sparta, Thebes and Pella, the seat of Philip of Macedon, but the remains of their past glories would fit into a corner of the Archaeological Museum in Athens.

The city is called after Athena, goddess of wisdom and daughter of Zeus, who fought a legendary contest with Poseidon, the sea god and brother of Zeus, to see who would be the city's patron. Poseidon offered the city water by striking the rock of the Acropolis to start a spring, but Athena won by creating an olive tree.

In its early days Athens must have been ruled by the Minoan dynasty on Crete and the Mycenaeans who led the siege of Troy. An early hero of the city, Theseus, is supposed to have freed Athens from the Cretan yoke by killing its mythical monster, the minotaur, and also united the towns and villages of Attica under Athenian rule. The Minoan empire sank in the eruption of the Santorini volcano around 1500 BC and Athens emerged as the leader of Attica between 850 and 750 BC.

The city's early history from 750 to 500 BC is dominated by a series of tough men like Dracon, who framed the laws, Solon, who devised the idea of a democracy of equal citizens, and Pisistratus, a tyrant who developed the city's commerce and a strong fleet. It emerged as a military power as a result of the Persian Wars of the 5th century after assisting Greek towns in Asia to revolt between 499 and 497 BC.

Darius, the Persian king who already ruled all Asia Minor, decided to punish the Athenians and to add Attica to his empire, so he invaded with a huge force in 490 BC.

The result was one of the most famous battles of history. A tiny lightly-armed Athenian army ran across the plain of Marathon at the Persians as they were embarking from their ships and swept the huge force into the sea. The soldier who ran the 26 miles back to Athens to report the victory inspired the Marathon races of today.

Darius' son Xerxes came back with even greater forces ten years later, cutting a canal through one of the peninsulars of Halkidiki for his fleet. This time Athens was united with other Greek city states and a small force of Spartans – legend says 300 – fought a delaying action with the Persian hordes at the pass of Thermopylae before they reached down as far as Attica. Although Xerxes briefly took Athens and burned it, the citizens had evacuated the city and the fate of the invasion was sealed by two battles.

Xerxes sat on a hilltop and watched the nimble Athenian ships destroy his huge fleet of galleys off the island of Salamis in 480 BC, then a Greek army led by Sparta finished off his land forces at Plataea in 479 BC.

The peace that followed gave Athens a chance to develop an Aegean empire by uniting the islands in the confederacy of Delos, and also to develop art and literature. The City enjoyed a Golden Age for 48 years, led by Pericles for 30 of them. It saw the building of the Parthenon and long defensive walls down to Piraeus. It bred writers and playwrights like Herodotus, Sophocles and Aeschylus, and sculptors like Praxiteles and Phidias. It also developed the concept of democracy – equality for all citizens. They were supported by a big population of slaves and democracy turned into 'the rule of the mob.'

The Golden Age ended with the outbreak of the Peloponnesian War between Athens and Sparta in 431 BC and ended in defeat for Athens and the demolition of its long walls 27 years later. The war raged back and forth between the Peloponnese and Attica and as far afield as Sicily where the Athenians mounted a disastrous siege in 415 BC, but the die was cast when the Spartans achieved better leadership and the aid of the Persians.

With the end of the war Athens lost its military superiority, but art continued to flourish through writers and philosophers like Euripides, Thucydides, Socrates, Plato, Aristophanes and Xenophon. Thebes emerged as the dominant power in central Greece until a much bigger power swept down from the north in 358 BC. Philip of Macedonia spent the next twenty years uniting Greece into something like the country it is today, then his son Alexander took over and extended the Greek empire as far as India and Egypt.

Macedonia was itself succeeded and Greece invaded by the Romans from 200 BC, becoming a province of the Roman Empire in 146 BC. The Romans ruled for five centuries and during much of the time Athens was the leading university of the Empire. Many famous Romans were educated in Athens and Hadrian loved the city enough to build his triumphal arch and complete the Temple of Zeus.

The Roman Empire split in 340 AD and Greece became a province of Byzantium or Constantinople for 900 years. It was then invaded by a series of raiders from Western Europe including the Crusaders, the Franks and the Normans until the Turks took Constantinople in 1453. They took Greece into their empire for nearly 400 years, although Athens was won by Venice for brief periods during that time.

Greece revolted against Turkey in 1821 and eventually won its War of Independence in 1833 with some foreign help. The following year the little town of Athens was proclaimed capital of Greece by the young Otto of Bavaria who was selected as king by other European powers. But the war scarred what remained of ancient Athens, the Acropolis and Parthenon suffered several assaults and explosions, and when Lord Elgin removed the marble frieze from the Parthenon to England in 1800 he was probably preserving it from a much worse fate.

The path of Greek history has hardly been smooth since then. The country has alternated between a royal family and dictatorship, has lost a skirmish with Turkey in the early 1920's – which resulted in over 1 million Asian Greeks flooding into Athens – has been occupied by the Germans and the Italians in World War II, and been torn by its own bloody civil war between 1947 and 1949.

But it finally seems to have emerged from the periods of dictatorships and monarchy after shaking off the 6-year rule of the colonels in 1973 and voting against the return of King Constantine, who lives in exile in London. Since then it has been a flourishing democracy in the West European style, which has enjoyed a big economic boost since it joined the Common Market in 1981.

The time has surely come for Britain to acknowledge this and to make a grand gesture to a fellow member of the EEC by returning the Elgin Marbles from the British Museum to the Acropolis in Athens where they were carved. It would give a big boost to the Greek people and the British Museum has enough treasures for them not to be missed. Those who are keen to see the marbles would have a good excuse to visit Athens.

Not to be missed in Athens
All roads in the centre of Athens seem to go up to the Acropolis and it is the best place to start a sight-seeing tour. First, because so many·of the architectural treasures are there and secondly, because it gives such a good view of the city.

177

The four temples of the rock are white by day and gold by night when they are floodlit. They were built separately and designed by different architects, but they fit together as if by design. They are outstanding wonders of the ancient world, and a fitting monument to the Golden Age of Athens in the 5th century BC.

The Parthenon, which is the biggest of the group and the most imitated, has lost its wooden roof, its giant statue of Athena to whom it was dedicated, and its decorative stonework, which is spread between the British Museum and the Acropolis Museum. But its remaining columns and frieze, all cunningly curved and tapered to give an illusion of straightness and symmetry, convey enough of the majesty of the original building.

It is remarkable that so much remains after centuries of neglect, Turkish gunpowder and modern pollution. The Propylaea or Gateway, has been carefully restored and the tiny temple of Athena Nike is an exchanting miniature that has also benefited from careful restoration. The six maidens or Caryatids who support the roof of the Erectheion today are copies of the originals, which are in the Acropolis Museum. But the scene still sets the imagination racing.

Only the crowds can spoil a tour of the Acropolis, and it is worth going early in the morning to catch it in bright sunlight. Complete the tour with a visit to the Acropolis Museum, which has some beautiful statues and other finds from the temples.

Beneath the rock of the Acropolis lie other wonders of the ancient world. The theatres of Dionysus, dating from the 6th century BC, and the relatively modern Herodus Atticus theatre, built in 160 AD, which still mounts regular performances today. They should be looked over when empty of action and audience.

Beyond the two theatres stand the Aeropagus Hill and the Pnyx, where assemblies of citizens used to take place and justice to be dispensed, where Demosthenes rallied the Athenians against Philip of Macedon and Pericles expounded his version of democracy. Nowdays they star in sound and light displays and make a pleasant daytime stroll.

On the opposite side of the Acropolis lies the ancient market or Agora, which gives a different glimpse of the old town from the temples perched above, since it was there that trade took place and people met to shop and gossip. It contains the pretty arcade of Attalus, a museum, and an appropriate temple, the 5th century Theseion or temple of Hephaistos dedicated to the fiery god of smiths and metal workers. It contains the remains of other temples, churches and an old university of Athens, Greek and Roman.

You are now three-quarters of the way around a circle of wonders of the ancient world, which is completed with the monument of Lysicrates, Hadrian's triumphal arch and the high pillars of the temple of Olympian Zeus, the biggest in ancient Greece, which was completed by Hadrian.

To conclude this classical tour you have to visit the National Archaeological Museum, a long walk or short bus ride along Patission via Omonia Square, which offers free entrance on Sundays and Thursday like many other treasures of ancient Greece.

It is more compact than its huge rivals in Western Europe like the British

Museum and has an amazing range of rich remains, including the golden death mask of Agamemnon from Mycenae, the massive bronze of Poseidon raised from the seabed off Sounion, the crouching jockey who starred in the movie as the 'Boy on a Dolphin', smiling kouroi, and the frescoes of plants and Minoan life from Santorini – kept in Athens lest that island's volcano misbehaves. These individual wonders are surrounded by rooms full of black pottery, statues, weapons and jewellery enough to keep anyone fascinated for an hour or two. It should be visited at 8 am in summer to avoid bad crowds.

If you are not tired of museums and want to see something of a different Greece, the Byzantine and Benaki museums, both on Vassilis Sofias Avenue, have rich collections of Byzantine art, icons, frescoes, gold ornaments, costumes and church treasures covering the period from Roman times to the present day. Combine them with visits to the 11th century church of Agios Apostoli, the 12th century Agios Eleftherios or the 11th century Agios Theodori.

Those who want to the see the city's development in more modern times can do so at the Museum of the City of Athens, which shows the development of the new city from the 1820's and is housed in the palace used by Otto of Bavaria, the first modern king of Greece.

No tour of Athens is complete without a stroll down the two one-way main streets of the modern city, Stadiou and Venezelou, and a coffee in one of the two main squares, Omonia and Syntagma. The latter is the modern centre of Athens and contains two of its plushiest hotels, the Grande Bretagne and King George as well as the Parliament buildings on the north side guarded by the evzones in their woolly uniforms. Beyond that is the National Park Gardens for a cool walk or rest from the frenzy and delights of the rest of the city.

If you just want a drink in a spectacular setting take the funicular up Lycabettus hill or try the rooftop bar of the Hilton Hotel.

Shopping and souvenirs

The Oxford Street of Athens is Stadiou Street. Department stores, fashion and jewellery shops and souvenir shops are all within easy walking distance of Syntagma Square, while cheaper versions of the same thing including Prisunic are closer to Omonia.

Mitropoleos is the best place to start looking for a flokati dyed wool rug, jewellery, furs or icons, but to find bargains and shops of a more ethnic nature you have to plunge into the 'Flea Market' of Athinas Street towards Monastiraki metro station. It only really lives up to its name at the weekend when it is taken over by antiques, copperware and miscellaneous junk, but during the week is the scene of a colourful food and drink market around the middle of Athinas and a great hunting ground for handicrafts around Pandrossou Street.

The food market is the place to buy herbs, olives, nuts, pickles, honey and fruit and around it are some of the cheapest wine and liquor shops in the world. You can buy by the bottle or bring in bottles to be filled by hoses connected to authentic oak barrels around the walls.

Pandrossou and streets and squares around it are lined with shops selling

Greek rugs, pottery, kebab skewers, worry beads, goat bells, woven bags, olive wood dishes and sandals. Leather, hand-made sandals are a speciality of Pandrossou and likely to be a bargain. If not, haggle over the price since that is the custom in this area where handicrafts spill out on to the pavements as if to snare the unwary tourist.

You may also find a bargain here in flokati rugs, furs or a leather coat. The showrooms and warehouses of the merchants who bring in such goods from northern Greece lie along Ermou and around Monastiraki.

Shops are usually open from 8 am to 1.30 pm and again in the evening from 4.30 pm or 5.30 pm to 8.30 pm, but if you want an English language newspaper, a bar of chocolate, a postcard or a phone call, they can all be bought at the little kiosks that lie around the main squares and along the main Streets, which open all hours.

Banks open from 8 am to 2 pm to change money and traveller's cheques, which can also be changed at big hotels through the day. The National Bank of Greece in Syntagma also keeps longer hours up to 8 pm at night and is situated conveniently next door to the Athens office of the National Tourist office of Greece. That is the place for free maps of Athens, Greece, and the islands, and ferry and bus timetables.

Most of the big airlines, including Olympic and British Airways, are on the opposite side of Syntagma. The central OTE office for international telephone calls at normal rates (big hotels charge a fancy premium) is on Stadiou Street. All of Europe and North America can be dialled direct and there are English-speaking operators on overseas call lines.

Everything within central Athens is within an area about a mile long by 1½ miles wide and so it is possible to walk. Otherwise, take a trolley bus going in the right direction or hail a taxi. Both will be a lot cheaper for the distance than comparable transport abroad.

Worth visiting outside Athens

Visitors to Greece in the days before package tour flights to the islands used to hit Athens before they went anywhere else in Greece. The big jets flying to Corfu, Rhodes and Crete have changed all that, but Athens remains the obvious transit stop for virtually the whole country, thanks to regular buses and planes from Athens and ships from the port of Piraeus.

It still makes sense to spend a few days in the city and then go on to explore other parts of Greece. If you are bitten by the culture bug, and want to go on dipping into the past, you are within easy reach of the east coast of Attica, Delphi and the Peloponnese, which is a treasure house of ancient and Byzantine sites. You might also consider visiting the spectacular cliff monasteries of Meteora for a glimpse of Medieval religious Greece or the Pelion peninsular to see early 19th Century villages clinging to the steep wooded hillsides.

If you are dying for sea, sand and the simple life after a week or a few days in the city, you should take a ship or a plane to the islands. Internal flights from Athens airport are the most painless way to get to distant islands with airports – there are about 20 of them. Other islands, notably these near Athens in the Saronis Gulf and the Western Cyclades are best reached by ship or hydrofoil from the port of Piraeus, while a handful off the east coast of Attica like Kea, Andros, Evia and Skiros have easy bus and ship connections via Lavrion, Port Rafti, Rafina and Kimi.

Piraeus, The Port of Athens

The islands are Greece and many of them are easily visited from Athens or the mainland. No-one should visit the capital, even for a long weekend, without taking a bus or metro train to Piraeus and hopping on a boat or hydrofoil for a short visit to one of the nearby isles of the Saronic Gulf.

Piraeus is an experience in itself. It has been the port of Athens for 3,000 years and nowadays the two have sprawled so far that they have joined up in one big conurbation and it is impossible to know when you are passing from one place to the other.

Piraeus is like a seaside bus station. It serves nearly a hundred islands, some with several ships a day, so they are tooting their arrival and departure every five minutes and passengers are rushing everywhere with bags, cases, bundles of food and even livestock. As if it wasn't frantic enough, the quayside is thronged with ticket touts directing passengers to boats leaving in the next ten minutes, cars and buses coming and going, cake shops, restaurants and a full-scale food and clothing market all serving the mass of travellers passing through the port.

It is not a peaceful place to stay, though it can be an easy stopover for one night between one island ferry and another. You can eat well, but the nightlife is tawdry with many clip-joints serving the passing sea trade. Jolly good-time girls like the one played by

Melina Mercouri in 'Never on Sunday' are rare and would never dream of diving into Piraeus harbour as she did in the closing moments of the film for fear of being caked in oil.

Check shipping schedules carefully with more than one agency and then don't believe them, and you will not go far wrong. Greek ships rarely run on time. However, the most reliable and frequent are those serving the islands of the Saronic Gulf, which depart every 15 or 30 minutes and compete with regular hydrofoils from nearby Zea Marina.

Attica

Cape Sounion, at the end of the Attic Peninsular 70 kilometres from Athens, is a stunning sight with its fifth century BC temple of Poseidon perched on a promontory lauding it over the coast road and the ships passing on their way from Piraeus to the Aegean islands. On a clear day you can see the island of Kea from the temple and most days in Greece are clear.

It is a good idea, if possible, to go out by the winding coast road to see the Apollo Coast – as the tourist authorities named it many years ago – and to return by the country route via Markopoulo. The return trip is through the heart of the Attic wine country, where most of the retsina drunk in Greece is produced, and also gives a glimpse of wooded hillsides and olive groves which make a pleasant contrast with the steamy life of Athens.

North of the wine country and even closer to Athens lies the battlefield of Marathon, where a tiny Athenian army saw its finest hour sweeping the Persian hordes into the sea. There is a burial mound to the Athenians who died in the battle and a museum nearby, but this trip is more notable for the atmosphere of the plain rather than the mound or the pottery collection of the museum.

You can combine it with a visit to Vravron, or Brauron close to Markopoulo where the white columns of a temple of Artemis rise from an olive grove. It also has a museum and traces of the old town which gave ancient Athens leaders like Cimon and Pisistratus. Ramnous, north of Marathon, has a temple of Nemesis perched above the sea like the temple at Sounion, but not in the same state of preservation.

West of Athens lies Elefsis, sandwiched between the dull island of Salamis and the mainland steelworks, and just off the motorway. Extensive excavations have unveiled traces of the buildings where important mysteries or festivals took place in the ancient world. There is also Dafni, only 20 minutes from Athens, which has a pretty little 11th century monastery with icons and other Byzantine trappings.

Delphi

Delphi on the slopes of Mount Parnassus is one of the wonders of the ancient world. It used to be regarded as its centre because Apollo slew a dragon there and the most famous oracle of all time spoke forth from a dark cleft between two rocks which ultimately rise to 4,000 feet.

If you want to experience the ancient Greek world in all its mystery, art and atmosphere, this is a good place, rivalling the best that Athens and the Peloponnese can offer.

Delphi can be approached either by car ferry from the Peloponnese to the port of Itea and then a steep road by bus or taxi, or a long winding road

from Athens which passes through spectacular scenery, but takes over three hours. It can be done in a day, but if possible take two, stay overnight in the village and pause at Arachova and Ossios Loukas on the way.

The road from Athens goes via Thebes, which is a modern dusty town showing nothing of its ancient splendour. It then winds up into the mountains, passing herds of goats, rows of beehives and awesome drops. Arachova is a pretty terraced hill village built in tiers which is famous for its wines, flokati rugs, furs and blankets. Buses to Delphi invariably stop and the village is out to fleece the tourist, but even so there are bargains to be had there given time and patience.

The vale of the oracle at Delphi is a grassy amphitheatre overlooking the blue Gulf of Corinth with wooded hillsides stretching down to Itea on the coast and rocky outcrops reaching up to Mount Parnassus above. The modern village of Delphi, like Arachova, is out for the tourist trade. It swings with music summer and winter, and hotels and restaurants are built along the main street with views of the Gulf and charges to match, but it still beckons to visitors to stay at least one night. Some stay longer in winter when Delphi is base camp for skiers on Mount Parnassus, a 30 minute bus ride away.

You need an hour or two to look over the vale and soak up the atmosphere. To see the sanctuary of Apollo, the temple of Athena, the treasuries, the Sacred Way, stadium, theatre and museum, to drink at the Castalian Spring and to consult the oracle. It will grant you a vision more precious than that offered by modern fortune-tellers. If its predictions are ambiguous, they always were in the ancient world too.

Delphi's remains are rich, as befits a place that was funded by every city in the ancient world, and its setting is so breath-taking it can make you believe for a minute in the oracle and the old pantheistic religion. Its museum also has its quota of treasures, including the proud Delphic charioteer, whose face graces many postcards, and a set of Caryatids rivalling those in the Acropolis Museum in Athens which once supported roof of the Siphnian treasury.

A turn off the road between Athens and Delphi leads to another famous relic overlooking the Gulf of Corinth. The isolated monastery of Ossios Loukas is also set in magnificent mountain scenery and is one of the great Byzantine monuments in Greece. Two churches, the Katholikon and the Theotikon, nestle together. They have marble walls and splendid mosaics showing scenes from the Bible such as the Nativity, Baptism and the Crucifixion. The monastery was built in the 10th and 11th centuries, but is still occupied and maintained by a handful of monks who seem delighted to show it off to visitors and live happily side by side with a modern restaurant/hotel complex.

Meteora

The cliff monasteries of Meteora are about equidistant from Athens and Thessalonika on the road that crosses central Greece between Ioanina and Larissa. They are one of the wonders of the Mediaeval world and one of its minor mysteries.

How and why were they built on grey rock pinnacles like eagles' nests pointing to the sky? Legend says that they were founded by a monk who

flew up on the back of an eagle, but it is more likely that monks who lived in caves among the rocks retreated to the peaks to protect their treasures and their solitude from brigands and invaders like the Franks and the Turks.

The rocks are the Dolomites of Greece. You can see them from ten miles away in almost any direction as you approach along a winding mountain road via Metsovon or Trikala. Perched on their stubby peaks are more than thirty monasteries and hermitages, many of them inhabited and welcoming visitors, all of them defying gravity and the rules of architecture.

Meteora can be reached in a day from Athens, Thessalonika or Corfu, but it is a sweat. It is a best to stay overnight in nearby Kalambaka or Kastrika, honest hill towns offering simple hotels, restaurants with steaming pots displayed in their windows and bars frequented by men in baggy pants with shepherds' crooks. Take the early morning bus or walk to the foot of the Great Meteoro built around the middle of the 14th century and separated by a deep valley from the Varlaam Monastery. At that time of day the sun seems to bounce off the peaks and light up the scene like a film set, and in fact Meteora has starred in two or three thrillers, which have used its dramatic setting to good effect.

Originally entry was only by climbing a rope ladder or being hauled up in a basket, which ensured the monasteries security and isolation. In recent years they have been supplemented by steps carved in the rock and bridges, but heavy items are still hauled up by basket.

The monastery chapels are covered with icons and frescoes of early saints and martyrs, many suffering nasty mediaeval deaths and torture. Some are beheaded or stoned, others sliced to death, boiled alive or strangled with fine rope.

The four big monasteries, Great Meteoro, Varlaam, Agios Stefanos and Agia Triada, all have displays of parchment bibles, icons, wood carvings and religious clothing. Great Meteoro also has a grisly memento to the monks who toiled over the centuries to produce these beautiful things – a room full of skulls lit only by candles. Varlaam boasts a peaceful monastery garden. But the other two monasteries have more sense of isolation because they are off the main tourist track.

Women were not allowed into the monasteries in the early days. They are now, but only in long skirts, not trousers. Men must wear long trousers. The splendour of the scene and the holy atmosphere, is spoilt a little by big notices to that effect, entry fees for the big monasteries and tourist shops inside them.

Even so, the rock chimneys of Meteora transcend those drawbacks and look as if they might have been tailor-made by God for monastic communities to worship him in a remote part of central Greece. They have also guaranteed this remote region a rich tourist trade for the rest of time.

Peloponnese

If you have a keen sense of history, the best place to savour the ancient world in the whole of Greece is the Peloponnese. It is a mountainous and fertile part of the mainland, which has the feel of a separate island and has far more fascinating historical remains than both Athens and Crete put together. It also has great atmosphere.

The Argolid area in the east boasts the citadel and beehive tombs of Mycenae, the ancient cities of Corinth, Tiryns and Argos, the amphitheatre of Epidavros and the old town of Nafplion, all of which can be reached in a day trip from Athens. The western Peloponnese has Olympia, site of the early games, plus Nestor's palace at Pylos, and two well-preserved sites at Vassae and Ithomi.

Go south through moody Arcadia and you can see the Mediaeval splendour of Greece in the deserted villages of the Mani, the Byzantine city of Mystras, the old town of Monemvasia and the castles of Methoni and Mystras.

And it has spectacular places to stay, great beaches and better food and wine than Athens or any island. It is a place to stay in and tour around rather than just a place to visit from Athens, and is not hard to get to.

Regular buses run to all the main towns from Athens and hydrofoils that ply the Saronic Gulf go on to Monemvasia and Kythera. Kalamata in the southern Peloponnese has an airport, with regular flights from Athens and a growing number direct from Britain.

The Peloponnese, as its name suggests, is technically an island, but is has been made so by man and only since the late years of the 19th century when French engineers built the narrow, steep-sided Corinth Canal. In the old days, ships were dragged across the isthmus by rope along a runway of wooden blocks between the Saronic Gulf and the Gulf of Corinth to avoid the stormy, long journey around the feared capes of Matapan and Maleas.

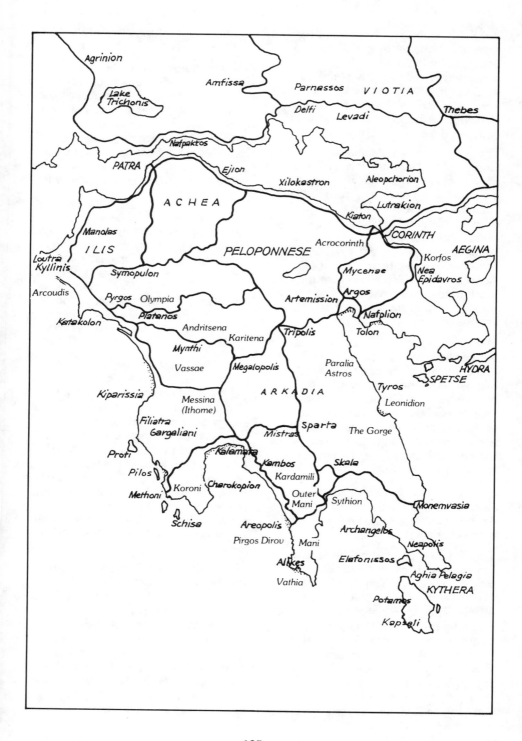

But the Peloponnese has always had a separate character from Athens and Attica, since the days when it contained proud rival city states such as Corinth, Sparta and Mycenae, which all ruled Greece for a time and challenged Athens at regular intervals between times.

The gateway to the Peloponnese is Corinth, a pleasant modern little town with seaside gardens a few miles from the canal and a few miles from the tall columns of ancient Corinth, which rise from an inland hill. They are the remains of a huge Doric temple of Apollo towering above the remains of a mainly Roman city at the foot of AcroCorinth, which had one of the most impregnable castles in Greece in the days of the Frankish and Venetian occupations.

Old Corinth is certainly worth a visit, but it is eclipsed by neighbouring Mycenae, half an hour or 45 kilometres to the south. This is the place where the German archaeologist Heinrich Schliemann discovered one of the wonders of the ancient world and the missing link between Greek legend and history when he opened a beehive tomb in 1882.

It contained the golden death mask of Agamemnon and led to other finds in a second beehive tomb next door and in the citadel up above.

The citadel is entered by the famous Lion gate and lies on a low hill giving a magnificent view down the Argive Plain to ancient sites at Argos and Tiryns. The old city of Mycenae is not brilliantly preserved, though you can clearly make out Agamemnon's throne room and palace, but the atmosphere is magic. If you climb the citadel early in the morning or at twilight, always the best time to visit ancient sites, you can imagine Agamemnon striding up the hill after his victorious return from the siege of Troy.

The next two ancient cities of the plain, Tiryns and Nemea, call for much imagination to be recognisable as such from the piles of old stones that remain, but they are notable as the birthplace of another legendary hero, Hercules, who must have been useful in their building. Argos and Epidavros, further down the plain, have more to offer.

Argos, which gave its name to the peninsular, is a dusty town nowadays, but the hill towering over the town has an impressive Frankish castle and at the foot are some interesting remains of the ancient city, mostly Roman, comprising a market place, odeon, baths and theatre, which is bigger than its more famous counterpart at nearby Epidavros.

However, Epidavros, set in a cool, green glade, is the best-preserved and the most famous ancient theatre in Greece. Built in the 4th century BC, it still gives regular shows of Greek dramas during a festival in the summer months and the acoustics are as good today as they were in the time of Alexander. If the site is not crowded, it is a good place to exercise your vocal cords, whispering a passage of Shakespeare to see if the sounds can be picked up easily by someone in the back row.

All the sites of the Argolid peninsular can be readily visited from Athens or from the isles of the Saronic Gulf such as Spetsai, Hydra or Poros. If you want to stay in this part of the Peloponnese while doing the sites good places are the pretty seaside resort of Tolon, which has a sand dune beach and boats running to two islands in the bay, or nearby Nafplion, which is well worth visiting anyway.

This bustling town at the top of the gulf was the capital of modern Greece for a few years after it first won its independence. It is dramatic in appearance with its houses tumbling down both sides of a steep hillside in tiers and its streets often giving way to steps, while the summit of the hill is crowned with a Venetian fortress set on a rocky headland. It has plenty of hotels and restaurants, regular buses to Athens, Mycenae, Argos and Epidavros, and also a swimmable pebble beach, but keen swimmers would be well-advised to take a bus 10 kilometres to Tolon for a better one.

South of Nafplion on the west side of the Argolikos Gulf lie a series of pretty seaside resorts with restaurants, rooms and beaches like Paraka, Astros, Agios Andreas and Tirou. Leonidon is a spectacular harbour and the gateway to one of the unsung wonders of the Peloponnese – a steep gorge running up to the plain of Sparta, containing pretty welcoming mountains villages.

The main site of Western Greece is Olympia, a few miles inland from the ugly town of Pyrgos. The sacred grove of the original Olympic Games – they are staged at Athens in modern Greece – is green and fertile and reminiscent of Delphi.

The layout of the site is well-preserved, though you have to use your imagination on the fallen columns to raise some of the buildings from the dead. You can still run or walk around the arenas where the athletes of the city states competed every four years, even when they were at war with each other. The games ran from 776 BC to 393 AD when a Roman Emperor ordered the sanctuary destroyed.

The inland road from Olympia to Kalamata, another sprawling

Peloponnesian town, passes through the wooded hills and valleys of Arcadia, where you can hear Pan playing his pipes if you strain hard enough, and it also connects with two other spectacular sites. The amphitheatre of Ithomi rivals that at Epidavros, not for its state of preservation or acoustics, but for its isolated setting amid grand hills and cypress trees. And the old town built by the Theban General Epamonidas in 368 BC as a bulwark against the Spartans is surrounded by huge walls 9 kilometres long which seem to stretch to the horizon. The Doric temple at Vassae is well-preserved and is a twin of the Parthenon in Athens. Again the setting is isolated and natural compared with the Athenian temples.

In recent years it has been encased in a tent to preserve it from the elements and it has a surrealistic appearance as you drive the 10 kilometres along the mountain road from Andretsina.

It is a good idea to combine visits to Ithomi and Vassae with one to Megalopolis, which lies between and boasts one of the biggest amphitheatres of the ancient world, now sadly covered in grass.

Pylos in the south-western Peloponnese, is a pretty little town with a Mediaeval castle looking out on the bay of Navarino where the combined fleets of Britain, Russia and France sank over 50 Turkish galleys in 1827 and helped set Greece on its way to independence. You can hire a boat to see the skeletons of the wrecks underwater in the bay.

It is also the legendary capital of Nestor, the wise old king who fought in the Trojan Wars and was visited by Telemachus seeking word of his father Odysseus. Sure enough an ancient palace has been found on a low hill 20 kilometres north of Pylos. It has a neat layout like that at Mycenae and boasts an old bathtub and jug for pouring in the water.

Pylos is a good place to stay with adequate swimming. So are Methoni and Koroni, on the same western peninsular of the three that hang down from the Peloponnese. Both have well-preserved Mediaeval castles and reasonable sandy beaches.

To savour the Mediaeval splendour of Greece, though, you have to travel through Tripolis and the modern town of Sparta – which curiously has scant remains of its premier place in the ancient world – to the nearby Byzantine city of Mystras just 3 miles from Sparta on the edge of the Taygetus Mountains.

It was launched by the Frankish prince, William Villehardouin, in 1249 when he built a fortress on the hill overlooking ancient Sparta, but brought to its magnificence by his Byzantine successors. They built a series of palaces, monasteries and churches, richly-bricked and frescoed on the hill site. At its peak in the 14th and 15th centuries the Byzantine city housed over 40,000 people and you can sense its glorious past strolling through the ruins today.

It is a strange sight in modern Greece and equally odd is the Mani region south of the Taygetus on the middle peninsular of the three that hang down from the Peloponnese. This is a haunting area of turreted villages set in wild, mountainous scenery between Gythion and Areopolis in the north and Gerolimin in the south. The villages and their watchtowers are largely deserted today and they stand as monuments to a feudal period when they were occupied by warring clans,

who built them up by night and pelted their enemies with stones by day.

They are gaunt, grey villages, overgrown with prickly pear and gnarled olive trees, and the nearby towns seem to match. The atmosphere is eerie and charged with a pregnant silence, broken occasionally by the barking of a dog or the braying of a donkey on the loose among or near the ruins.

It is a good area to motor through staying perhaps in Gythion, which is a colourful harbour town with good sandy beaches nearby.

A less gaunt, but prettier area is what is called 'the Outer Mani', between Kalamata and Areopolis, which contains pretty beach resorts at Kardamili, Stoupa and Agios Nikolaos. Also a good base for touring the Mani peninsular.

Be sure to visit Vathia, which the National Tourist Office has tried to preserve as a traditional settlement and guesthouse. Its towers rise like natural crags on a spectacular site overlooking the sea. Also make a stop at Pyrgos Dirou, where a path near the sea leads down to a labyrinth of natural caves festooned with stalactites and stalagmites which can be viewed from the comfort of a small boat. On the eastern peninsular, and reachable by ships and hydrofoils that run down the east side of the Peloponnese, lie the third wonder of the Mediaeval world in the southern Peloponnese, Monemvasia. It is an old Byzantine town of churches, houses and castle built on a rock in the sea and reached only by a narrow causeway. This is the Mont St Michel of Greece and has attracted a community of painters as well as summer visitors in recent years.

You can stay on the landward side of the town and swim from beaches either side, but it is best to eat in the town in the evening when its narrow winding streets are lit in a way that evokes something of its splendid past.

Two other splendid relics on the Medieval past are the villages of Karitena and Andretsina in the Western Peloponnese. The first is perched on a high rock with a castle on top, while the second is a jumbled delight of alleyways, plane trees, squares and some of the cheapest restaurants in the Peloponnese.

The Peloponnese is not famed for its beaches, but you can swim almost everywhere around its long coast – which is longer than that of Crete. Tolon in the east is a thriving beach resort with the usual modern accompaniment of windsurfing and water-skiing. Corinth and Porto Heli are two other centres in the east where you can find modern hotels and good beaches within convenient striking range of the sites of the Argolid peninsular. Costa, opposite the island of Spetse, also boasts a fine sandy beach.

Korfos is a quiet, get-away-from-it-all resort with rooms, restaurants and good swimming 30 kilometres south of Corinth. And there are plenty of small swimmable coves on the west side of the Argolikos Gulf south of Nafplion.

You can also find a superb sandy beach north of Neapolis and south of Monemvasia, opposite the island of Elafonissos.

In the west Koroni and Methoni both have sandy beaches and further north between Patras and Olympia there are a series of beautiful dune beaches all with names beginning with 'K'.

Katakolo, Kyparissia, Kyllini and Kolagria. Kyllini and nearby Loutra Kyllini have an easy ferry connection to the Ionian isles of Zante and Kefalonia.

The western coast of the Peloponnese is almost uninterrupted beach, as is the east side of the Messina peninsular between Koroni and Kalamata. Stay at Arcoudis just south of Loutra Kyllini, or Gialova in the bay of Pylos.

Halkidiki

East of Thessalonika and west of Turkey, northern Greece narrows into a thin strip of coastal plain with two big ports, Kavala and Alexandroupolis, and bulges out into the Aegean in a slanting three-pronged peninsular called Halkidiki. It looks a bit like a crab with three pincers, and also like a smaller version of the Peloponnese with two long inland lakes almost cutting off all land in the north to make it into an island.

Halkidiki is the outstanding holiday and beach area of mainland Greece. It cannot rival the Peloponnese for ancient sites, but it totally eclipses it for long sandy beaches and pretty ports, flanked by fertile meadows, pinewoods and grand hillsides. Strategically-placed hotel developments along all three of its prongs or peninsulars lay on watersports and other modern diversions without spoiling the intrinsic beauty of the area.

It has strong links with the Orthodox church, which took sanctuary on the eastern peninsular, Athos, for centuries of Turkish invasion, and with the Asian Greek community, settling many Greeks when they were thrown out of Turkey after the 1919–1922 war. This helps to account for the prosperity of the area and the use of the word 'Nea' ('New') in so many of the place names on the other two peninsulars, Kassandra and Sithonia.

Halkidiki's only drawback for the holidaymaker is that its position in mainland northern Greece cramps its hot season into four months, June to September, whereas Athens, Rhodes and Corfu bask in Mediterranean heat from April to the end of October.

Each of its three peninsulars have an island atmosphere not unlike that of Corfu or Rhodes and, in the best Greek tradition, each feels totally different from the other two. Kassandra in the west is the lowet peninsular, a land of low hills and meadows sweeping down to pretty ports in every bay. Sithonia in the middle is higher, grander and greener with fewer ports, yet it boasts the modern wonder of Porto Carras. Athos in the east is high, remote and rocky, a monastic republic culminating in a holy mountain nearly 7,000 feet high.

The National Tourist Organisation of Greece has sponsored dozens of hotels and campsites along the coasts of Kassandra and Sithonia, and northern Athos. Yet it has never become Greece's 'No 1 tourist resort' and it is still possible to find a beach to yourself in high summer.

No part of the peninsular is more than 150 kilometres from the main city of northern Greece, so it is the natural gateway to the area.

Thessalonika is about 3¼ hours' flying time from London, and 40 minutes from Athens. It also has good rail and bus links with Athens and rail to Western Europe. Onward coach or bus travel to the Halkidiki resorts then takes between 1½ and 3 hours,

allowing for the odd stop and roads that wind over mountains and around the bays of the peninsulars.

There is a Halkidiki bus service to all three peninsulars from Thessalonika with a stop just 2 kilometres down the road from Thessalonika Airport, and two good restaurants a few yards away, which can save the cost and hassle of a long taxi or bus ride into the bustle of the city.

The main bus routes from Thessalonika run either via Poligiros, the capital of Halkidiki 70 kilometres away with an archaeological museum and good views of the three-pronged peninsular, or via Arnea, a pretty hill village which does a big trade in mountain honey, flokati rugs and carved wooden walking sticks.

Apart from the main bus connections, which are not that frequent, local connections tend to be thin on the ground and it often pays to have your own transport, to take taxis, or to take boat trips to see more of this scenic area. It is a good area to sail around and big hotels and package tour companies usually lay on a selection of coach tours and boat trips to other beauty spots on the peninsular, to Mount Athos, Thessalonika and ancient sites like Pella, Vergina and Philippi.

Beaches

The beaches are Halkidiki's crowning glory. As you drive along the coast roads around any of the three peninsulars, they emerge one after another around each promontory. Sand sometimes gives way to pebble, notably on Athos, but the majority are long, golden and gently sloping as if made for easy bathing.

You can swim almost anywhere along

the coasts of Kassandra and Sithonia and along the coast road between Thessalonika and Kassandra, which runs past beach and campsite developments at Nea Epivates, Agia Triada, Nea Mihaniona and Epanomi almost as soon as it passes the airport.

The swimming is also good on the Athos peninsular up to the point where you hit the border of the monastic republic. The roads around each of the three peninsulars run conveniently around the coasts, so that access to beaches is no problem so long as you have transport.

The hotel developments and campsites that have sprung up over the past twenty years have all the water sports, tennis courts and beach activities that modern man could ask for, often including bicycles, small motor boats and yachts for hire. Kassandra has a string of big hotels like the Ammon Zeus, the Athos Palace, the Pallini Beach, the Alexander Beach, the Kassandra Palace and the Pella Hotel on its eastern shore and the Sani Beach and Mendi on its western shore. There are two more developments at Sermili and Gerakina Beach at the head of the Gulf of Kassandra, Sithonia has the big development of Porto Carras with its three hotels, the Meliton Beach, the Sithonia Beach and the Village Inn, and the north end of Athos has the Eagles Palace and the Xenia just outside Ouranoupolis.

Porto Carras has the best complex of tennis courts in Greece, including floodlit courts, and a well-watered 18-hole championship golf course.

The hotels have been sited along some of the best stretches of beach in Halkidiki, but any short trip along the coast will reveal many more swimmable coves.

Nea Moudania and Nea Kalikratia at the thin end of Kassandra have spectacular beaches, then the peninsular is reached through Potidea with its ancient canal which cuts the peninsular into a man-made island. There are beaches all the way down the eastern shore from Potidea to Hiroussou via Kalithea, Kriopigi and Pefkohori, while the loop road around the southern tip takes you to yet more on the western shore via Skioni, Possidi and Siviri to Sani Beach and Nea Fokea.

Sani has the best windsurfing scene and good sandy beaches either side of the big hotel, but Siviri is a pleasant little resort with good sand, Paliouri has an amazing curve of sand beside a landing stage for boats to the other peninsulars – though, curiously, no restaurant. One of the best stretches on the east coast is a long shingle beach stretching from Pefkohori up to Hanioti, arguably the best area to stay on Kassandra.

Sithonia's beaches start at the head of the Gulf at Gerakina and Sermili and run down the west coast to Nikita, Nea Marmaras, Porto Carras and Porto Koufo. Porto Carras alone claims 33 sandy coves at a distance of 100 kilometres from Thessalonika Airport and Port Koufo is a big enclosed harbour with a sandy beach running half the way around it. On the east coast of Sithonia there are more beaches in partially hidden coves at Kalamitsi, Sarti, Vrouvourou and Panagias.

But the most spectacular beach on the east coast of Sithonia is the long curved sweep of Sikia, 3 kilometres from the pretty inland village of the same name. It is a good place to stay for a few days because it also has easy access to the best west coast beaches between Toroni and Port Carras.

At the north end of the Athos peninsular Ierissos has a beach and Ouranopolis has two or three good stretches of sand snaking around towards the Eagles Palace Hotel, and more on a sprinkling of Caribbean-style offshore islands including Amouliani which can be reached and explored by tiny hired motor boats from the beach at Ouranopolis.

There are yet more good beaches on the east coast of Halkidiki at the pleasant little beach resorts of Staroni, Olymbiada, Stavros and Asprovalta.

Nightlife and dining out

In this area of Greece you can have a choice of nightlife in the West European mode, in nightclubs, bars and discos in the big hotels, and typical Greek nightlife, which is walking and dining out in the open air.

Most of the big hotels have bars, discos and smart restaurants, plus trips to a 'typical Greek taverna' with floorshow and 'authentic bouzouki music' and barbecues by the pool with live music.

But the prices will be on a par with those in Western Europe too and there is a lot to be said for going out for a typical Greek evening when you can 'do the town' for a fraction of the price a meal and drinks will cost in the hotel. You will certainly be able to view an impromptu display of mass walking and possibly join in impromptu dancing too if you pick a crowded square rather than a quiet back-street restaurant.

Nea Marmaras, Nea Fokea and Ouranopolis are three ports that teem with this kind of life and have amazing selections of bars and restaurants, while Porto Carras has its own smart, modern version of a Greek port where you can dine within view of millionare yachts and in company with their inhabitants for a modest premium over prices in Nea Marmaras a mile away.

In fact, the outdoor life at Porto Carras seems to have developed so well that it has smothered some of the indoor pursuits. Neither its much-vaunted casino nor its theatre were operating during a recent high summer visit.

There are some first-class fish restaurants in Halkidiki, by the harbours at Nea Fokea and Porto Koufo and Nea Mihaniona, which is halfway on the journey to and from Thessalonika and seems to have the biggest fishing fleet in these parts.

It has its own wine factory too at Chateau Carras, just beyond Port Carras where shipping millionaire John Carras has copied some French methods and is always open to visitors.

Not to be missed in Halkidiki

Northern Greece and Halkidiki have a powerful history, but not so many spectacular archaeological sites as the Peloponnese and Athens. However, there is enough in this area to keep history buffs happy for more than a day or two.

Halkidiki is known to be one of the oldest inhabited places in the world, thanks to finds in a cave at Petralona west of Poligiros and close to the road that runs down from Thessalonika to the Kassandra peninsular. Apart from its impressive stalactites and stalagmites, the cave boasts bones, primitive tools, traces of fire and the skull of a man estimated to be around 200,000 years old.

Santorini —
A volcanic view

KALYMNOS

"Pothia harbour by night.

N. EAST AEGEAN

A painter's scene: Molyvos
on Lesvos.

KOS

Panorama of the grand
harbour.

PELOPONNESE
A cut below the rest: the
steepsided Corinth Canal.

ATHENS

Mistress of all she surveys:
The Parthenon by day.

FROM ATHENS TO ZAKYNTHOS THE WIDEST SELECTION OF HOLIDAYS TO GREECE

For Summer no one offers a better selection of holidays to Greece than Thomson - a selection of islands and mainland areas from a range of 9 brochures. Something to suit all tastes. So whether you're looking for the classical splendours of Athens or the golden beaches of Zakynthos, Thomson has the Greek holiday for you.

There are 9 brochures to choose from offering everything from luxury hotels in "A La Carte" to the freedom of your own holiday home in "Villas & Apartments".

And for those who prefer to sample the truly Greek way of life, none could be better than Thomson Simply Greece - the no. 1 specialist to Greece.

So many islands .... so many holidays.

Let Thomson help you decide

"Where to go in Greece"

Simply Greece

Skytours

VILLAS AND APARTMENTS

Small & Friendly

AIR FARES

YOUNG AT HEART

A LA CARTE

Summer Sun

Winter Sun

 **THE NUMBER ONE SPECIALIST TO GREECE**

The Athos peninsular came into its own in the Persian wars. A storm off the peninsular sank Darius' fleet on its way towards central Greece in 492 BC. That persuaded his successor, Xerxes, to cut a canal for his fleet across the head of the peninsular between Ierissos and Tripiti when he invaded and you can still see clearly where the land is flattened across the neck of the peninsular to this day.

Northern Green has always been a rich mining and agricultural area, its broad plains fed by fast-flowing rivers from the northern hills. As a result, it became the heartland of Macedonia, ruled by Philip, who first united Greece by conquest in 338 BC, and his son, Alexander the Great, who conquered and ruled the known world from the Adriatic to the Indus over the next 15 years.

Little remains of important Macedonian towns like Olynthus and Potidea, except for the latter's ancient canal. Olynthus is a magnificent setting on a hill set back from the coast, but the remains are little more than piles of stones. Even Pella, the site of the royal palace where Philip ruled, Alexander was born and which served as the first capital of a united Greece, does not yet seem a major site and is a bit out of the way 30 miles north-west of Thessalonika. However, Pella is still being excavated and is worth visiting for its mosaics and what has emerged of the royal palace and state buildings of the old capital of Macedonia. Its tiny museum has one of the best-known and often reproduced mosaics of Dionysus riding a panther.

Philip chose to be buried 45 kilometres south-east of there at Vergina, a short way from the town of Veria and the ski resort of Mount Vermio, if

archaeologists are right about the rich royal tomb they found there with huge marble blocks and gold caskets. It is believed to be ancient Aigai, the early capital of Macedonia and its royal burial place. The gold caskets are now on display in the museum of Thessalonika, but visitors to Vergina can look over two large tombs, a Macedonian palace and a well-preserved ancient theatre.

The Royal Tomb has now been rebuilt under its original mound with large glass skylights to allow easier viewing of the underground system.

Thessalonika or Salonika was called after the sister of Alexander the Great and emerged around the end of the fourth century BC. It clearly flourished under the Romans after they annexed Macedonia in the second century BC. Their amazing walls still circle the modern capital of northern Greece and the second biggest city in the country. Its main monuments to Roman occupation are from the empire period, the Arch of Galerius resplendent with cavalry, elephants and chariots charging to victory against the Persians, the same emperor's mausoleum or Rotonda plus Roman baths, theatre and marketplace.

The city's charming little museum near the trade fair centre has Roman finds, but its true splendours are the finds from Vergina, especially the gold caskets bearing the star emblem of the Macedonian royal family, silver ornaments and massive iron armour, which is believed to have been Philip's.

East of Halkidiki is another important Roman site in northern Greece at Philippi 15 kilometres north of Kavala. Philippi was named after Philip, but flourished as a link town in the eastwards spread of the Roman world. It came to fame in 42 BC when Julius Caesar's assassins, Brutus and Cassius fought Mark Anthony and Octavian at Philippi. The battle settled the fate of the known world and laid the foundation stones of the Roman Empire. Philippi is an impressive Roman hill site with forum, theatre and the remains of two early Christian basilicas.

The apostle Paul visited Philippi, Kavala and Thessalonika, later writing an epistle to the Thessalonians.

Under the Roman occuption from 148 BC northern Greece enjoyed a rich Byzantine culture, despite constant invasions from the north, and it reached its peak in the 10th century when the first monasteries were established on the rocky shores of Mount Athos as refuges from invaders. The Orthodox church and the national spirit of Greece were kept alive in that mountain fastness during the later centuries of Turkish occupation and strangely respected by the Turks, who allowed Athos to develop first into a Holy Mountain and gradually into a monastic republic.

Thessalonika stayed under Turkish rule until it was liberated in the first skirmishes between Greece and Turkey in 1912–1913. More of northern Greece was won during World War One, but many of the present-day families of northern Greece did not settle the area until the 1919–1922 war, which resulted in the resettlement of 1½ million Greeks from Turkey. Hence names like Nea Moudania, Nea Marmaris and Nea Roda, which you find all over Halkidiki.

Halkidiki is a beautiful area to explore and has a network of good roads, which make it easy if you have a car or can find the right bus connections; many start from Thessalonika and most go back to Poligiros, the capital of Halkidiki. It is also easy to go by sea from one prong of the peninsular to another and most of the big hotels run boat excursions, which are well worth sampling.

If you have a car, a great drive is through the centre of Halkidiki via Poligiros and Arnea to the east coast around Olymbiada. The winding road runs through spectacular forests with chestnuts, pines and a wide variety of wild flowers and blossoms.

Kassandra's attractions are mainly its beaches and pine-fringed coves at places like Sani, Haniotis, Paliouri and Kriopigi, but it is worth visiting the ancient canal at Potidea and the cave at Petralona about 27 kilometres north. Nea Fokea has a Byzantine watchtower giving character to its waterfront and Kallithea the ruins of a temple of Zeus Ammon on its seashore.

Sithonia rivals Kassandra for beaches all the way from Pirkadikia at the head of the Gulf of Agiou Orous to Porto Koufo and Kalamitsi on the tip of peninsular. Porto Koufo has a good beach, but more besides as it is a calm harbour, nearly land-locked, which houses a sizeable fishing fleet and serves good fish at tavernas along the seashore.

Nea Marmaris is a delight of a port with three bays and dozens of restaurants, while nearby Port Carras is worth visiting to see Greece's answer to France's Port Grimaud and Spain's Porto Banus – a modern port complex with hotels, a yacht harbour, shops, restaurants and most sports from riding, tennis and golf to windsurfing and paragliding.

Sithonia also has a satellite isle called Diaporos off its east coast, which can be visited by boat from the peninsular opposite or on an excursion from the big hotels. It has lovely little inlet beaches and tiny satellite isles connected by shallow reefs to Diaporos.

Athos is the most dramatic peninsular and a must for visitors to Halkidiki. Ouranopolis (or 'city of the sky'), called after the Byzantine watchtower which rises over the harbour, has grown into a flourishing seaside resort with hotel, restaurants and watersports in recent years. It has good sandy beaches and many more are accessible by small hired motor boat on a series of offshore islands, including Amouliani, a dreamy place to stay, which can be reached by caique from the harbour three or four times a day.

Ouranopolis also has the easiest boat access to Europe's only monastic state and Greece's answer to Tibet and the Vatican – Mount Athos. It is possible to take boats from there and Ierissos to view the twenty monasteries from the sea, which is the only way women can see them. There are also boats from Ouranopolis to Daphne, the monastic state's only port halfway along the east coast of the peninsular.

Mount Athos

The monks' republic sits serene, remote and mysterious on the third prong of the trident that makes up Halkidiki, nestling beneath the holy mountain or Mount Athos, which reaches over 6,000 feet and often wears a halo of cloud. It is a treasure house of religious history with more relics of the New Testament story than are displayed in all the Catholic churches of Spain and Portugal.

The holy mountain is almost unknown outside Greece, seldom visited in the past, and only rarely filmed. It is a land locked in time, free from pesticides and cars, overgrown with trees and wild blossoms, and teeming with insects and butterflies. It is a marvel to view from the sea and etches deep in the memory of anyone who visits for a few days.

With biblical symmetry, each coast of the peninsular has ten monasteries clinging to its shore and rising from the rocks. Almost all of them can be viewed from the boats that run along the two coasts. This is just as well for half the human race because women and even female animals have been banned from the mountain for ten centuries, and boats with women on board have to stay 500 yards offshore. Even so, you often see a merry monk or hermit waving at boats from the seashore and the monks do have shore leave via Ouranopolis once in a while.

If you want to visit for a few days you need to be male and to have a visa from the Ministry of Foreign Affairs in Athens or the Ministry for Northern Greece in Thessalonika. You can then take a boat from Ouranopolis to Daphne. Remember that cine cameras, like women are forbidden.

The scene of departure for Athos is a strange one. Two boats stand at the quayside, one loaded entirely with men en route for Daphne, the other with both sexes, making a trip along the coast to view the monasteries from the sea. On the quayside stand a group of monastic widows, waving goodbye to their menfolk for anything from one to four days.

The boat to Daphne takes two hours with stops at monastery harbours on the way. Then comes a bone-shaking bus trip to Karye, the village capital of Mount Athos were the Greek visa is exchanged for a residence permit, to be handed over to the receptionist monk at each monastery visited. It bears the seal and stamps of Athos.

It is fascinating, and a little disturbing, to see how inflation and the march of tourism is changing Mount Athos. The rule is that only ten foreigners are allowed there at a time, but dozens take the boat some days and in high season one monastery alone had 35 visitors sleeping there, including 15 foreigners. The monasteries provide simple board and lodging without charge, and will even supply a basic packed lunch – maybe just bread and olives – to anyone taking the long haul around Mount Athos itself, which can involve walking five or six hours between monasteries. The average is nearer two hours.

The paths between are rough, varying from first-class riverbed to stony track and there is no transport, apart from a few boatmen who ply the coastal routes in summer. So you need a strong pair of shoes.

The welcome from the monks is always friendly, but the board and lodging can be spartan and the atmosphere far from relaxing. Mount Athos is no holiday camp.

Beds are in small dormitories and are hard. The sheets and blankets are not washed too often. Bathrooms are primitive and without toilet paper and mirrors. You can always recognise returning pilgrims by the stubble on their chins. Curfew is at dusk, the monastery gates are locked, and the only light for reading is a shared oil lamp.

Long before first light there is a dawn chorus of monks going to early services, summoned by bells and wooden drums at hourly intervals from around 3 am our time.

Mount Athos time is uncannily different. The day starts at dawn or dusk, depending on the monastery, and some ancient clocks stubbornly tick away their own time, which bears no relation to either the monastic schedule or the world outside. There is a charming vagueness about dates too. When I last visited Athos in mid-October my residence permit was stamped 'September 26.'

Breakfast is a small, simple, meal. Often coffee, water and a piece of turkish delight. Evening meals, taken just before dusk, do not go much further than a plate of beans or soup, bread and olives, spiced with a glass of thick, fruity monastery wine.

The culinary event of the day is lunch which can run to three courses with cheese and fruit. But it too is simple.

For the dedicated, this is a small price to pay for the freedom to wander for four days in a land locked in time – or different times – with no cars, TV or women to divert the mind and endless religious relics to see. The monasteries are like fortified museums teeming with frescoed chapels and row upon row of mediaeval icons.

In one I visited the monks jokingly referred to their refectory as 'the bank' and carefully locked it behind visitors. Its walls were covered with golden icons dating back to the 10th century, all numbered like those in the churches. There are no doubt rich men who wouldn't mind swopping their numbered bank accounts in Zurich for one of these.

The monasteries started in the 10th century, though there were hermits on Athos before that. They reached their zenith in the 16th century when there were 40,000 monks living in forty monasteries.

They survived plundering raids by the crusaders and by pirates and a surprising number were burnt down or swept away in landslides to be rebuilt on the same spot. They flourished during the long period of Turkish occupation as an outpost of free Orthodoxy and Greek thought, buying their independence with silver.

What the march of history could not destroy is now gradually being eroded by an understandable lack of enthusiasm on the part of Greek youth to submit to the monastic discipline and isolation. There are now upwards of 1,000 monks in twenty monasteries, including one Bulgarian, one Serbian and one Russian community.

A typical monastery resembles a small walled village with nine or ten separate churches and five-storey blocks of living quarters, but only twenty or thirty monks scattered about its spacious wings.

Every church is festooned with icons and greater treasures, such as pieces of the Holy Cross, solid gold bibles and pieces of clothing worn by the saints and Virgin Mary.

The Russian monastery, easily recognised by its green oriental bell towers and within easy walking distance of Daphne and Karye, claims to have the second biggest bell in the world. Cast in Moscow, it weighs in at 13,000 kilogrammes. Iviron, also close to the capital, boasts a solid silver lemon tree sent by the Tsar of Russia and a miraculous icon reputedly painted by one of the apostles, which fell in the sea on arrival at Mount Athos. One of the monks was given a special dispensation, so the story goes, to walk on the water to retrieve the floating treasure.

Wondrous tales abound for patient listeners, but they are sometimes hard to believe. I asked a dozen times to see the miraculous icon while staying at Iviron, but somehow was never understood, even though I pointed to pictures in the lobby showing a monk walking the waters bathed in a heavenly light.

Is it a legend or are the monks reluctant to unveil their holiest treasures for fear of unwanted publicity or theft? There have been cases of looting in recent years and the local police force is clearly not up to dealing with anything beyond a simple traffic accident or stamping papers.

The capital, Karye, is a pretty village with two small restaurants and two hostels. It also houses the Government building, where the council of monks meets, and Protaton church, which is richly frescoed.

The southern part, where the holy mountain slopes down to the sea, is a steep cliff where hermits and artists live. It is almost sheer and one look explains how the Persian invasion fleet was destroyed on the rocks in 483 BC. But there is a navigable track around the headland.

Athos is more than a giant museum of Greek religious history. It has a lush landscape, full of fruit trees and blossoms where insects fly free of the risk of insecticides, and a dramatic coastline with a monastery or church hanging over most large bays above white pebble beaches.

Worth visiting outside Halkidiki

Halkidiki is sandwiched between Thessalonika, the second biggest city in Greece, and Kavala, the grandest port of northern Greece. If you tire of beaches and yearn for something more urban for sight-seeing or shopping, a day trip to one of them makes good sense. Organised coach tours run to both places and there are also easy bus connections.

Thessalonika is a smart city with a university, wide streets and a port, rather like Athens and Piraeus rolled into one, though not so busy or frantic as its southern rivals and it has a cooler, wetter climate. Although the city was called after Alexander's half-sister, the big Macedonian sites are elsewhere, but the treasures of Vergina are in the city's small museum and there are Roman remains in evidence.

The modern city resembles a book opening on to the Gulf of Thermaikos. At its spine is the 15th century white tower and the black statue of Alexander on his horse. A rich residental and park area runs east and to the west lies the harbour, railway station, squares and hotels. It is usually easy to find a hotel room in Thessalonika, but book in advance if you plan to stay in September when the city's big trade fair fills the exhibition area in the middle of the city.

You can easily see the sights of Thessalonika in a day, including one or two of its fine Byzantine churches which date back as far as the 7th century, and leave enough time over for shopping and possibly a bus trip to Pella or Vergina.

Kavala is roughly equidistant from Halkidiki and the old Roman town of Phillipi is only a few kilometres from there. It is a pretty, bustling port teeming with fish restaurants and fishing boats nipping between flat ferries which run to the islands of Thassos and Limnos.

Peter Ustinov sold souvenirs on the quayside here in the film 'Topkapi' and it is a colourful port surrounded by an amphitheatre of buildings and crowned by a Byzantine castle and a Turkish aqueduct.

It is no great chore to drive to Kavala because the road is first-class and lined with good sandy beaches. Kavala has beaches of its own stretching from Kalamitsi in the west to Keramoti in the east.

Central Greece

This is a land of mountains, lakes and rivers, and some surprisingly big towns. It is a land that can be both wild and mysterious. No wonder the Ancient Greeks sited their oracles in these echoing hills and accredited the biggest of all, Mount Olympus, with the seat of the Gods. When the tips of the mountains are cloaked in cloud, you can see them still ruling and protecting all they survey. Something to think about when winter skiing at the tiny resort on Olympus.

The road network in central Greece is one of the best in the country, but beware of reading or trying to write postcards when travelling by bus. The roads wind and wriggle like snakes, twisting the intestines at every turn. There is plenty to see on and around the roads. Apart from spectacular scenery, you can spot some exotic wildlife; giant tortoises, birds of prey and storks, which rest on the steeples of churches as if they know they are on protected ground. If the fur shops are any guide, there are wolves here and there too. Everything is larger than life. On a scooter trip across Epirus from Corfu, I was surprised to feel the shadow of a small plane across my tiny vehicle. But I was not prepared to see a hungry-looking fish eagle with red beak and black and white markings, at least six-foot across the wings. He must have taken the scooter for a sheep in fourth gear and showed no fear as he landed on the road 20 yards away. There he stayed until thankfully an oncoming Metaxa lorry hooted him back into the air.

The first port on the west coast of central Greece is Igoumenitsa, a major ferry link with Italy and Corfu. Despite its role as a port, it is a delightful little seaside town with a long curving beach. Not at all a bad place to be marooned in for a few hours or overnight while waiting for a ferry or bus connection.

If you take the coast road south from Igoumenitsa, you soon hit the seaside resort of Parga, the jewel of western Greece. It has three sandy beaches on separate bays fringed by islands. Above each bay stands a castle, and Parga looks more like an island port than a mainland resort. It is a good place to linger in on this coast and the advent of tourism has brought good restaurants, wind surfing, discotheques and daily excursions to the isle of Paxos and to Necromanteion, the mythical entrance to the underworld.

The Necromanteion itself is a vaulted underground room where the oracles of the dead were pronounced. It is upstream from the pretty coastal village of Amoudia at the mouth of the River Acheron – the fabled river of the Underworld.

The entrance to Hades is the Gorge of the Acheron 20 miles upstream close

to the village of Gliki. There is a welcoming restaurant under the plane trees by the bridge for visitors who are not in too much of a hurry to reach the other side.

Further south the road forks inland for Arta, a pretty town boasting a 13th Century castle and church to match, and south for Preveza, the main port of Epirus with a ferry link across the straits and a right turn for the island of Lefkas, linked to the mainland by a narrow road along a causeway.

Messolonghi, on the mouth of the gulf of Patras, has a special place in modern Greek history, for its heroic role in the 19th Century War of Independence. Here the English poet, Byron, came with funds and new hope during a four-year siege. He died for the cause – from fever – and his statue stands proud in modern Messolonghi. The town is now approached over a lagoon, which serves as a fish hatchery and attracts storks to the town's rooftops. In every way this stretch of water gives Messolonghi character it might not otherwise have.

A prettier town in itself is Nafpaktos, on the north side of the Gulf of Corinth. It rises white from the blue sea with a harbour guarded by two Venetian towers and with passable stony beaches.

Halfway along the north shore of the Gulf lies the port of Itea, which can also be reached by ferry from the Peloponnese, by far the least painful route for visitors to Delphi. The alternative is a long winding bus or car journey from Athens, but with the compensation of some spectacular scenery on the way.

Back in Igoumenitsa, the other main road goes eastwards to Ioannina. Approached from the other direction or the air, this smart, bustling town can be seen at its best, reflected in the lake with its island in the foreground. The castle promontory of the self-seeking Turkish governor, Ali Pasha, looks like a second island. There is now a restaurant on the island and many more along the shore, where they serve frogs legs and eels and trout from the lake. You can wash these all down with sparkling Zitsa wine – the not-so-bad Greek answer to champagne. If you visit Zitsa itself, a few kilometres away, you will be treading in the footsteps of Byron, but don't expect a shrine or posh cafes.

A little further away to the south is Dodoni, site of the oldest oracle and best amphitheatre in Greece. Its magical setting is well worth a visit if you are in this area.

Half an hour north of Ioannina is a spectacular country of deep gorges and limestone cliffs called the Zagori or Zagorohoria, which is a national park containing 46 traditional villages with slate-roof houses, stone walls and frescoed churches.

The central feature of the area is the Vikos Gorge, sometimes called 'the Greek answer to the Grand Canyon', which boasts 3,000 foot rock walls and attracts organised hiking groups for holidays.

The Vikos Gorge links up around a dozen villages. It is carpeted with wild flowers including cyclamens, crocuses and helibores.

The best way to see the gorge is to stay in one of the stunning villages on its lip and walk along it to another. The two most dramatic villages are Monodendri and Papingo. You can walk from Monodendri to Papingo in around 8 hours or do a round trip to a nearer village like Kipi or Koukouli in 6 or 7.

You need to be just average-fit to tackle the descent by steps into the gorge, which itself takes an hour, and to walk the riverbed, which is mostly dry in summer. But you do need to allow a little extra time for directions because signposts and good maps are extremely rare. Anyone who is daunted by the walking should still visit the villages and take a short walk of about 10 minutes from Monodendri to the monastery of Agia Paraskevi, which is perched on the lip of the gorge.

Epirus is not short of beaches. If you find Parga a trifle busy, try Sivota to the north, Amoudia to the south or – if you really want a long sandy stretch of beach to yourself – a magnificent stretch of around 20 kilometres that reaches from Preveza past Kanali to Riza. There are some lovely little beach hotels and welcoming restaurants near Kanali.

This province also has a spectacular old Roman town in Nikopolis 7 kilometres east of Preveza along the land-locked Gulf of Ambracia or Aktion, which sometimes doubles for the name of the airport.

Nikopolis was built by Octavian when he became the Emperor Augustus to celebrate his victory over the combined fleet of Anthony and Cleopatra at the battle of Actium in 31 BC and literally means 'Victory City'.

The original town stretched for miles and the ruins still do. If this makes them a little hard to appreciate, at least take a long look at the walls, the baths, the early Christian churches and the massive amphitheatre and stadium site for some idea of the power that once ruled the known world in the name of Rome.

The Far North

The mountainous far north of Greece, west of Salonica, is an area few tourists penetrate by choice, though some encounter it when coming into Greece from Yugoslavia. The most spectacular town of the area, and the most colourful to stay in, is the fur-making centre of Kastoria, built on a peninsula bounded on two sides by a lake, which the locals fish from oblong punts. The lake is lined by tall houses with wooden bays projecting over the water.

In summer it becomes the 'Greek Lake District' between Kastoria and Edessa, a bustling town with canals and parks set on a high cliff, where the canals gather into two mighty waterfalls that shoot out on to the valley below.

Naoussa is the wine centre of the north and two or three of its wine factories, including that of Boutari, throw open their doors to visitors. Three kilometres down the road at Lefkadia are two of the best-known Macedonian tombs to rival that of Philip at Vergina, which lies 15 kilometres to the south beyond Veria.

Visitors with cars can do a pleasant round tour west of Thessalonika, taking in Pella, Edessa, Naoussa, Lefkadia and Vergina, which can be extended for another day by taking in the lakes between Edessa and Kastoria. A good place to stay on the coast south of Thessalonika is the tiny seaside resort of Makrigialos, which has a couple of hotels, a strip of restaurants and a passable beach.

Campers or motorists staying along the coast between Platamonas and Paralia must be tempted to try to climb Mount Olympus and commune with some of the world's most ancient gods. They should be warned that the peak is 9,500 feet above sea level, is permanently snow-capped and the last 2,000 feet is strictly for rock climbers with ropes and ice-picks. You can, however, climb 3,600 feet up by car, driving along a winding road via Litochoro and the Dionysius monastery – called after the Athenian friend of St Paul, not the god – to a spectacular little camp site and cafe, where the mountains provide shelter from the winds and there are mules for hire for the next stage of the ascent. That goes up a rough path nearly 4,000 feet to an Alpine Federation hostel, bookable from Litochoro. This site sits proudly at the base of Zeus' throne, a huge curved basin of scree stretching up to the celestial summit. It is a hard climb, but the views and atmosphere are ample reward. The whole journey can be made by the fit in a day from the coast.

Pelion

Pelion is a peninsular paradise hanging from Volos, halfway between Athens and Thessalonika, which has something of the feel of an island and is unique on the mainland.

It is wooded and hilly, rising as high as 5,500 feet on Mount Pelion above Volos, and abounds with streams, flowers, fruit trees, birdsong and beautiful 18th century villages. They have grand squares shaded by plane trees, winding cobblestone streets and tall stone mansions with painted wooden windows, coats of arms and grey slate roofs.

Pelion also boasts a better selection of sandy beaches than you find on most islands and a good variety of swimming on both sides of the peninsular. The beach resorts of the limpid Pagassitic Gulf on the west coast, like Kala Nera, Afissos, Kalamos, Horto, Koukouleika and Milina, offer swimming in calm lagoon-like waters. Those of the exposed east coast like Korefto, Mylopotamos, Agios Ioannis and Platania, often have surf.

The best way to see Pelion is by car. Volos, which is the gateway to the peninsular, has no civil airport, though you can travel there by rail. Alas, the picturesque little mountain railway, which used to run from Volos to Milies, stopped running in the early 1970's and can only be used as a scenic footpath nowadays.

Volos is about 5 hours' motoring from Athens by the national highway and a little longer if you take the scenic route via the long island of Evia.

Motoring through Pelion in the summer and autumn is akin to touring a giant orchard. Apples, pears, chestnuts and peaches rain down on the roads between its spectacular hill villages.

If there are just six showpiece villages, they are Makrynitsa and Portaria just above Volos, with panoramic views of the city, Milies and Vizitsa overlooking the Pagassitic Gulf above the beach resorts of Kata Nera and Afissos, and Zagora and Tsangarada, which are conveniently situated above the beach resorts of Korefto, Agios Ioannis and Mylopotamos.

Mylopotamos is a dramatic little sand beach between two rocks where big waves keep the shore clean, while Agios Ioannis is a developing resort with a strip of hotels and restaurants and a good sand beach. The most homely seaside resort is the rather strung-out village of Korefto, which has good, modestly-priced eating and rooms to match.

Everywhere there seems to be a perfect combination of stunning hillside villages to visit and eat in, and a beachside resort to stay and swim in. Afissos is a perfect base for the whole peninsular, though afficionados of old buildings should think of staying one night in either Makrynitsa or Vizitsa in one of the hostels restored from a 200-year old mansion. It is not that cheap, but it is comfortable.

The architecture is a northern Greek style, which survived in a pure form in the remote, high villages of Pelion when it became a refuge for patriots fleeing the Turkish occupation. The churches are different too; white squat structures with wooden cloisters, separate bell towers and wide courtyards.

These villages have good restaurants in spectacular settings, serving a wide variety of herby stews and bubbling local wine. Try the station restaurant at Milies, where the old railway line used to terminate, or one of the eateries in the main square of Zagora.

The two sides of the peninsular are connected by a good road, climbing in hairpin bends across the spine of the peninsular through Hania, which doubles as a ski resort in winter. It is a touristy place with more souvenir shops than all the rest of Pelion, but stop for a yoghurt and honey.

The eastern shore is different in character because the pine and chestnut trees thin out to expose open countryside not unlike parts of Britain. Platania at the tip has good sands, rooms and restaurant and an occasional boat to Skiathos.

The easy way to the Sporades islands, though, is via ship or hydrofoil from Volos. It is a busy commercial port and not a place to linger for long. Its main claim to fame is that it is the gateway to Pelion.

13. Shopping and Souvenirs

People don't go to Greece for a shopping expedition as they might to London, Paris or the Far East. Yet, it is stacked out with souvenir shops winking with bright colours and only the most insensitive or world-weary will pass them all by.

So long as you keep a completely cool head, inspect a few shops before you make up your mind and then buy only what you really want, you may end up with some treasures and a few bargains.

There is a temptation to buy the first painted heroic plate, icon, or rug for the wall at home because it looks such a beautiful piece of art, until you see the 300th such item and realise they are the height of Greek kitsch and no longer look faintly attractive. Sponges, Greek-pattern shirts and dresses and worry beads all have local appeal too, but will you ever use them at home?

Most of the best buys in Greece are outside the souvenir shops in specialist food, drink, fur, pottery, leather, jewellery, hardware and clothing shops.

You will never go wrong buying olives. Or olive oil, especially the dark green unrefined variety that is sold neat from a barrel. It is the best in the world. So is much of the local fruit, melons, peaches, grapes and the like, though they may not travel well. Greece is one of the great aromatic countries of the world and herbs sold in food shops or supermarkets are worth buying if

you can't find your own crop on a scented hillside. So are nuts and Greek (or Turkish) delight.

Local wines are surprisingly cheap and good on big wine-producing islands like Crete, Rhodes, Samos, Kos, Kefalonia and Paros. And on the mainland in the vicinity of Athens, Salonica, Patras or Porto Carras, which are all major wine-producing centres.

If you buy in a shop rather than at the airport, you can almost double your duty-free allowance. Wines from around 400 drachmas are great bargains. This includes retsina which travels and keeps perfectly, just as it was designed to. Brandy, ouzo, liqueurs and gin, from 900 drachmas a bottle are also amazingly inexpensive. Cigarettes are similarly cheap if you can take the harsh taste, which is somehow never so appealing once back in Britain.

Fur rugs and coats, made mainly in the north around Kastoria, are best bought in a fashionable shop, or other sophisticated centres like Rhodes and Mykonos. There you can get a cut to match the skin and not end up looking like an overfed bear.

The same rule goes for pottery, jewellery and leather, although many islands have specialist local potters, who have always made cooking and fancy pots for local consumption.

Greek jewellery, whether silver, gold

or simple costume, is up with international standards and rarely overpriced, though that does not mean local shops will drop below the international gold price. In the hardware shops there are some good buys in local lamps, Greek coffee pots and ornamental kebab skewers and, on the islands, the same shops will stock local snorkelling and spear-fishing equipment at much lower prices than Regent Street or Fifth Avenue.

Greek clothing is not always high fashion, but you can find light cotton dresses and patterned headsquares which are ideal for the climate, don't look out of place at summer parties back home and cost less than Woolworth's. Men can usually find denim shorts that fit and are cheap, though they can shrink on their first wash.

Corfu is the Olive isle and olivewood bowls, trays and plates are as good there as anywhere.

It is also a fertile island abounding in food and drink products. It hardly makes sense to bring back yoghurt, but local honey is delicious. So are Loukoumi (Turkish delight elsewhere), nuts, olives and crystallised fruits. Corfiot olive oil has to rank among the best in the world, especially the dark green kind that you can't buy in Western Europe.

Corfu has its own wines and liqueurs, including Koum Kouat, made from tiny Oriental oranges, but try it locally before buying a bottle as it is very, very sweet.

Local sandals, boots and locally-woven cloth are all worth looking out for. Sandals and boots are often made by the shoe-maker on the premises and you can have a pair made to order,

especially on big islands like Crete, Paros and Corfu.

Hand-knitted island sweaters are another item worth hunting down. Most of the Cyclades stock them the year round as a natural protection against the driving winds that hit the islands in both mid-summer and mid-winter. They also stock thick fishermen's vests, which have been taken up as high fashion items by many visitors to the Greek islands in recent years.

Mykonos has a whole horseshoe-shaped street of shops selling smart furs, leather jackets and high fashion clothes beside the standard island sweaters and sandals.

Fur never comes cheap, but you are likely to get a better bargain in Rhodes than anywhere in Western Europe, thanks to its duty-free status and the hot competition between different shops to drive a bargain. You may also find the fit on the generous side, though, to suit a fuller Greek figure, so don't be in a hurry to buy until you find the cut that is right for you.

The same goes for handbags and high fringed boots, which are a speciality of the village of Archangelos and stand in rows along the village street there. They are sometimes called 'snake boots'.

When it comes to handicrafts you have to look at Rhodian pottery – jugs, bowls, plates, plant pot covers, tiles and drink coasters decorated with fish, flowers, trees, ships and mermaids. In fact, after being on the island for a week or two you certainly will have done because there are pottery factories along the main roads and stalls selling it everywhere including Lindos.

Tour buses regularly make stops at

one or more pottery workshops or factories. But it is probably better to buy in town where there is a wider selection and you might be able to bargain more than at the factory.

Much of the pottery is made around Lindos and the same town specialises in lacework table cloths, shawls and table mats. Again you should cast your eye around a good selection rather than jump at one hung outside a house on the main donkey steps winding through Lindos Town.

Rugs are a tricky subject. There are some beauties in skin and wool, notably the flokatis which have featured in Sunday colour mags in recent years. But they can be as dear in Greece as in Britain. The only golden rule is to know what one is worth to you and bargain like crazy for the right price. Or settle for a woven bag.

You can't bargain at the kiosks. Found everywhere, these are a unique Greek invention, open far beyond the usual morning and evening shopping hours, and seem to stock everything you might need urgently, from a ball-point pen to a stamp, a sticking plaster, a telephone, newspaper and sun-glasses.

14. Eating and Drinking

A typical meal in the Greek islands is skewered kebab or souvlakia accompanied by a Greek salad of tomatoes and cucumber topped with feta cheese and black olives. This is true whether you choose to eat in a pistaria (or grill house) or a conventional restaurant.

But in any restaurant in a town or port you will find pre-cooked alternatives like stuffed tomatoes, moussaka, keftedes or meat balls, vegetables in oil and soups. In any restaurant within a mile or two of the sea you are almost certain to be offered fish, most commonly fried squid, grilled marithes or whitebait and barbounia or red mullet.

There is likely to be a sprinkling of Italian dishes too, especially spaghetti and increasingly pizza, reflecting the tastes of the islands' medieval occupants. Chicken and omelettes are also available in most places.

First-time visitors tend to jump at fish when it is offered, and it can be a good choice when it is genuinely fresh and not over-priced, but it pays to check on both points before ordering, remembering that fish kept in a deep freeze for weeks is not fresh and you should not pay £5 a plate when you should be paying £1 or £2. Fish can be the big rip-off of restaurants throughout Greece.

Better to stick to chicken and omelettes, which are always made from fresh ingredients with a natural flavour that you never find in Western Europe rather than be lured into an expensive, disappointing fish dish simply because the sea breeze is blowing and you are watching a marvellous Mediterranean sunset.

The best place to eat fish is where it is a speciality like a harbourside restaurant where the catch comes in each day or a small beach taverna run by a fisherman's family. In the same way, the best and cheapest places to eat souvlakia or kebab are the specialist grill houses or pistarias you find in the most big ports.

Greeks usually drink either retsina, the ubiquitous resinated wine, or beer with such meals, but there is often a local wine available on the big islands.

There are also plenty of snacks eaten in other places that make a good supplement to or substitute for a full meal if the weather is hot. Most islands have yoghurt, which is especially delicious with honey. Many of the islands have local honey.

Cheese and olives also make a great snack, whether it is the ubiquitous feta or goat's cheese, graviera or Greek gruyere, or local cheeses like the superb mizithra, a soft white cheese found in central Crete.

Whatever island you are on, try seasonal fruits like strawberries, peaches, apricots, oranges, melon and grapes. Greece has some of the best fruit in the world and the islands are no exception.

MENU

ΤΙΜΟΚΑΤΑΛΟΓΟΣ

Κατάστημα ΕΣΤΙΑΤΟΡΙΟ – ΨΗΣΤΑΡΙΑ ΛΙΑ
ΠΙΤΣΑΡΙΑ – ΚΑΦΕΤΕΡΙΑ

Greek	English	χωρίς φπά	με φπά
Κουβέρ	Couvert		100
Ψωμί	Bread		100
ΟΡΕΚΤΙΚΑ	**STARTERS**		
Ελιές	Olives		350
Ρώσικη σαλάτα	Russian salad		350
Ταραμοσαλάτα	Tarama salad		350
Μελιτζανοσαλάτα	Eggplant salad		350
Τζατζίκι	Tzatziki		350
Σκορδαλιά	Garlic sauce		350
Πιπεριές	Green peppers		500
Ντολμάδες	Stuffed vine-leaves		500
Τυροπιτάκια	Cheese pie		300
Τυρσοαλατα τηγ	Cheese Salad		
πατατες τηγ	French Fries		350
Κολοκάκια τηγ	Marrow Fries	600	
Παπουτσάκια τηγ	Potato Pack	600	
Ποικιλία	Variety	1600	
ΠΙΤΣΑ	**PIZZA**		
ΠΙΤΣΑ ΚΑΘΙΕΛΗ PIZZA – κατσινα			
ΖΥΜΑΡΙΚΑ	**PASTES**		
Μακαρόνια με σάλτσα	Spaghetti Napoliten		600
Μακαρόνια με κιμά	Spaghetti Bolognese		800
Παστίτσιο	Pastizzo		900
Πιλάφι	Rice		500
ΛΑΔΕΡΑ	**COOKED IN OIL**		
Ντοματες γεμιστές	Stuffed tomatoes		800
Φασολάκια	Green beans		600
Μπάμιες	Okra		
Αρακάς	Green pees		
Γίγαντες	Beans		
ΚΙΜΑΔΕΣ	**MINCED MEATS**		
Μουσακάς	Moussakas		900
Μελιτζάνες παπουτσάκια	Aubergines special		900
Κεφτέδες	Meat balls		900

ΠΙΑΤΟ ΗΜΕΡΑΣ	DISH OF THE DAY	χωρίς φπά	με φπά
ΚΥΡΙΑ ΦΑΓΗΤΑ	**MAIN DISHES**		
Μοσχάρι κοκκινιστό	Veal with tomato sauce		1100
· με πατάτες	· with potatoes		1100
· με πιλάφι	· with rice		1100
Μοσχάρι στιφάδο	Veal stew with onions		
Αρνί γιουβέτσι	Lamb with pasta		
Αρνί φρικασέ	Lamb with lettuces		1100
Κοτόπουλο κοκκινιστό	Chicken with tomato sauce		1000
Κοτόπουλο	Chicken		1100
κοτόπουλο πανέ	Meriland Chicken		1200
ΨΗΤΑ	**ROASTS**		
Μοσχάρι	Veal		
Αρνί	Lamb		
Χοιρινό	Pork		
ψητό κατσίκας	Roast beef	1600	
ΤΗΣ ΩΡΑΣ	**GRILLED**		
Μπον φιλέ	Fillet steak		1500
Παϊδάκια	Lamb chops		1300
Μπριζόλες μοσχαρίσιες	Veal steak		1200
Μπριζόλες χοιρινές	Pork chops		1100
Σουβλάκι	Souvlaki		
Συκωτι σχάρας	Grilled liver		900
Μπιφτέκια	Beef burgers		
ΨΑΡΙΑ	**FISH**		
Γαρίδες	Shrimps		
Καλαμαράκια	Squids		
Μπαρμπούνια *	Red mullets		1800
Αθερίνα *	Mullets		900
Τσιπούρες *	Tsipoura		
Συναγρίδα *	Gurnet		
Σφυρίδα *	Red snapper		
Γλώσσα	Sole		
Γάλεος τηγανητός	Fried galeos		1100
ΣΑΡΔΙΝΑ	SARDINA		

ΜΑΡΙΔΑΚΙ	1000
ΚΟΛΙΟΣ	1000
ΧΤΑΠΟΔΙ – ΟCTAPUS	1100
ΓΑΒΡΟΣ	
ΞΙΦΙΑΣ	
ΣΑΡΔΕΛΛΕΣ	
ΑΣΤΑΚΟΣ *	

ΣΑΛΑΤΕΣ	SALADS	χωρίς φπά	με φπά
Σαλάτα εποχής	Season's salad		
Τοματοσαλάτα	Tomato salad		
Αγγουροτομάτα	Cucumber-Tomato salad		
Χωριάτικη	Greek salad		
Χόρτα	Vegetables		
Λάχανο	Cabbage		
Μαρούλι	Lettuce		
ΤΥΡΙΑ	**CHEESES**		
Φέτα	Feta		300
Κασέρι	Kasseri		
Γραβιέρα	Gruyere		500
Γιαουρτ-Μέλι	Yoghurt-HONEY		
ΦΡΟΥΤΑ	**FRUITS**		
Μήλα	Apples		
Πορτοκάλια	Oranges		
Αχλάδια	Pears		
Καρπούζι	Water melon		
Πεπόνι	Melon		
Σταφύλια	Grapes		
Ροδάκινα	Peaches		
ΓΛΥΚΑ	**SWEETS**		
Κρεμ καραμελέ	Cream caramel		300
Κανταΐφι	Kataifi		400
Μπακλαβάς	Baklavas		400
ΑΝΑΨΥΚΤΙΚΑ	**REFRESHMENTS**		
Λεμονάδα	Lemonade		200
Πορτοκαλάδα	Orangeade		200
Κόκα-κόλα	Coca-Cola		200
Σέβεν Απ	Seven Up		200
Σόδα	Soda water		200
Εμφιαλ. νερό	Mineral water		200
TONIC	TONIC-WATER		

ΚΡΑΣΙΑ	WINES	χωρίς φπά	με φπά
RETSINA LEFKAS 375ml			650
» » 750ml			1200
CAMBAS 750 ml			1200
CAVA LOGOTHETIS 750 ml			1800
VERTZAMO 375 ml			650
VERTZAMO 750 ml			1200
ICANTALI ΑΓΙΩΡΓΙΤΙΚΟ			2200
ICANTALI ΜΑΚΕΔΟΝΙΚΟ			2200
LAC DES ROCHES			1500
ΛΑΥΚΟ ΛΕΥΚΑΔΟΣ			550
RETSINA CAMBAS			1200
ΜΠΥΡΕΣ	**BEERS**		
AMSTEL 500 ml			300
HEINEKEN 500 ml			350
HOLSTEN 375 ml			350
ΠΟΤΑ	**DRINKS**		
ΟΥΖΟ ΠΟΤΗΡΙ	OUZO - GLASS		250
ΟΥΖΑΚΙ	OUZO - BOTTLE		600
ΚΑΦΕΔΕΣ	**COFFEES**		
ΚΑΦΕΣ ΦΡΑΠΕ	CAFE FRAPE		300
ΝΕΣ ΚΑΦΕ	NES CAFE		200
ΕΛΛΗΝΙΚΟ	GREEK COFFEE		300
ΕΣΠΡΕΣΣΟ	ESPRESSO		300
ΚΑΠΟΥΤΣΙΝΟ	CAPUCCINO		300

Υπεύθυνος σύμφωνα με το νόμο

Το κατάστημα υπόκειται σε αγορονομικό έλεγχο ως προς τις τιμές
Prices are subject to police control.

Greek food is loved by some and hated by others. They slate it for its lack of variety, over-use of olive oil, and being served lukewarm. You even hear people say: 'I would go to Greece but for the food. And the wine tastes like disinfectant.'

They have either suffered too much of the bland international package tour food served up by some hotels, or they have not taken the trouble to explore Greek food and wine carefully. An average Greek menu contains a vast variety of dishes and wines. They are pure and healthy, free from cloying preservative and, like so many of the best things in life, improve on acquaintance.

They suit the climate and convey an unusual sense of luxury for a modest price because in Greece you can eat out in the open air and that much closer to nature, including the fields where the food was raised or the sea where it was caught.

Look at the menu illustrated in this book. It immediately tells you four things. It is in two languages – Greek and English. There is a huge variety of dishes, in a dozen different categories. Most of them are amazingly cheap, taking the drachma at 350 to the pound for easy reckoning and the second price column, which includes service. And the most expensive items are fish, which is often priced per kilo.

Clearly it pays to explore the menu rather than jumping at the first thing offered, which is often fish and is often a rip-off in tourist areas. If there is no written menu, have a look around the kitchen, which is an accepted custom in Greece, or examine the glass-fronted refrigerator in front of the kitchen, which is a standard item in Greek restaurants.

Order there and then, because service can be slow if you are too shy to follow the Mediterranean custom of waving and shouting at the waiter to attract his attention.

Appetizers or starters: These are a mixture of dips like taramosalata (cod's roe), tsajiki (garlic, yoghurt and cucumber) and melitzanasalata (aubergine), soups, which are often more like a stew, and octopus, which is strictly an acquired taste. The first thing to try are the dips, eaten with bread.

Pasta: A legacy of the Italian occupations of Greece, but not usually up to Italian standards.

Fish: Usually good and fresh, but usually expensive too, so tread warily. Greek lobster and shrimps are nothing special and can cost more than the same items in Western Europe without such good dressings. Red mullet is also dear for no good reason, but it is worth trying a small fish or two. Squid and small fish like whitebait, called marithes, are delicious and bargains. Swordfish is usually worth a small premium.

Vegetables cooked in oil: They are delicious when you have acquired the taste, especially beans, but are often served cold and are not the first thing to choose if you are new to Greek food. When you have been in the country a while, though, look out for fried aubergine and marrow.

Pre-prepared meat dishes: These can be delicious when you are used to the way they are cooked early in the day and served lukewarm later. Especially stuffed tomatoes, stuffed aubergines and moussaka.

Grills and A La Minute dishes: This is where people new to Greece should look for their main course, if they want meat because it will be served hot and freshly-cooked. Roast meat, like fish, is often charged by the kilo, but it is not so expensive. Chicken is always good in Greece because it is cheap, and is not reared in a factory and fed on fishmeal. Pork cops and skewered meat are also good buys.

Salads: These are another safe and rewarding area for people new to Greece, whether they fancy a plain tomato salad, plain cucumber or a Greek salad with onions, olives and chunks of cheese added. Don't expect to see lettuce, but try raw cabbage salad if you find it.

Cheese: The main Greek cheese is feta, which is goat cheese. It is rich and creamy, but can be strong for newcomers. There is often an alternative.

Fruits and desserts: Greek fruit is amazingly tasty, especially melon, watermelon, peaches, apricots and grapes, thanks to the climate and its freshness. Apples are the exception that taste better in Britain. Greek ice-cream is also superb, a legacy of the Italians that has lost nothing in the translation.

Drinks: You have probably never read a wine writer praising Greek wines and they are all too often associated with retsina, the golden wine which is laced with pine essence. Personally, I love it to death. It is the cheapest wine in Europe served in a restaurant for just over £1 a 500 centilitre bottle, and a perfect match for Greek food once you get to know it. But there are many other good wines, both local and national, which may better suit a new visitor.

Demestica from Patras comes red and white, is found almost everywhere in Greece and is moderately-priced. The same can be said of other brands like Kamba and Boutari. But be prepared to try local wines, especially on wine-producing islands like Kefalonia.

If you can get along with none of them, try beer, but make sure it is cold. Greek beer tends to be fizzy and chemical compared with English beers. Not a refreshing taste when warm. Greek mineral water is always good.

Ouzo, the aniseed spirit that resembles pernod and turns white in water, may be an acquired taste, but Greek brandy is acceptable to most tastes, so long as it is taken in sparing quantities.

You will not find them on many restaurant menus, but Greek restaurant and bars can turn out superb omelettes. They taste good because the eggs are fresh and they are cooked in olive oil. An omelette and sald with a bottle of wine followed by fresh fruit and coffee can be one of the most satisfying and healthy meals you can eat in the hot noon temperature of Greece.

Coffee is not on many restaurant menus either because it is usually served at separate bars, cafés, pastry shops and coffee houses. In fact drinking coffee is a great ritual in Greece. The standard cup looks like a thimble full of grounds laced with sugar to reduce its bitterness, which is exactly what it is, but is cheap and taken with a glass of water can be lingered over for hours. If you can't take it, ask for 'Nescafee' with milk, which is the standard expression for a big instant coffee.

It often makes sense when dining out in the evenings to eat a main course, or mixture of savoury dishes, in a restaurant and retire to a pastry parlour or cafe for dessert, coffee and after-dinner drinks. They serve some delicious treacly cakes with eastern names like baclava, kadifi, galaktoboureko and loukoumades, plus yoghurt and honey, chilled rice puddings and custards, but beware of fluffy cream cakes, which are all appearance and taste like cardboard.

It is easy to see that anyone can wine or dine in style in Greece on anything from one simple dish to a 12-course banquet. Either will be good value so long as it is eaten in a typical Greek restaurant.

Unfortunately, their prices bear no resemblance to those of some isolated package tour hotels, which can charge up to two or three times those in the town and turn out worse fare.

15. Helpful Hints

Customs
Visitors entering Greece face normal customs regulations on personal belongings and duty-free goods. When leaving Greece, the duty-free allowances for UK residents are like those for the rest of the EC area. If you can carry it, you can now bring back 10 cases of wine and 1 of spirits for your own consumption.
Cigarettes 300
Cigars 75
Tobacco 400 grams
Spirits 1½ litres
Wine 5 litres
Perfume 75 grams
As for souvenirs, you can take out virtually what you like, **except** for any antiquities or works of art (however small) found in Greece. The penalties for illegal export of antiquities are severe, and permits for export have to be obtained from the Archaeological Service, 13 Polygnotou Street, Athens, or the Ministry of Culture and Sciences.

Time change
Greek Standard Time is two hours ahead of GMT. Greek Summer Time corresponds almost exactly with British Summer Time (March–October) so the two-hour difference applies virtually all year round.

Information
On places, maps, accommodation and festivals. The National Tourist Organization of Greece (NTOG) is the most obvious source of further information. Its worldwide offices will provide leaflets and maps on individual regions, plus lists of all hotels down to C grade. Make use of it, too, for up-to-date information on travel, festivals, museums and special festivities.

Books
There are many books that have been written about Greece over the years. Everyone has their own tastes in travel literature, but in London, for a wide selection of books on Greece, we suggest you try the Hellenic Book Service, 91 Fortress Road, London NW5 Tel: 071-267-9499, Zeno Greek Bookshop, 6 Denmark Street, WC2. Tel: 071-836-2522 and Chapter Travel, 102 St John's Wood Terrace, NW8. Tel: 071-586-9451.

Addresses in Britain
National Tourist Organisation of Greece,
4, Conduit Street, London W1R 0DJ. Tel: 071-734-5997.

Thomson Holidays,
Greater London House,
Hampstead Road,
London NW1 7SD
Tel: 071-387-9321
Leading tour operator in Greece.

Tourist Police
In Greece there's a helpful branch of the police called Tourist police. They have the same powers and duties as regular police, but their special authority is to help foreigners. Many have a knowledge of English and can give all kinds of assistance, ranging from accident emergencies to just finding accommodation. It is for the latter that Tourist police are especially

useful. Their job is to know where accommodation exists, and in towns and on the islands they will have lists of people with rooms to let.

Remember, wherever you are in Greece the Tourist police telephone number is the same – 171.

Where to change money
Banks
Open Monday to Friday 0800–1400. In main tourist centres some banks open in the evenings and at weekends as well.

Banks will change foreign currency and travellers cheques. Eurocheques backed by a Eurocard guarantee, can also be cashed in almost every branch of the Bank of Greece and other banks displaying the EC sign. Credit cards are sometimes accepted. For any transaction your passport will be needed.

Hotels and Tavernas
Often even the smallest taverna in holiday centres will change foreign currency and travellers cheques. Usually only the large international hotels will take Eurocheques and credit cards for payment.

Shops
Most shops catering for tourists will accept foreign currency or travellers cheques as payment. The rate of exchange won't be particularly good, though, and any change will be in drachmas.

Travel Agencies
Tickets can usually be paid for in foreign currency or travellers cheques or credit cards.

Tipping
Tipping is much the same as in the UK, but on a more modest scale. On the menus of most restaurants you will notice two prices for each item, the first is without service, the second with service. In most cases the second price is always charged so you only need to leave a few drachmas as tip after your meal.

Health
Full medical insurance is strongly advised for all visitors to Greece. In most cases you have to pay for the treatment at the time of illness/accident and then claim back the money from the insurance company after your return home.

Insurance
It is usually cheaper to buy a comprehensive insurance which covers medical expenses, baggage loss or theft. If you do lose any of your personal belongings report it immediately to the police or Tourist police (Tel: 171).

Telephones
The Organismos Telephikinonion Eliathos (known as OTE) run the Greek telephone service. In small towns and villages there are public telephones at most post offices, in large towns the OTE offices are completely separate. Use kiosks, tavernas and shops for local calls. The owners are usually very obliging and will charge the standard rate. Whether at a public telephone, or those at hotels or tavernas, you pay for your call after you have made it, so you don't need a handful of small coins or tokens.

Useful Telephone Numbers

Directory enquiries	131
General information	134
International operator	161
Time	141
Medical care	166
City police	100
Country police	109
Coastguards	108

Tourist police	171
Fire	199
Roadside assistance (24 hours)	104

Post
Opening hours: 0800–1300 (APPROX). Buy your stamps at post offices or from kiosks and shops selling postcards. Post boxes are yellow and can be found in all towns and villages.

Shopping
Except in supermarkets and large shops there are definitely no set shopping hours in Greece. The rule to follow is that on the islands and country areas most provision shops open very early, close from approximately 1300–1600, and then open again for a few hours in the evening. On Sunday afternoons and Saints Days almost every shop is closed.

Travel
Ferries
In a country that's made up of over 1,000 islands, boats are obviously one of the main forms of internal transport. There are about 250 Greek ports in total, all with scheduled ferry connections. To find a comprehensive list of ferry timetables is not often easy, but the NTOG will usually be able to give some advice or a rough timetable.

Aeroplanes
Olympic Airways internal flights provide a magic carpet to distant islands and mainland. You can fly to over 30 destinations from Athens, a few more from big islands like Crete and Rhodes. Check with a timetable from Olympic.

Hydrofoils and Catamarans
A long ferry journey can eat considerably into your holiday time and there are now several fast hydrofoil and catamaran services, cutting sea travel times by anything up to 70 percent. These operate from Piraeus to the Saronic Islands and eastern Peloponnese; and in the Dodecanese from Rhodes to Kos, Nissiros, Patmos and Samos. Others link up to the Northern Sporades islands of Skiathos, Skopelos and Alonissos with Volos and other ports on the mainland. There's a speed boat service in operation from Patras to Zakinthos and Kephalonia.

Driving
A British driving licence is sufficient – you do not need an international one to drive in Greece.

As in the rest of Europe, drive on the right and overtake on the left are the rules to remember. Otherwise road signs and signals are standard international and can easily be followed. Front seat belts are compulsory and there are now strong 'Drink and Drive' laws.

Taxis
On the islands taxis are an important form of transport and are used for even quite long journeys. Fares are low by our standards. In towns fares will be shown on a meter. In country areas you pay by the kilometres, though for longer journeys it is wiser to try and arrange the fare in advance to save any misunderstanding later.

Car Rental
Many British package tours organise special car rental deals for their clients. If you can arrange this, it is usually the cheapest way of hiring a car when on holiday. Rates vary, but renting a car in Greece is not a cheap exercise. Rates quoted hardly ever include the 18 per cent charged for local taxes and collision damage insurance.

Scooters and Motorbikes

Scooters are an ideal way of summer holiday travel. Especially on the islands where the distances aren't great. Most islands and mainlands centres organise scooter hire and the rates are not expensive. On a scooter or motorbike, you can explore small paths and tracks vetoed to cars and often discover the unspoilt and unknown beaches. But, take out a good insurance policy and drive carefully on the unmadeup roads.

Bicycles

Cycling has never really caught on in Greece. The terrain is too mountainous and the summer climate too hot and deters all but the real enthusiast. However, you can usually rent a biycle cheaply on the developed islands and, if you have your own, ferries hardly ever charge for transporting it.

Language

In Athens, main towns and all but the smallest islands, English (of sorts) is spoken. So, you can really get by on a holiday in Greece without knowing much Greek. However, it is always useful to understand, or recognise, some words and phrases in any language, and we have selected what we consider are the essentials. For anything more specific, buy a good phrase book and/or a dictionary.

SOME USEFUL PHRASES...

How are you?	Ti kanete	Τί κάνετε;
Fine, thank you, and you	Kala, efkaristo, kee sees	Καλά, εὐχαριστῶ, καί σεῖς
What is that?	Ti, eeneh afto	Τί εἶναι αὐτό;
Do you speak English?	Milate Anglika	Μιλᾶτε Ἀγγλικά;
How much is it?	Poso kani afto	Πόσο κάνει; ὑτό
That's too expensive	eeneh poli ahkreeva	Εἶναι πολύ ἀκριβά
I don't understand Greek	Then katalaveno hellinika	Δέν καταλαβαίνω Ἑλληνικά
I want to go to . . .	Thelo na pao sto . . .	Θέλω νά πάω στό ...
Where is . . .	Pou ine	Ποῦ εἶναι
What time is it?	Ti ora ine	Τί ὥρα εἶναι
Can I have . . .?	Boro nah ekko	Μπορῶ νά ἔχω...;
Please give me . . .	Parakalo, dhoste mou	Παρακαλῶ, δῶστε μου
Could you speak more slowly, please?	Boreetah na milate pio siga, parakalo	Μπορεῖτε νά μιλᾶτε πιό σιγά, παρακαλῶ
a single room	ena mono dhomateeo	ἕνα μονό δωμάτιο
a double room	ena diplo dhomateeo	ἕνα διπλό δωμάτιο
with twin beds	meh dio krevatia	μέ δύο κρεββάτια
with balcony, shower	meh balkoni, doos	μέ μπαχλόνι, ντούς
Where are the toilets?	Pou ine i toualettes	Ποῦ εἶναι οἱ τουαλέττες
I'll be staying three days	Tha meeno tris imeres	Θά μείνω τρεῖς ἡμέρες
I am, we are	eemi, eemaste	εἶμαι, εἴμαστε
I have, we have	echo, echoume	ἔχω, ἔχουμε

English	Phonetic	Greek
I don't know yet	Then ksero akoma	Δέν ξέρω ἀκόμα
No, I don't like it	Okhi, then mou aresee	Ὄχι, δέν μοῦ ἀρέσει
Have you any stamps	Echete grahmatosemah	Ἔχετε γραμματόσημα
Walking	meh ta podeea	μέ τά πόδια
Can we camp here?	Boromeh na kataskenosomeh edo	Μποροῦμε νά κατασκηνώσουμε ἐδῶ;
Where is the tourist information centre?˙	Pou eeneh to touristiko grafeeo	Ποῦ εἶναι τό τουριστικό γραφεῖο;
The bill, please	Ton logaryasmo, parakalo	Τόν λογαριασμό, παρακαλῶ
This is not fresh	Afto then ine fresko	Αὐτό δέν εἶναι φρέσκο

SOME USEFUL WORDS . . .

English	Phonetic	Greek
Yes, no	neh, okhi	ναί, ὄχι
Yes (more formal or with emphasis)	malista	μάλιστα
Please, thank you	parakalo, efkaristo	παρακαλῶ, εὐχαριστῶ
Thank you very much	efkaristo polie	εὐχαριστῶ πολύ
Welcome, excuse me, pardon, what, watch out (no exact English meaning)	oriste	ὁρίστε
Good morning, day	kaleemera	καλημέρα
Good evening	kalee spera	καλησπέρα
Good night	kaleenikta	καληνύχτα
Excuse me, I'm sorry	signomi	συγνώμη
Hello	yasou	γειά σου
Goodbye	adio	ἀντίο
The (singular and plural)	o, ee, to	ὁ, ἡ, τό
	ee, ee, ta	οἱ, οἱ, τά
Where, when	pou, pote	ποῦ, πότε
How, who	pos, pios	πῶς, ποιός
Why, because	yiati, dioti	γιατί, διότι
What, nothing	ti, tipota	τί, τίποτα
Good, bad	kalos, kakos	καλός, κακός
Big, small	megalo, mikro	μεγάλος, μικρός
left, right	aristera, dexia	ἀριστερά, δεξιά
cheap, dear	fthino, akrivo	φθηνός, ἀκριβός
hot, cold	zesto, krio	ζεστός, κρύος
open, closed	anikto, klisto	ἀνοικτός, κλειστός
fast, slow	grigora, sigar	γρήγορα, σιγά
very good	poli kalo	πολύ καλός
new, old	neo, palio	νέος, παλιός
far, near	makria, konta	μακρυά, κοντά
Entrance, exit	issodos, exodos,	εἴσοδος, ἔξοδος
Museum, post office	mousseo, takidromio	μουσεῖο, ταχυδρομεῖο
Hotel, restaurant	xenodokio, estiatorio	ξενοδοχεῖο, ἑστιατόριο
Bank, church	trapeza, ekleesia	τράπεζα, ἐκκλησία
Ruins, toilet	archea, tooaleta	ἀρχαία, τουαλέττα
Bus, stop	leoforio, stasis	λεωφορεῖο, στάσις
Train, station	traino, stathmos	τραῖνο, σταθμός
Danger, take care	kindino, prosekete	κίνδυνος, προσέκετε
Upper, lower	ano, kato	ἄνω, κάτω
Beach, sea	paralia, thalassa	παραλία, θάλασσα

Aeroplane, airport	aeroplano, aeroporto	ἀεροπλάνο, ἀεροδρόμιο
Ship, small boat	vapori, varka	δαπόρι, δάρκα
At, in (side)	sto, mesa	στό, μέσα
To, from	pros, ahpo	πρός, ἀπό
After, before	meta, prin	μετά, πρίν
And, or	ki, ee	καί, ἤ
Here, there	edo, eki	ἐδῶ, ἐκεῖ
Now, then	tora, tote	τώρα, τότε
With, without	meh, horis	μέ, χωρίς
One, two	ena, dio	ἕνα, δύο
Three, four	tria, tessera	τρία, τέσσερα
Five, six	pende, exi	πέντε, ἕξι
Seven, eight	efta, okto	ἐφτά, ὀκτώ
Nine, ten	ennea, deka	ἐννέα, δέκα
Twenty, fifty	ikosi, peninda	εἴκοσι, πενήντα
Hundred, thousand	ekato, hilia	ἑκατό, χίλια
Sunday, Monday	kiriaki, deftera	Κυριακή, Δευτέρα
Tuesday, Wednesday	triti, tetarti	Τρίτη, Τετάρτη
Thursday, Friday	pempti, paraskevi	Πέμπτη, Παρασκευή
Saturday, today	Savato, simera	Σάββατο, σήμερα
Month, week	mina, evdomada	μήνα, ἑβδομάδα
Morning, evening	proi, vradi	πρωΐ, δράδυ
food and drink	fayita kee pota	φαγητό καί ποτά
table, menu	trapezi, katalogos	τραπέζι, κατάλογος
glass, bottle	potiri, bukali	ποτήρι, μπουκάλι
beer, wine	bira, krassi	μπύρα, κρασί
salt, pepper	alahti, piperi	ἁλάτι, πιπέρι
oil, lemon	lahdi, lemoni	λάδι, λεμόνι
bread, butter	psomi, vutiro	ψωμί, δούτυρο
coffee, tea	kafes, tsai	καφές, τσάϊ
jam, honey	marmelada, meli	μαρμελάδα, μέλι
eggs, fried	avga, tiganita	αὐγά, τηγανητά
milk, sugar	gala, zahkaree	γάλα, ζάχαρη
water, lemonade	nero, lemonada	νερό, λεμονάδα
ice cream, yoghurt	pahgoto, yaouriti	παγωτό, γιαούρτι
soup, fish	soupa, psari	σούπα, ψάρι
mullet, lobster	barbouni, astakos	μπαρμπούνι, ἀστακός
meat, cheese	kreas, tiri	κρέας, τυρί
beef, veal	vodino, moskari	δοδινό, μοσχάρι
pork, chicken	hirino, kotopoulo	χοιρινό, κοτόπουλο
lamb, suckling pig	arnaki, gurunopoulo	ἀρνάκι, γουρουνόπουλο
ham, sausage	zambon, loukaniko	ζαμπόν, λουκάνικο
salad, tomatoes	salata, tomates	σαλάτα, ντομάτες
potatoes, beans	patates, fasolia	πατάτες, φασολ
omelet	omehletah	ὀμελέττα
fruit, apples	fruita, milia	φρούτα, μῆλα
grapes, melon	stafilia, peponi	σταφύλια, πεπόνι
resinated wine, ouzo	retsina, uzo	ρετσίνα, οὖζο

16. Main Dates in Greek History

Greek history is a story of countless invasions and occupations, reflecting the country's position on the ancient anvil of civilisation and the modern crossroads of Europe and Asia. These ebbs and flows of wars and conquests gave birth to European civilisation.

Greek history is well documented because writers like Homer and Herodotus recorded events at length. Their contemporaries in Egypt and Mesopotamia were using their papyruses mostly for palace inventories and limiting their versions of great events to brief inscriptions on stone.

The first 1200 years from around 1500 BC to 300 BC were largely concerned with the unification of Greece, with the city states sometimes fighting among themselves, sometimes uniting to fight the eternal war with Asia. Most of the time from then to the Second World War, Greece has been occupied by a series of foreign invaders; the Romans, the Crusaders, the Venetians, the Turks, the Italians and the Germans. It is only since 1949 that the country has been really free and united, and even during the last 30 years there has been the shadow of military dictatorship, the troubles in Cyprus and the arguments with Turkey over Aegean oil rights.

It is no wonder that the Greek people are so fatalistic, and only surprising that they still offer such warmth and hospitality towards strangers.

BC

3000–1500 The Minoans rule the Eastern Mediterranean from Crete.

1150 Mycenae, dominant in Greece, leads the siege and sack of Troy supported by Sparta, Pylos and the Ionian Islands.

850 Homer of Chios composes 'The Iliad' and 'Odyssey'. City states such as Athens, Corinth, Samos, Mytileni and Samos emerge.

776 First Olympic games between city states.

734 Greek colonisation of Corfu, Sicily, Asia and Black Sea.

664 First sea battle between Corinth and her colony Corfu.

650 Age of tyrants and law-makers, including Dracon in Athens.

546 Persian conquest of Asiatic Greeks.

512 First Persian invasion of Europe. Darius conquers Thrace.

499–497 Ionian revolt and burning of Sardis.

490 Darius invades Greece, and is beaten by Athenians and allies at Marathon.

483 Persians under Xerxes hew canal through Chalcidice.

480 Xerxes invades Greece. Spartans die delaying Persians at pass of Thermopylae, but Persian fleet is destroyed by Athenians at Salamis.

479 Greek army led by Sparta wins battle of Plataea.

478 Athens founds confederation of Delos to unify Greeks. The Golden Age or Age of Pericles begins, with writings of Herodotus, Sophocles, Aeschylus;

concept of 'democracy' and colonisation of Aegean.

459 Athenian expedition to Egypt. Building of long walls to Piraeus.

454 Egyptian expedition fails. Transfer of treasury of Delos to Athens.

448 Peace with Persia. Athens loses Thebes at battle of Coronea.

431 The Peloponnesian War breaks out between Athens and Sparta. First Peloponnesian invasion of Attica.

429 Death of Pericles.

422 Battle of Emphipolis leads to peace of Nicias and defensive alliance between Athens and Sparta.

418 Sparta wins battle of Mantinea. Athens isolated.

415 Athenian expedition to Sicily. Siege of Syracuse.

405 Battle of Aegospotami decides fate of Peloponnesian War.

404 Athens surrenders and long walls demolished, but culture flourishes under Socrates, Europides, Plato, Aristotle, Aristophanes, Thucydides and Xenophon.

401 Cyrus revolts against Artaxerxes with 10,000 Greek troops, but is killed at Cunaxa. The 10,000 march back.

395 Alliance of Thebes and Athens against Sparta.

374 Peace between Athens and Sparta.

371 Emerging power of Thebes nearly defeats Sparta at Leuctra.

369 Thebans invade Peloponnese

364 Thebes defeats Athenian allies at Cynoscephalae.

362 Peace after Thebes defeats Spartan and Athenian armies.

358 Philip of Macedon starts conquest of northern cities. Aegean isles revolt against Athens.

356 Birth of Alexander.

351 Demosthenes rallies Athenians against Philip.

342 Philip conquers Thrace.

338 Philip defeats combined Greek armies at Chaeronea.

336 Macedonians invade Asia, but Philip is murdered. Accession of Alexander, who is elected general of the Greeks.

334 Alexander invades Persia. Battle of Granicus. Conquers Asia Minor.

333 Alexander at Gordion, cuts the sacred knot.

332 Alexander conquers as far as the Hindu-Kush.

323 Death of Alexander. Greece revolts against Macedonia.

300 Hellenistic Age starts. Colossus of Rhodes erected.

200 Roman legions on the borders of Greece.

146 Corinth invaded. Greece becomes a Roman province with Athens the leading university of the Empire.

AD

340 The Roman Empire divides into East and West. Greece becomes a province of Byzantium or Constantinople.

527 Justinian becomes Emperor and law-giver, wins back Italy, Spain and North Africa. The great age of Byzantium follows.

1204 The Crusaders invade Greece. Many islands fall to Venice and parts of the mainland to the Franks and Normans. Sack of Constantinople.

1261 Greeks retake Constantinople

1309–1523 The Knights of St John occupy Rhodes and Kos.

1453 Emerging power of Turkey takes Constantinople. Scholars flee to Italy. Greece in eclipse for four centuries.

1466 and Venice briefly win back Athens
1687 from Turks while ruling Crete.

1716 Venice retains Corfu after Turkish assault, but again loses Athens, other Ionian isles and Peloponnese to Turks.

1770 Russia captures some Aegean isles from Turks.

1797 France wins Venice and with it Corfu.

1813 Treaty of Paris gives Corfu and Ionian isles to Britain.

1821 Greece revolts against Turkey in

War of Independence which lasts 12 years.

1822 Turks crush revolt on some islands, massacre of Chios.

1824 Death of Lord Byron during Greek War of Independence.

1833 Last Turks evicted from Athens, which becomes capital of Greece.

1863 Ionian isles ceded peacefully to Greece.

1912 Italy defeats Turks and wins Dodecanese under Treaty of Lausanne.

1913 Crete and north-east Aegean isles join Greece after Balkan Wars.

1914–1918 Greece on Allied side in First World War, wins back more territory.

1919 The Greek take Izmir (Smyrna) and war with Turkey follows.

1922 Kemal Ataturk retakes Izmir.

1936–1940 Greece under military rule of Metaxas, who says 'no' to Mussolini.

1939–1945 Greece again on the Allied side in World War Two. Occupied by Italians and Germans for much of war.

1945–1948 Dodecanese liberated by British forces and reunited with Greece.

1947–1949 Savage civil war ending in Communist defeat.

1967 Military dictatorship of Colonels under Papadopoulos suppresses democracy. King Constantine leaves Greece after abortive attempt to restore democracy.

1973 Restoration of democracy under Karamanlis, but Greeks vote against return of king and Turkey invades northern Cyprus, redividing island with Attila line, so that Turkish part includes Kyrenia and Famagusta.

1981 Greece joins Common Market. First Socialist Government under Papandreou's Pasok party.

KEY TO SERIES

Each book is absolutely up-to-date and all are a convenient wallet shaped 200 x 100 mm with maps/illustrations and many personal tips.

EGYPT 1994	£8.95 hard	1 872876 09 9
by Reg Butler	£4.60 paper	1 872876 10 7

An easy to read guide to the treasure house of Egypt.

DOMINICAN	£8.95 hard	1 872876 11 0
REPUBLIC 1994	£4.60 paper	1 872876 12 9
by Reg Butler		

An up to date account of this increasingly popular Caribbean destination.

BARBADOS,	£8.95 hard	1 872876 13 7
ST. LUCIA AND ANTIGUA	£4.60 paper	0 907070 14 5
1994 by Reg Butler		

How to choose? Each island has its individual charm and appeal. This book provides you with personal guidelines.

JAMAICA 1994/5	£8.95 hard	1 872876 15 3
by Reg Butler	£4.60 paper	1 872876 16 1

A vivid account of this splendid colourful destination.

KENYA 1994/5	£8.95 hard	1 872876 17 X
by Reg Butler	£4.60 paper	0 907070 18 8

An exploration of the beautiful beaches and game parks, with illustrations of the wildlife.

Buy them at your local bookshops or send in this coupon to:

....

SETTLE PRESS (Reader Service Dept.)
10 Boyne Terrace Mews, London W11 3LR

Please send me the book(s) I have ticked. I am enclosing £
(prices cover postage and handling in UK).

Mr/Mrs/Miss...

Address ....

....

....

NEW GUIDEBOOK AND TRAVEL TITLES (All 9" x 6")

WHERE TO GO IN AMERICA £14.00 hard 0 907070 73 6
by Ken Westcott Jones   £8.99 paper 0 907070 74 4

A comprehensive guide to the attractions of each part of America, interlaced with historical and geographical detail. Many personal recommendations from a well established writer. Extensive crystal clear maps.

'American guide packed with useful information' – *E.Anglian Daily Times*

WHERE TO GO IN ROMANIA £9.99 paper 1 872876 19 6
– NEW EDITION
by Harold Dennis-Jones

An up-to-date post-revolution guide book from an author whose recent journeys in Romania are the culmination of 26 years of visits. Major value for anyone interested in Romania. First printing sold out in 3 months.

'An attempt to unravel the country's history is balanced by practical advice on travelling through the country' – *Sunday Telegraph*

'You know he must be correct' – *Charity Magazine*

WHERE TO GO IN TURKEY £8.99 paper 1 872876 02 1
– A NEW LOOK
by Reg Butler

The first edition sold out in UK and overseas within 6 months of publication amid rave reviews.

'Contains resort rating tables with vivid descriptions of every region in this tourist haven' – *The Bookseller*.

'It is a first class no nonsense, travel book – *The Glasgow Evening Times*.

WHERE TO GO IN   £14.00 hard 0 907070 67 1
THE CANARY ISLANDS £8.99 paper 0 907070 68 X
by Reg Butler

"Anything you could need to know for a holiday in the Canaries" . . . The Press and Journal. "The perfect companion for the traveller who wants to sightsee but not be bogged down with details" . . . Travel Trade Gazette.

WHERE TO GO IN TUNISIA £14.00 hard 0 907070 48 5
by Reg Butler   £8.99 paper 0 907070 49 3

This is an essential guide to a country which now offers such a wide variety of entertainment, scenery, sport and cultural development. Whether you want a superb lazy beach holiday or prefer to visit desert retreats, Roman remains and Arab markets, this book enables *you* to choose or, if you prefer, rely on the author's unique resort and site rating tables.

WHERE TO GO IN SPAIN £9.99 hard 0 907070 42 6
A guide to the Iberian peninsula £8.99 paper 0 907070 43 4
by H. Dennis-Jones

Adding to the wide canvas of the Settle Press travel series, it contains rating guides for all the Spanish coastal regions and colourful descriptions of the interior, including the cities.

Buy them at your local bookshop or use the coupon overleaf.